Dick Leonard is an historian, journalist and author, and a former Labour MP. For many years he was Assistant Editor of *The Economist*, and headed their office in Brussels, where he was later a correspondent for the *Observer*. He also worked for the BBC, and contributed regularly to leading newspapers across the world. His publications include *A History of British Prime Ministers: Walpole to Cameron*, *The Routledge Guide to the European Union*, *Elections in Britain*, *A Century of Premiers: Salisbury to Blair*, *Nineteenth-Century British Premiers: Pitt to Rosebery* and *Eighteenth-Century British Premiers: Walpole to the Younger Pitt*.

Benjamin Disraeli and William Ewart Gladstone are without doubt the two most iconic figures of Victorian politics. Their distinctly different personalities and policies led to 28 years of bitter political rivalry. For the first time, this book provides the full story of their rivalry and its origins, comparing the upbringing, education and personalities of the two leaders, as well as their political careers. Dick Leonard considers the impact of religion on the two men, their contrasting oratorical skills, their attitudes to political and social reform, foreign affairs and imperialism as well as their relations with Queen Victoria. In their private lives he sheds new light on Gladstone's guilt-ridden obsession with 'reforming' prostitutes, and Disraeli's almost completely successful efforts to conceal the existence of two illegitimate children. Providing important new perspectives on the two towering political characters of the Victorian Age, this book will be essential reading for anyone interested in nineteenth century British history and politics.

'…a solid and well-told primer…[brings] out splendidly the hilarious priggishness of [Disraeli's] arch-enemy…'
Sam Leith, *The Spectator*

'…Leonard has the journalist's nose for a telling anecdote and a plain, unpompous style…*The Great Rivalry* is his crowning achievement…written with captivating panache, packed with well-chosen quotations, full of psychological insight…readable, entertaining and illuminating.'
David Marquand, *New Statesman*

'Riveting'
Patrick Cormack, *House Magazine*

'admirably informative…and a pleasure to read'
Roy Hattersley, *The Oldie*

'Fascinating book about two people whom I know less about than I should…it combines insight with wit and brevity.'
David Owen, former Foreign Secretary

'Dick Leonard has produced masterful portraits of these two remarkable figures. His book, packed with shrewd assessments of the issues and personalities of the Victorian period, will delight and enlighten all lovers of British political history.'
Mark Garnett, Senior Lecturer in Politics, University of Lancaster

'Dick Leonard has a real feel for how Parliament works'
Denis MacShane, *Tribune*

'an unfailingly engrossing read from cover to cover'
*Journal of Liberal History*

'[The author] has the good journalist's enviable ability to assimilate and digest complicated material and to reproduce it as a clear brief or historical analysis.'
*Conservative History Journal*

# THE
# GREAT
# RIVALRY

## GLADSTONE

## DISRAELI

## DICK LEONARD

LONDON · NEW YORK

New paperback edition published in 2016 by
I.B.Tauris & Co. Ltd
London • New York
www.ibtauris.com

First published in hardback in 2013 by I.B.Tauris & Co. Ltd

ISBN:  978 1 78453 637 4
eISBN:  978 0 85773 337 5

A full CIP record for this book is available from the British Library
A full CIP record is available from the Library of Congress

Library of Congress Catalog Card Number: available

Typeset in Minion by Dexter Haven Associates Ltd, London

# Contents

# List of plates

# Preface

Benjamin Disraeli and William Ewart Gladstone are two of the most iconic of British premiers, and millions of words have been written about both of them. Each of them had formidable achievements to their credit, and they were undoubtedly among the most distinctive and complex characters ever to reach the top of the 'greasy pole' (as Disraeli described it) of British politics. Their long rivalry, as leaders respectively of the Conservative and Liberal parties, endlessly fascinated both their contemporaries and later generations. Both have been exceptionally fortunate in the biographers who have chosen to write about them. Each was the subject of multi-volume lives, written by distinguished authors, within a few years of their deaths, John Morley in Gladstone's case, W.F. Monypenny and G.E. Buckle jointly in Disraeli's. These works remain of great interest, but do not – of course – benefit from the results of modern scholarship – notably the editing of the 14 volumes of Gladstone's diaries by M.R.D. Foot and H.C.G. Matthew, and the publication of Disraeli's correspondence by the editors of the Disraeli Project at Queen's University, Ontario. Much more accessible to modern readers are biographies of Gladstone by Roy Jenkins (1995), H.C.G. Matthew (two volumes, 1986 and 1995) and Richard Shannon (two volumes, 1982 and 1999) and of Disraeli by Robert Blake (1966), Sarah Bradford (1982) and Stanley Weintraub (1993). These are all works of the highest quality. There have been many more biographies, and numerous other authors have written more specialist works on various aspects of their careers. Despite this great outpouring, interest in these two long-dead Victorian statesmen seems not to have abated, and it has been suggested that there was now a need for a single volume, of moderate length, which would constitute a *comparative* biography of the two men. The present work is an attempt to meet this demand. It is intended both for the general reader and for students of history and politics.

Although it is largely focussed on the intense rivalry which dominated the two men's lives for three decades, it is designed to cover, at least in broad outline, the entire period of their lives and careers, and it touches on virtually all the important political events and controversies of their time. These include electoral reform, the struggle between free trade and protectionism, the great split in the Tory Party in 1847 and the creation of the Liberal Party in 1859, the reform of the budgetary system, the Crimean War, the admission of Jews to Parliament, the Eastern Question and the expansion of British imperialism, the struggle for Irish Home Rule and the looming battle to curb the powers of the House of Lords. In all of these events one or both men were leading participants. It may not perhaps be too presumptuous to claim that the book could be read as a political history of the nineteenth century, or at least its final seven decades.

This book is dedicated to my two very young grandchildren, Jakob and Noa, while I also wish to acknowledge the love and support of my wife, Irène, and of our children, Mark and Miriam, and their respective partners, Gabrielle and Phiroze, without whose constant encouragement this book would never have seen the light of day. I am also deeply grateful to my brother, Dr John Leonard, who – as with several of my earlier works – read the entire manuscript with great care and made many valuable suggestions for improvements, as did Dr Mark Garnett, of the University of Lancaster. My warm thanks are also due to Jo Godfrey, of I.B.Tauris, my able and sympathetic editor. Responsibility for any surviving errors or misinterpretations is mine alone.

Dick Leonard
London, November 2012

# Prologue

## The night of 16–17 December 1852

I t was 10p.m. on the evening of Thursday, 16 December 1852. A packed House of Commons waited expectantly to hear the Chancellor of the Exchequer reply to the four-day debate which had followed the introduction of his budget a week earlier. The Chancellor was the Tory MP for Shrewsbury, Benjamin Disraeli, and the task facing him was formidable. For the Conservative government, led by the 14th Earl of Derby, was in a minority, and Disraeli needed to win over the votes, or at least the abstentions, of a dozen or more opposition MPs to carry his budget, which was the centrepiece of the government's programme. The opposition was itself deeply divided, between Whigs, Radicals, assorted Irish Members and dissident Conservatives, known as Peelites. They were named after the former Tory Prime Minister Sir Robert Peel, who had been repudiated by his own party for his action in repealing the protectionist Corn Laws in the face of the Irish famine in the late 1840s.

Disraeli was also the Leader of the House of Commons, and the key figure in the government after the Prime Minister. His budget comprised a complex and ingenious mixture of proposals, and though the sums did not really add up he had presented them with his customary *panache*. During the debate his proposals had been heavily criticised by opposition spokesmen, including several former chancellors of the exchequer, but none of them had really succeeded in exposing their flaws and inconsistencies. Disraeli, in fine fighting form, now set out to demolish the arguments which they had put forward. In his winding-up speech, which lasted three hours, he attacked his critics with great ferocity, arousing immense enthusiasm among his followers on the Tory benches. It is doubtful, however, if these were good tactics, as his sharpest barbs were directed at three of the most respected members of the House – two former chancellors, Sir Charles Wood and Henry Goulburn, and a former Home Secretary, Sir James Graham.

When Disraeli finally sat down at 1 a.m. on Friday 17 December, the House prepared to vote on his proposals. But the MP for Oxford University, William Ewart Gladstone, who had already spoken earlier in the debate, leapt to his feet and demanded the floor. A former Tory cabinet minister, he sat with the Peelites, but was widely regarded as something of a maverick. Gladstone was immediately ruled out of order by the Deputy Speaker, who was in the chair, but Gladstone blandly ignored him, and launched into a two-hour tirade against Disraeli. After overcoming noisy interruptions from irate Tories, he proceeded to spellbind the House. He began by rebuking Disraeli for the boorish and vulgar, not to say 'unparliamentary', way in which he had attacked his opponents. In his most patronising tone, he directly addressed the Chancellor in the following terms:

> I must tell the rt. hon. gentleman that whatever he has learned – and he has learned much – he has not yet learnt the limits of discretion, of moderation, and of forbearance, that ought to restrain the conduct and language of every Member of this House, the disregard of which is an offence in the meanest of us, but is of tenfold weight when committed by the leader of the House of Commons.[1]

Gladstone then proceeded masterfully to a forensic dissection of the budget proposals, in all their details, succeeding in convincing every member of the opposition that they were ill-considered and unworkable.

Outside the House, a tremendous thunderstorm was raging, with repeated flashes of lightning illuminating the gloomy chamber through its high Gothic windows – and adding to the high drama of the occasion. When Gladstone finally resumed his seat, after 3 a.m., the House proceeded to vote on the budget, which it rejected by 305 votes to 286, with only Tory MPs voting for it. Later the same day, the Earl of Derby travelled down to the Isle of Wight to present the government's resignation to Queen Victoria, who was already installed at her country residence,

Osborne House, preparing to celebrate Christmas. Within a few days a new government was formed – a coalition of Whigs and Peelites, with the support of the Radicals, and with the Peelite Earl of Aberdeen as Prime Minister. Gladstone became Chancellor of the Exchequer, almost entirely on the strength of his speech in the budget debate. Thus began 28 years of bitter rivalry between Disraeli and Gladstone, who repeatedly succeeded each other, first as chancellors of the exchequer and later as prime ministers, throughout this time, ending only with Disraeli's death in 1881.

# One

# Benjamin Disraeli, early life, 1804–41

T he determining event in the life of Benjamin Disraeli occurred on 31 July 1817. On that day, aged 12, he was taken to St Andrew's Church, Holborn, by a Gentile friend of his father's, and baptised in the Church of England. Nobody could have foreseen it at the time, but it was only this which enabled him to pursue a political career, and – after many vicissitudes – attain the premiership. Had he remained a Jew, he would have been ineligible for membership of the House of Commons, at least until 1858, when the law was changed.

Benjamin was born at 5.30 a.m. on Friday 21 December 1804 in the Bloomsbury district of Central London. The house in which he was born, overlooking Gray's Inn Gardens, is still standing – 22 Theobald's Road – though at the time the address was 6 King's Road, Bedford Row. He was the second child and eldest son of Isaac D'Israeli and his wife Maria Basevi. Isaac was a second generation immigrant, his father, Benjamin D'Israeli, having emigrated to London in 1743 from the obscure little central Italian town of Cento, near Ferrara, in the Papal States. The elder Benjamin, who set himself up as a merchant importing Italian straw hats, flourished, becoming a stockbroker and, in 1801, one of the founder members of the London Stock Exchange. He expected his son to follow him in his business, but Isaac aspired to be a poet and man of letters, and after several years of desultory activity, was delighted to receive a large legacy from his maternal grandmother, which left him as a man of independent means. He established himself in James Street, near Covent

Garden, and began to frequent the Reading Room at the British Museum, where he met a wide range of writers, publishers and other literary men. Most of his own literary work, which included poems, essays, novels, a biography and several historical works, was of little merit, but he struck gold with the publication in 1791 of *Curiosities of Literature*. This was a compendium of literary gossip and biographical anecdotes which went through 13 editions and was much admired by Lord Byron, Sir Walter Scott and the publisher John Murray, all of whom became his friends. He was subsequently a well-respected figure on the British literary scene.

In February 1802, aged 36, Isaac contracted what proved to be a happy marriage, and moved house to Bedford Row, where all his five children were born – Sarah (1802–59), Benjamin (1804–81), Naphtali (born and died in 1807), Ralph (1809–98) and James, known as Jem (1813–68). Their mother, Maria, came from another Italian Jewish immigrant family, and was the aunt of the well-known Victorian architect George Basevi. Benjamin grew up loving and admiring his father, but remained distinctly cool towards his mother, whom he felt had neglected him, while lavishing affection on his two younger brothers. All the children were named according to traditional Jewish customs, and the boys were circumcised, but Isaac D'Israeli became progressively less happy as a member of the Sephardic Bevis Marks Synagogue in the City of London. Its teachings were highly Orthodox, and D'Israeli's sympathies were more in line with the Reform Judaism movement established in Germany at the beginning of the nineteenth century. Although he contributed to the funds of the synagogue on an annual basis, he ceased to attend its services. In 1813, the elders elected him a warden, in the expectation that he would decline to serve, and pay a fine instead. But D'Israeli reacted sharply, saying that the office was 'repulsive to his feelings…he could never unite in your public worship because, as now conducted, it disturbs instead of exciting religious emotions'.[1] When the elders imposed a fine of £40, he refused to pay, and after a prolonged argument eventually resigned his membership. While never converting himself, he had his daughter and three surviving sons baptised into the Church of England. This was on the advice of his friend, the historian Sharon Turner, who argued that it would be socially to their advantage.

The young Benjamin was immensely proud of his Jewish heritage, which he had a strong impulse to glamorise. He greatly embroidered his father's lineage, in later written accounts, maintaining that he came from an aristocratic line of Sephardic Jews who had left Spain in 1492 and established themselves in Venice for several centuries before Isaac's father emigrated to England in 1748. Actually, the family, originally known as Israeli, almost certainly came from the Levant, and went not to Venice but – as stated earlier – to Cento in the Papal States. Ironically Benjamin's mother, though unknown to him, had comparable antecedents to those he attributed to his father. She was a direct descendant of Isaac Aboab, the leader of the Jewish community in Castille, who in 1492 led twenty thousand followers into exile in Portugal.[2] Her family had lived in Britain since the seventeenth century. Benjamin's parents provided him with a well-appointed and comfortable home, liberally staffed by domestic servants, both in Bloomsbury and later in the country, when Isaac, solicitous for the delicate health of his eldest son, moved in 1829 to a spacious mansion in Buckinghamshire – Bradenham House, near High Wycombe. Despite the family's relative affluence, however, Benjamin's education was badly neglected. He was the only nineteenth-century prime minister – apart from the Duke of Wellington – not to receive a university education. More remarkable was that he was the only one not to have been educated at a prestigious 'public' school. Instead he was sent to a 'dame school', run by a Miss Roper, in Islington, and subsequently to two little-known private schools, run by clergymen, in Blackheath and Walthamstow. This despite the fact that his younger brothers, both clearly far less intelligent than himself, were enrolled at Winchester. Isaac, according to an account which Benjamin gave to a would-be biographer in 1860, had intended him to go to Winchester, but was dissuaded by his mother, who perhaps felt that he was too delicate to face the rigours of an English 'public' school. So, he finished up as an unhappy boarder at Higham Hall, Walthamstow, where the headmaster, the Rev. Eli Cogan, was a Unitarian minister. It was a small establishment, with fewer than sixty pupils, and hardly calculated to expand the minds of its young charges, who were recruited from 'what was then termed "the middling class", sons of prosperous but unaristocratic fathers'.[3]

Some idea of Disraeli's schoolboy experiences may be gained from his two thinly disguised autobiographical novels, *Vivien Grey* and *Contarini Fleming*. From these it appears that he felt a profound sense of difference between himself and his fellow pupils, whom he felt to be both less intelligent and less sensitive than himself. As Robert Blake commented, 'It is certain that throughout his adult life he was conscious of dwelling apart from other men and it is probable that this awareness first came upon him when he was a schoolboy...To the end of his days he remained an alien figure.'[4]

In part, the difference was no doubt due to his physical appearance; he did not look a typical Anglo-Saxon, as most of his schoolfellows probably did. Benjamin may not have gone to a 'public' school, but he did not miss out on at least some of the experiences usually associated with them. He appears to have fallen deeply in love with one of his fellow pupils at Walthamstow, though whether the relationship was physically consummated is not clear. Disraeli certainly had feminine traits in his character, and may perhaps have been bisexual. One of Disraeli's biographers refers to 'the latent homosexual element in Disraeli's friendships with younger men'. She refers specifically to Lord Henry Lennox, an amusing but essentially frivolous younger son of a duke, who was unsuccessful both as a politician and as the would-be husband of an heiress, once lamenting to Disraeli that 'It is always the same thing; either the lady has too little money or I am too old.' Disraeli long appeared to be besotted with Lennox, whom he habitually addressed as 'beloved' in his many letters, and once wrote, 'I can only say I love you.' Even so, Sarah Bradford concludes that 'the relationship was almost certainly not physical'.[5]

At the age of 15, Disraeli left Higham Hall, convinced that it was not able to teach him anything relevant to his vast but still inchoate ambitions. The school authorities were not sad to see him go, writing to Isaac D'Israeli that Ben appeared to be 'of foreign and seditious mind, incapable of acquiring the spirit of the school'.[6] He returned to live in the parental home, now transferred to more spacious premises at 6 Bloomsbury Square, following the death of his grandfather, Benjamin, whose legacy enabled Isaac to upgrade his lifestyle. Ben spent the next two years luxuriating in his father's well-stocked library, reading widely, but in an undisciplined fashion. His father made periodic attempts to direct his reading, and apparently gave him some instruction in Greek and Latin, but he was largely left to his own devices. He did not acquire a deep knowledge of the classics, but accumulated a good stock of Latin tags, with which, as was the custom of the day, he later embellished his parliamentary speeches. Uncertain of the precise course which he wished his life to follow, his main ambition was to acquire fame, and he scrawled on the endpaper of the *Historical Almanac for 1821* a quotation from Petrarch: 'I desire to be known to posterity; if I cannot succeed, may I be known to my own age, or at least to my friends.'

Isaac D'Israeli gave frequent dinner parties for his literary associates, and the young Ben was encouraged to participate. He impressed the guests with his intelligence, precocity and gift for repartee, though not all of them accepted his self-evaluation as a genius. John Murray, in particular, took him very seriously, and began to send him manuscripts which he was considering for publication for his opinion, which elicited sharp, witty and pertinent comments. When he was nearly 17, Isaac suggested that he should go to Oxford, but Benjamin demurred. Already convinced that his self-evident gifts would very quickly win him both wealth and fame, the idea of spending several years in what he then apparently regarded as an academic backwater held little appeal for him. So, just short of his seventeenth birthday, on 10 November 1821, he was articled to the law firm of Messrs Swain, Stevens, Maples, Pearce and Hunt, based at 6 Frederick's Place, Old Jewry, near the London Guildhall. It cost his father 400 guineas (£420), and it was apparently informally understood between Isaac and one of the partners, Thomas Maples, that Benjamin might well, in the fullness of time, marry his daughter. This daughter, Disraeli was later to recall, 'was by no means without charm, either personally or intellectually'. Yet he was to prove a gauche and inexperienced suitor, and 'his visits to the Maples household, with Ben dressed in his finest black velvet suit, from Byronic ruffles to black silk stockings decorated by red clocks, came to nothing. Eventually the young lady would tell Ben, "You have too much genius for Frederick's Place; it will never do."'[7]

Without unduly exerting himself, Ben appeared to give satisfaction to his employers, and made many useful contacts through his work. Yet his desire to become a solicitor soon waned. It was generally agreed that he should aspire to higher things, and in November 1824, not quite 20, he was admitted to Lincoln's Inn to read for the bar. He joined the chambers of his uncle, Nathaniel Basevi, in Old Square, later transferring to those of a family friend, Benjamin Austen. Even then, Disraeli – who had by now dropped the apostrophe from his name – did not give the impression of having his heart set on the law. He had already sent Murray the draft of a novel which he had written, but when he received no early response concluded that Murray was too embarrassed to tell him it was no good, and so sent him a message to burn it. Now he set out self-consciously to present himself as a bohemian, dressing in a very dandyish style, modelling himself on Byron, while attempting to build a quick fortune by gambling on the stock exchange with money he didn't have. He drew friends, including Murray, into his speculations, particularly in South American mining shares. Indeed, at the urging of Murray, and at the expense of the promoter of these investments, J.D. Powles, he wrote three 'largely fraudulent pamphlets, apparently unaware of the extent of the fraud perpetrated on the investing public by Powles or of the fact that he was describing in the most laudatory terms, mines and companies which existed only on paper'.[8]

These three pamphlets, all published by John Murray, appeared in 1825, and are the first three items of an extensive bibliography of Disraeli's writings appended to Robert Blake's biography.[9] They are, by a wide margin, the most slender and meretricious of his works. Disraeli clearly hoped that the impact of the three pamphlets would greatly boost the value of the shares which he and Murray had jointly bought, and yield him an enormous profit. Instead, after a short initial rally, the shares fell vertiginously, and he was left heavily in debt. This did not seem to diminish the high regard in which he was held by Murray, who, in September 1825, responded enthusiastically to a proposal by his still only 20-year-old friend that he should launch a new daily newspaper, *The Representative*, as a rival to *The Times*. Murray agreed to put up 50 per cent of the capital, the remainder to be supplied equally by Disraeli and Powles. Murray sought to associate Sir Walter Scott with the venture, and hoped to recruit his son-in-law, J.G. Lockhart, as editor of the new paper. He dispatched Disraeli to Scotland to interview the two men, armed with a letter of introduction which could not have been more laudatory:

> I may frankly say that I never met with a young man of greater promise. He is a good scholar, a hard student, a deep thinker, of great energy, equal perseverance, and indefatigable application, and a complete man of business. His knowledge of human nature, and the practical tendency of all his ideas, have often surprised me in a young man who has hardly passed his twentieth year.[10]

Neither Scott nor Lockhart were, however, overly impressed by the young emissary, and were lukewarm about the projected newspaper. Lockhart in fact used the encounter to manoeuvre himself into the post of editor of Murray's *Quarterly Review*, an influential high Tory journal, which he rightly assessed to be a more solid venture. Unabashed, Disraeli returned to London, flinging

> himself into the work of organisation with headlong energy. Premises had to be taken, offices to be planned, a printing establishment to be fitted up; reporters and sub-editors had to be interviewed and engaged, contributions to be secured from commercial authorities in the City, and home and foreign correspondents to be appointed and instructed. In all he was indefatigable.[11]

He was also wildly extravagant, making reckless promises to many of those whom he sought to associate with the paper. Launched two months behind schedule, in January 1826, it was a total failure from the start, and crashed the following June, leaving Murray £26,000 the poorer, Powles on his way to bankruptcy, and Disraeli with debts which he had not fully discharged a quarter of a century later.

Disraeli lost no time in trying to recoup his losses, embarking – at double-quick speed – on writing a *roman-à-clef*, in which he mercilessly satirised his leading collaborators in the affair, including the long-suffering Murray. The novel, entitled *Vivien Grey*, appeared anonymously, but with the false suggestion that its author was a leading figure in high society. It was, initially, a *succès de scandale*, but when its true authorship emerged, it attracted universally hostile reviews. *Blackwood's Magazine* for July 1826 referred to him as 'an obscure person for whom nobody gives a straw', while the *Monthly Magazine* suggested that the author should 'content himself with sinking into total oblivion'.[12] Disraeli made £750 from the book, but it ensured the lasting enmity of Murray and of many others, who felt they had been duped by him. The whole episode did him enormous damage, as Blake recounts: 'He acquired a reputation for cynicism, double-dealing, recklessness and insincerity which it took him years to live down.'[13]

He also suffered a nervous breakdown, from which he partially recovered by embarking on a short 'grand tour', on borrowed money, to France, Switzerland and Italy. On his return, he was still feeling low, and Isaac D'Israeli thought a spell of country air would do him good, and moved the whole family to a beautiful Queen Anne house which he rented at Bradenham, near High Wycombe. Benjamin remained there for nearly a year, making only occasional furtive trips to London, fearful of running into creditors who would dun him for his debts. He continued his legal studies, but only fitfully, and soon polished off another novel – one of his slightest, *The Young Duke*, which was moderately well received, and earned him £500. He then departed, together with his sister Sarah's fiancé, William Meredith, on a far more ambitious foreign journey, which took him to Spain, Malta, Albania, Turkey, Palestine and Egypt. Altogether he was away for 16 months, and it would have been longer if it had not been for the tragic death of Meredith, from smallpox, in Egypt. This prompted his early return to comfort his sister, who henceforth devoted her life almost exclusively to her brother's interests. They maintained an almost daily correspondence when Benjamin was away from home, and he regularly reported to her on all his doings, and confided in her in a way which he did with no one else, his parents certainly included.

Disraeli's direct encounter with 'the gorgeous east' fired his imagination, reawakened all his fanciful dreams about the exotic origins of his family, and installed a lasting prejudice in favour of the Turks against the Greeks, which was to be reflected in his later policies as Prime Minister. He lapped up the luxury and the indolence of the Turkish court, writing to Edward Bulwer-Lytton:

> To repose on voluptuous ottomans and smoke superb pipes, daily to indulge in the luxury of a bath which requires half a dozen attendants for its perfection; to court the air in a carved caique, by shores which are a perpetual scene; this is, I think, a far more sensible life than all the bustle of clubs, all the boring of drawing rooms, and all the coarse vulgarity of our political controversies … I mend slowly but I mend.[14]

His general health and sense of well-being did improve markedly during the journey, with one unfortunate exception. On his return, he had to undergo painful treatment for a venereal infection. In May 1832, he published a further autobiographical novel, *Contarini Fleming*, and the following year two adventure stories, *The Wondrous Tale of Alroy* and *The Rise of Iskander*, inspired by his journeys in the Middle East.

By this time, he had finally renounced the bar. Yet he began to harbour doubts as to whether writing was the surest route to the fame and fortune he craved. His works had, at best, been only moderately successful, and their quality was very uneven. His style was lively, and he wrote with great facility, but his language was unduly florid, his characterisation poor, and his plots implausible. He began to form political ambitions, beginning the slow process of trying to re-ingratiate himself with respectable society. He suffered the indignity of being blackballed by several London clubs, including the Athenaeum and the Travellers'. It was his friendship with Bulwer-Lytton, a fellow (but far more successful) novelist whom he had met shortly before his oriental tour, which finally opened doors for him. Lytton, who had been elected to Parliament as an Independent Radical in 1831, hosted, with his wife Rosina, a political salon, to which the cream of aristocratic and political society was invited. He encouraged Disraeli to attend, and he leapt at the opportunity, making an immediate impression, both by the extravagance of his dress and the quality of his repartee. Lytton's brother Henry Bulwer recalled him as wearing 'green velvet trousers, a canary coloured waistcoat, low shoes, silver buckles, lace at his wrists, his hair in ringlets'.[15] This – together with his arrogance and conceit – repelled the more staid of Lytton's guests, but others found him amusing, and he probably gained as many admirers as critics during the course of his many visits to the Lytton household. Women in particular were charmed by him, and he became something of a *gigolo*, or in modern terms 'toyboy', to a series of somewhat older ladies, accepting their sexual favours while borrowing money from their complaisant husbands. His most notorious liaison, which lasted some three years, was with Lady Henrietta Sykes,

> the dark-haired bosomy wife of Sir Francis Sykes. A baronet whose family had become wealthy in the East India trade, he possessed a country house, Basildon Park; a yacht on which he spent much time, allegedly for his health; and a town house in Upper Grosvenor Street, a short walk from Disraeli's bachelor quarters at 15 Duke Street…the sultry Henrietta had married Sir Francis in 1821, when Ben was not yet seventeen, and had borne him four children, the eldest then eleven, and all of them usually kept out of sight in the country.[16]

Apart from Lytton, Disraeli's closest friend at this time was probably Count Alfred d'Orsay, the French artist and notorious dandy, reputed to be 'the handsomest man in England'. D'Orsay was living in a bizarre *ménage à trois* with the Earl of Blessington and his beautiful wife Marguerite, who made a precarious living by writing popular novels.

She also presided over a very popular salon boycotted by all respectable women, but not by their husbands. When the Earl died, in May 1829, he left much of his rapidly depleting fortune to d'Orsay, on condition that he married one of his young daughters from a previous marriage. This d'Orsay did, but only for form's sake (soon separating from her), and carried on his relationship with Marguerite for the remainder of their lives.

Disraeli was encouraged in his own dandyism by d'Orsay's example. By then, Disraeli had already set out on the tortuous trail which, after several setbacks, led to election to the House of Commons. In June 1832, a vacancy occurred at Wycombe, where his family home at Bradenham was situated, and he resolved to present himself as a candidate. His main problem was to decide in which political interest he should stand. He had developed a marked aversion to the Whigs, but otherwise had no settled political convictions. As a recent biographer, Christopher Hibbert, puts it,

> Realising that it might prove fatal to attach himself to a falling star, he shied away from the Tories, whose influence was rapidly waning; and he made up his mind to present himself as a Radical. 'Toryism is worn out,' he told [a friend], 'and I cannot condescend to be a Whig…I start in the high Radical interest.'[17]

In fact, like Bulwer-Lytton in 1831, he presented himself as an Independent Radical. His sole opponent in a constituency with a tiny electorate was a son of the Whig Prime Minister, Earl Grey. The result was:

| | |
|---|---|
| Hon. Charles Grey (Whig) | 23 |
| Benjamin Disraeli (Independent Radical) | 12 |

He tried again six months later in the general election following the passage of the 'Great' Reform Bill, which substantially enlarged the electorate of the constituency. This time he did rather better, the result, in the two-member constituency, being:

| | |
|---|---|
| Hon. R.J. Smith (Whig) | 179 |
| Hon. Charles Grey (Whig) | 140 |
| Benjamin Disraeli (Independent Radical) | 128 |

Each time he was defeated by opponents whom he had confidently expected to beat, flattering himself – no doubt justifiably – with being a vastly better orator, and certainly possessing a great deal more *chutzpah*.

In 1834 appeared a political novel, *A Year at Hartlebury or The Election*, written jointly with his sister Sarah, who was in fact the principal author, and published under the pseudonyms Cherry and Fair Star. It was not until 1979, with the publication of letters between Disraeli and his sister, that it became known that they were the authors, and the novel was republished, under their own names, by John Murray in 1983, with commentaries by two modern scholars, John Matthews and Ellen Henderson. In an attempt – remarkably successful – to protect their anonymity, Benjamin and Sarah had passed themselves off as a married couple, declaring in a Preface that 'Our honeymoon being over, we have amused ourselves during the autumn by writing a novel. All we hope is that the public will deem our literary union as felicitous as we find our personal one.'[18]

It is a short – and fairly slight – volume, but one which gives interesting insights into Disraeli's own views at the dawn of his political career. Apparently Sarah was the author of the first half of the book, and of the highly melodramatic final chapter. Written in the style of Jane Austen, though much inferior in quality, it is taken up with descriptions of the life and loves of the lower gentry in the village of Hartlebury, based very exactly on Bradenham. The main female character, Helen Molesworth, is an idealised portrait of Sarah herself, while the hero, Aubrey Bohun, a fabulously wealthy aristocrat and self-defined 'genius', is clearly based on Benjamin. Disraeli himself contributed most of the second half, which is devoted to a closely contested election held in the immediate aftermath of the passage of the 'Great' Reform Bill. He drew freely on his own experience of contesting elections in High Wycombe, and his contribution is notable for the deep disdain he felt for the Whigs, and his conviction that the 'old Tories', whom he admired, were 'finished', and could only prosper by adopting the ideas of the Radicals.

Disraeli was to contest High Wycombe a third time in 1835, still as an Independent Radical, when he came no closer to winning. By now, it had occurred to Disraeli that if he was to prosper in politics he needed to find a powerful political patron, and with this in view he sought out Lord Melbourne, who was Home Secretary in Earl Grey's Whig government. Disraeli himself recounted the occasion many years later, telling his secretary, Lord Rowton,

> Lord Melbourne asked how he could advance me in life, and half proposed that I should be his private secretary, enquiring what my object in life might be. 'To be Prime Minister.' It was then that Lord Melbourne, with a gravity not common with him, set to work to prove to me how vain and impossible to realise, in those days was this ambition ... You must put all these foolish notions out of your head; they won't do at all. Stanley will be the next Prime Minister, you will see.[19]

Melbourne was wrong: to his astonishment, he himself succeeded to the premiership when Grey resigned a few months later. As for Edward Stanley, he had resigned from the government and defected from the Whigs shortly after Disraeli's meeting with Melbourne. He was later, as the 14th Earl of Derby, to be three times Prime Minister of minority Tory governments, with Disraeli as his right-hand man, and eventual successor.

Disappointed by his interview with Melbourne, Disraeli now approached the veteran Tory politician and three times Lord Chancellor Lord Lyndhurst. He was the son of the American artist John Singleton Copley, well known for his painting (now in the National Portrait Gallery) of the Elder Pitt (Earl Chatham) addressing the House of Lords for the last time. Lyndhurst was a brilliant lawyer who enjoyed a somewhat louche reputation. They met at a dinner party given by Henrietta Sykes, and took immediately to each other. Lyndhurst opened many doors for Disraeli in Tory Party circles, and arranged for him to contribute articles to Tory-supporting newspapers. In return, Disraeli readily agreed to share Henrietta's charms with him, and later passed her on to him when his own ardour began to cool. With his customary insouciance, he then proceeded to write a further novel, *Henrietta Temple: A love story*, published in 1837 and based partly on his affair. With Lyndhurst's aid, he succeeded in being chosen as the Tory candidate for a by-election in Taunton in April 1835, caused by the appointment of the sitting member, Henry Labouchere, to a cabinet post. According to the law at the time, this necessitated him seeking the approval of his electors. Disraeli descended with haste and a great deal of panache on the constituency, and

> a vivid account of his appearance and manner of speaking survives from the pen of a contemporary journalist. He was more dandified than ever, loaded with glittering chains on his waistcoat and rings on his fingers. 'Altogether the most intellectual looking exquisite I had ever seen.' But the observer was impressed by his powers of speech. 'The dandy was transformed into the man of mind ... a practical orator and finished elocutionist.'[20]

He was soundly defeated by Labouchere, but the campaign was noteworthy for provoking a bitter feud with the Irish Nationalist Daniel O'Connell. He had written a letter of commendation to Disraeli when he fought Wycombe, and now reacted angrily to his switch from Radical to Tory. He read a newspaper report which alleged that 'Dizzy', as he was by now widely known, had branded him 'an incendiary and traitor'. In fact, Disraeli was not giving this as his own opinion, but was citing an earlier accusation of the Whigs, who had now formed a parliamentary alliance with O'Connell. O'Connell reacted with extreme violence, describing Disraeli at a meeting in Dublin as 'a vile creature', 'a living lie', 'a miscreant' and a 'reptile'. He continued, 'His name shows that he is of Jewish origin. I do not use it as a term of reproach; there are many most respectable Jews. But there are as in every other people some of the lowest and most disreputable grade of moral turpitude; and of those I look upon Mr. Disraeli as the worst.'[21]

Disraeli felt he had no alternative but to challenge O'Connell to a duel, but the Irishman had once killed an opponent and had vowed never to fight another. So Disraeli challenged his son, Morgan O'Connell, instead, and added the provocation of publishing an open letter to his father returning all his insults with interest. Morgan was not at all anxious to fight, but the police intervened and Disraeli was arrested and bound over to keep the peace. He seemed very pleased with himself, writing in his diary, 'Row with O'Connell in which I greatly distinguished myself.'[22]

It was about this time that Disraeli encountered Gladstone for the first time. Both were guests at a dinner given by Lord Lyndhurst. Gladstone, five years Disraeli's junior, had already been a Tory MP for several years, and had served as a junior minister in the shortlived government of Sir Robert Peel in 1834–5. There was probably no direct conversation between the two men, but Disraeli noted in a letter to Sarah describing the dinner that 'Young Gladstone was there.' Gladstone made no mention of Disraeli's presence in the voluminous diary which he kept, but many years later recalled the occasion, remarking that his only clear memory was of 'his amazement at the foppery of Disraeli's dress'.[23] Disraeli's conversion to Conservatism was cemented in March 1836 by his election to the Carlton Club, the 'holy of holies' of high Toryism. After his earlier experiences of being blackballed at the Athenaeum and Travellers', he was apprehensive of a further setback, and carefully prepared the ground, being proposed and seconded by two senior Tory peers, and enrolling the services of Lady Blessington to lobby on his behalf.

Disraeli went on to write his first political book, entitled *A Vindication of the English Constitution in a Letter to a Noble and Learned Lord* [Lord Lyndhurst] by 'Disraeli the Younger', an action which delighted his father Isaac. He also wrote a series of articles, notable for the venom with which they attacked leading Whigs, under the pseudonym 'Runneymede', which appeared in *The Morning Post*. He continued these in *The Times*, and – while he unconvincingly denied authorship – his fame spread and also his approval rating among the Tories. He lived extravagantly, contemplating moving into Byron's former chambers in the Albany, but he was always only one step ahead of his creditors, his debts now exceeding £20,000 (perhaps £650,000 in today's money). He was in daily dread of being thrown into a debtors' prison, and once had to hide down a well when a sheriff's officer came to arrest him, and on another occasion bribed the officer to go away. He importuned many of his friends and acquaintances for help, with varying degrees of success, and more than once called on his father to bail him out, while concealing the full extent of his debts.

Disraeli was now absolutely desperate to secure election to the House of Commons, and thus ensure the parliamentary immunity which would keep him out of prison. The death, on 20 June 1837, of William IV opened an opportunity to him, as it precipitated an immediate general election. He now received a number of invitations to stand as a candidate for the Conservatives. From at least nine possibilities, he chose Maidstone in Kent, which turned out to be an inspired choice. The other Tory candidate was one of the retiring members, Wyndham Lewis, a wealthy landowner who was entranced by Disraeli, and took him under his wing, paying the bulk of his election expenses. Mrs Wyndham Lewis was even more impressed, describing him in a letter to her brother as 'one of the greatest writers and finest orators of the day – aged about 30'.[24] When an unexpected Radical candidate, a former MP, entered the lists and a despairing Disraeli, already shaken by repeated antisemitic jibes, resigned himself to defeat, Mrs Wyndham Lewis was reputed to have summoned the Conservative agent, given him a large sum of money, saying, 'Spend that, and more if you want it – all that is necessary; but Mr. Disraeli must be returned.'[25] 'Maidstone electors expected to be bribed handsomely,' Weintraub commented. In the event, the Wyndham Lewis *largesse* proved sufficient to secure the election of both Tory candidates. The result, announced in mid-July 1837, was:

| | |
|---|---|
| Wyndham Lewis (Conservative) | 782 |
| Benjamin Disraeli (Conservative) | 668 |
| Col. T.P. Thompson (Radical) | 559 |

Disraeli's first emotion at being elected was profound relief that the immediate threat of prison had been lifted, though his creditors continued to press him hard. His friend d'Orsay sent him a message, hinting at a more permanent way out of his difficulties: 'You will not make love! You will not intrigue! You have your seat; do not risk anything! If you meet with a widow, then marry!'[26]

The newly elected Parliament did not meet until 15 November 1837, and Disraeli did not wait long to make his maiden speech. On 7 December he rose from his seat, determined to take the House by storm. It did not work out like that, being described by the diarist Charles Greville in the following terms: 'Mr. Disraeli made his first exhibition the other night, beginning with florid assurance, speedily degenerating into ludicrous absurdity, and being at last put down in inextinguishable shots of laughter.'[27]

Disraeli's first mistake was in the choice of subject matter. MPs normally choose non-controversial subjects for their first appearance, but Disraeli was determined to pursue his vendetta against O'Connell, who was the immediately preceding speaker. He launched into an elaborate assault on the electoral malpractices of the O'Connellites in the general election, accusing them of 'majestic mendicancy', and it was hardly surprising that he was soon the object of 'hisses, hoots, laughter and catcalls' from a claque of O'Connell's supporters. So extravagant was Disraeli's rhetoric and so bizarre his attire that the bulk of the House soon joined in the merriment and Disraeli could no longer make himself heard. He abruptly broke off his speech, with the defiant words, 'Though I sit down now, the time will come when you will hear me.'[28]

This has gone down as one of the most famous – if least successful – maiden speeches in history. It was not quite a total disaster, as

Disraeli related in a letter to his sister. He received some sage advice from R.L. Sheil, a veteran Irish MP who was not one of O'Connell's men. 'Now, get rid of your genius for a session,' he said. 'Speak often, for you must not show yourself cowed, but speak shortly. Be very quiet, try to be dull…and in a short time the House will sigh for the wit and eloquence they know are in you; they will encourage you to pour them forth, and then you will have the ear of the House and be a favourite.'[29]

Disraeli told Sarah, 'I think that altogether this is as interesting a *rencontre* as I have ever experienced.' He was sensible and humble enough to agree to follow Sheil's counsel. Within a month or two of this fiasco, however, an event occurred which had a profound effect on his future prospects – the unexpected death in March 1838 of his fellow member for Maidstone, Wyndham Lewis, from a heart attack. Lewis's heir was his brother, but he left his widow, Mary Anne, a life interest in his London home, in Grosvenor Gate, overlooking Hyde Park, and an income of between five and six thousand pounds a year. A good-natured but ill-educated woman, and a notorious chatterbox, she was – at 45 – Disraeli's senior by 12 years, and her undoubted charms were already fading. Yet – following the earlier advice of d'Orsay – within four months he proposed to her. He was on record as having said that 'I may commit many follies in my life, but I shall never marry for love,'[30] and it was almost universally believed that his motive was pecuniary. He made no very strenuous effort to deny this, but it was also evident that he was genuinely fond of her, and may also have been looking for a mother-substitute (with a single exception all the women in whom he was known to have taken a romantic interest during his life were older than him). Mary Anne insisted on waiting for a year after her husband's death before giving him an answer, but they were duly married at St George's, Hanover Square on 28 August 1839, with Lord Lyndhurst as best man, and Disraeli moved into her fashionable Grosvenor Gate home. Shortly before the marriage, Mary Anne had written down in parallel columns the qualities she detected in her bridegroom and herself. This revealed more discernment and self-knowledge than she has usually been credited with:

| *Him* | *Her* |
|---|---|
| 'His eyes they are as black as sloes, But oh! so beautiful his nose' | |
| Very calm | Very effervescent |
| Manners grave and almost sad | Gay and happy when speaking |
| Never irritable | Very irritable |
| Bad-humoured | Good-humoured |
| Warm in love but cold in friendship | Cold in love but warm in friendship |
| Very patient | No patience |
| Very studious | Very idle |
| Very generous | Only generous to those she loves |
| Often says what he does not think | Never says anything she does not think |
| It is impossible to find out who he likes or dislikes from his manner. He does not show his feelings | Her manner is quite different, and to those she likes she shows her feelings. |
| No vanity | Much vanity |
| Conceited | No conceit |
| No self-love | Much self-love |
| He is seldom amused | Everything amuses her |
| He is a genius | She is a dunce |
| He is to be depended on to some degree | She is not to be depended on |
| His whole soul is devoted to politics | She has no ambition and hates politics |

So it is evident they sympathise only on one subject: Maidstone, like most husbands and wives about their Children.[31]

Against expectations, it turned out to be a successful marriage; they became a devoted couple, and Disraeli was devastated when she died nine years before him. This, however, had not prevented him from embarking on a number of extramarital affairs, and he appears to have fathered two illegitimate children during the 1860s (see Chapter 6, below). As for her money, it turned out not to be enough to settle all of Disraeli's debts, though Robert Blake estimates that, altogether, she shelled out some £13,000 to his creditors.[32] This at least considerably eased the pressure on him, while as an MP he was now safe from arrest for debt.

Disraeli proved to be a very active MP, speaking frequently in the House, and showing at least spasmodic evidence that his earlier Radical sympathies were far from dormant. He criticised the implementation of the 1834 Poor Law, which introduced the horrors of the workhouse, and was one of only five MPs to vote against harsh punishment for Chartist leaders following the massive demonstrations and disturbances of 1839. Robert Blake wrote in his biography that 'politically at this time he could be described as a Tory Radical standing well to the left of centre.'[33] Shortly after his election, however, he had failed to support a motion to extend the right to sit in the House of Commons to members of all religious denominations. This would have included Jews, and 'Disraeli quickly realised that not a Tory vote was likely to be cast in favour – unless it was his.' He voted against, and the motion was defeated by 12 votes. 'In his first month in Parliament,' Weintraub comments, 'his timidity had totally overwhelmed his loyalties.'[34] Later on he showed more courage, voting in favour of similar motions in 1841 and 1845, speaking in favour during a further debate in 1847, and strongly supporting all further attempts until the ban was finally lifted in 1858. He also made a point of forging close relations with a number of prominent Jews, including several members of the Rothschild family, and made no attempt to disguise his Jewish origin, in spite of suffering from persistent antisemitic slurs. The only alteration he made to his name was to drop the apostrophe, which hardly disguised his antecedents. By contrast, another baptised Jew, Francis Cohen, the son of Isaac D'Israeli's stockbroker and an eminent lawyer, ended his days as Sir Francis Palgrave.[35]

# Two

# William Ewart Gladstone, early life, 1809–41

One of the many paradoxes in the long life of William Ewart Gladstone was that the economic basis of the political career of the great Liberal leader was a fortune largely rooted in the slave trade. That fortune was made by his father, John Gladstone (1764–1851).

Born John Gladstones, he came from Leith, in Scotland, and dropped the final 's' from his name after he moved to Liverpool in 1787. He came from a long line of Scottish Presbyterians, mostly small tradesmen, who had settled in the little market town of Biggar, in the Southern Uplands. The family was deeply pious, and in each generation included elders of the Church, and sometimes ministers, among its members. The first member of the family to achieve any level of prosperity was John's father, Thomas Gladstones. Apprenticed in his youth to a wine merchant in Leith, he rose to become 'a middle-ranking corn dealer in Edinburgh and Leith'.[1] Thomas's elder brother, the Rev. James Gladstones, joined him in Leith, where he became the rector of Leith Academy. Thomas Gladstones was to have 16 children, of whom four died in infancy. Much the most intelligent and enterprising was the eldest son, John, who after working alongside his father for several years left at the age of 22 to seek his fortune in Liverpool. Here he entered into partnership with a much older Scot, Edgar Corrie, who had become 'both a substantial brewer and a senior partner in a firm of corn factors'.[2] Corrie was entranced by his young countryman's unbounded energy and quickness to learn, and under his avuncular tuition John Gladstone rapidly became one of the most successful traders on Merseyside, soon branching out into other fields of activity, including property, shipping and West Indian sugar, cotton and slavery, acquiring in the process extensive plantations both in Jamaica and Demerara (Guiana), and the ownership of more than 1500 slaves. His wealth expanded almost exponentially, rising, according to his own very careful calculations, from £15,900 in 1795 to £40,000 in 1799, £333,600 in 1820, £502,550 in 1828 and £636,200 in 1833.[3]

In his early years in Liverpool, John Gladstone mixed socially almost exclusively with fellow Scotsmen, one of whom, William Ewart, became his closest friend. In the absence of a Scots' Kirk, they worshipped together at the Unitarian Chapel in Renshaw Street, but in 1792, 'young and still zealous in the faith of their fathers',[4] they clubbed together to establish a Kirk in Oldham Street. In the same year, John Gladstone, now aged 27, got married to Jane Hall, daughter of a Liverpool merchant. It was not an auspicious match. Aged 26, a year younger than her husband, Jane's health was very fragile, and 'within less than a year she was taking medicinal baths and visiting the spas.'[5] There were no children, and by 1798 Jane was dead. John, now a prosperous businessman, rapidly rising in local society, lost little time in seeking a replacement. In 1800, aged 36, he married his second wife, Anne Mackenzie Robertson, daughter of a Scottish lawyer who was Provost of the Highland town of Dingwall. She came from much higher in the social scale than the modest Gladstones family. For generations her family had been of the Highland gentry, and she could trace her ancestry back to King Robert the Bruce. Many years later, when Gladstone was Prime Minister, genealogists demonstrated that he was, through his mother, a remote blood relative of Queen Victoria. The author of a family history of the Gladstones described her in the following terms:

> Anne was twenty-eight, a beautiful dark-eyed woman. It seems surprising that she had been unwed for so long. Perhaps her shyness had kept her secluded for she had never been brilliant in company. Perhaps it was her intense religious dedication for she was strongly Evangelical, much concerned for the state of her soul and the souls of those whom she loved. Perhaps it was her health for like Jane Hall she was not strong. John Gladstone fell in love with the frail and beautiful Anne Robertson and she with him.[6]

They set up home in the house at 62 Rodney Street, Liverpool, where John had lived with his first wife. It was a substantial property, with room for a fair number of live-in servants. It was three years before they began a family, but on 24 December 1802, their elder daughter Anne Mackenzie (1802–29) was born. Three sons followed over the next five years, Thomas (1804–89), Robertson (1805–75) and John Nielson (1807–63). Two years later, on 29 December 1809, the fourth and most famous son was born, and was named after his father's close friend William Ewart. The family was completed four-and-a-half years later, with the birth of a second daughter, Helen Jane (1814–80).

By the time that William was born, his parents were no longer members of the Church of Scotland. Some time before 1804, when John Gladstone bought two seats at the newly built Anglican Church of St Mark's for £203, they had transferred their membership to the Church of England. The reason for the switch is unknown. It may have had something to do with their dissatisfaction at the level of preaching in the Kirk which John Gladstone had helped to establish, but more likely it was an indication of their upward social mobility. The higher ranks of the business community were solidly Anglican, and as John's affluence and standing increased, he naturally gravitated towards them. A similar movement was reflected in his political affiliation. In 1806, the prominent Radical William Roscoe stood for Liverpool in the general election, and John Gladstone was one of his strongest supporters. But Roscoe, though successful, soon disappointed his constituents, and bowed out the following year, when a further general election was held. By 1812, when he was well on the way to becoming one of the wealthiest and most influential figures in Liverpool, John Gladstone took the lead in inviting the leading Pittite Tory, and recent Foreign Secretary, George Canning to contest the city, personally guaranteeing his election expenses, estimated at £10,000. It proved a titanic struggle, with the Whigs responding by putting up the famous lawyer and orator Henry Brougham. John Gladstone effectively acted as Canning's election agent, and proved to be brilliant at the job (which largely consisted of the discreet handing out of bribes). Canning and his Tory running-mate were duly elected. Gladstone now developed political ambitions of his own, and dreamt of representing his adopted city in future parliaments. But nothing came of this, and he was reduced to buying his way into the House of Commons by way of a series of 'pocket' or 'rotten' boroughs, representing consecutively Lancaster, Woodstock and Berwick-upon-Tweed from 1818 to 1827, when he was unseated from the last of these for 'bribery, treating and other illegal transactions'. He was not a success in the Commons, and although he made two further unsuccessful attempts to be elected for other constituencies, he subsequently contented himself with being a major force in Liverpool, and buying himself a large estate at Fasque, in Kincardineshire, where he played at being a feudal landlord.

Despite his slave-owning and his resort to 'dubious electoral practices', he was generally perceived as a 'God-fearing man'. He was, according to H.C.G. Matthew, a classic Samuel Smiles character, 'mixing duty, probity and religion with materialism, initiative and a strong drive for worldly success'.[7] Smiles, the great Victorian apostle of 'self-help', indeed projected writing his biography, but was dissuaded by objections from within the Gladstone family. The home atmosphere in which the young William grew up is described by Matthew as

> moderately Evangelical, with the Evangelicals' strong emphasis on the reading of the Bible and on personal duty, family obligation, sin and atonement. Religion brought joy to the Gladstone women, but it weighed heavily on the men, and especially upon William … William's mother believed that he had been 'truly converted to God' when he was about ten.[8]

William was heavily influenced by his mother and his elder sister Anne, both of whom were very – but cheerfully – devout, and were regarded by him as saints. Anne was to die, still unmarried, at the age of 26. She and her mother possessed

> the Evangelical religious assurance, repose and sense of grace which Gladstone never throughout his life gained. For him, awareness of sin … was always uppermost, never its atoning opposite. His mother and sister represented to him, therefore, a quality of holiness which both inspired him and intensified his sense of inadequacy.[9]

Writing much later in life, in an undated note quoted in John Morley's monumental biography, first published in 1903, Gladstone reflected on his early childhood in terms which one can scarcely imagine any other prime minister employing:

> I wish that in reviewing my childhood I could regard it as presenting those features of innocence and beauty which I have often seen elsewhere, and indeed, thanks be to God, within the limits of my own home. The best I can say is that I do not think it was a vicious childhood…But truth obliges me to record this against myself. I have no recollection of being a loving or a winning child; an earnest or diligent or knowledge-loving child. God forgive me.[10]

He continued in this vein for several paragraphs, repeatedly emphasising how far he had fallen short of the standards which he believed the Almighty had expected of him. The young William's schooling began at a little school attached to the Anglican church which his father had endowed at Seaforth at the mouth of the Mersey estuary, some five miles from their Liverpool home. Here under the tutelage of the Rev. William Rawson, a Cambridge graduate who doubled up as the local priest, he studied with fewer than a dozen other boys, including initially his elder brothers. He later recalled,

> I have no recollection of being under any moral or personal influence whatever, and I doubt whether the preaching had any adaptation whatever to children. As to intellectual training, I believe that like the other boys, I shirked my work as much as I could. I went to Eton in 1821 after a pretty long spell, in a very middling state of preparation, and wholly without any knowledge or other enthusiasm, unless it were a priggish love of argument which I had begun to develop.[11]

John Gladstone, having amassed a considerable fortune, determined that his children should enjoy the privileges and opportunities open to the aristocracy, and wished all four of his sons to be educated at Eton. Three of them were, but the third son, John, insisted on going instead to the Royal Naval College at Portsmouth. Neither of William's other brothers distinguished themselves at Eton, but, in Roy Jenkins's words, 'William took to Eton like a duck to water.'[12] A tall, good-looking and ferociously hard-working young man who felt no sense of inferiority to his aristocratic schoolmates, he was a notable success, both academically and socially. He was soon to be co-opted to the school elite, becoming a member of the Eton Society (later known as 'Pop'), where, from the outset, he acquired a formidable reputation as a debater. Yet, comments Jenkins,

For an outstanding orator, which he was already on the way to becoming, he was singularly lacking in neatness of phrase … His force depended essentially on his flashing eyes and the physical authority of his presence. Thus the printed records of his speeches do not compare with those of Chatham [the Elder Pitt], or Burke or Canning or Abraham Lincoln, or even with the contrived epigrams of Disraeli, whose flippancy was so antipathetic to Gladstone.[13]

At Eton, he made a number of close friends, one of whom – Lord Lincoln, heir to the dukedom of Newcastle – was later to be instrumental in launching his political career. He also had a highly charged 'on–off' relationship with Arthur Hallam, the brilliant and dangerously attractive son of a leading constitutional historian, who was two years younger than Gladstone but was generally held to outshine him. Hallam was a promising poet who enjoyed a close friendship with Tennyson when they were both studying at Cambridge. He was to die tragically at the age of 22, and was the subject of Tennyson's famous poem *In Memoriam*. Jenkins commented that 'there is no evidence of any homosexual behaviour', but cites Tennyson's biographer, Robert Martin, who pointed out that 'sixty years after Hallam's death the Prime Minister and the Poet Laureate were still jealous of each other's place in his affections'.[14]

In his fourth year at Eton – on 16 July 1825 – he wrote the first entry in the diary which he was to continue until he was 85. His purpose, he later wrote, was 'to tell, amidst the recounting of numberless mercies … a melancholy tale of my inward life'.[15] In fact, it is largely a catalogue of the books which Gladstone read – over 20,000 in all – the events he attended and the people he encountered – some 22,000 in his long life, interspersed with agonising introspections as to whether he was truly acting out God's purpose in his life. The entire diary, brilliantly edited by M.R.D. Foot and, in particular, H.C.G. (Colin) Matthew, was published in 14 volumes between 1968 and 1994, under the title *The Gladstone Diaries: With Cabinet minutes and prime-ministerial correspondence*. Thanks to this Herculean effort, more is known of the private and public life of Gladstone than of any other nineteenth-century politician.

Gladstone left Eton at Christmas 1827, writing to his sister, Anne, 'I have long ago made up my mind that I have of late been enjoying what will in all probability be, as far as my own individual case is concerned, the happiest years of my life. And they have fled!'[16]

Yet Gladstone did not find the teaching at Eton very inspiring, and later wrote that the one thing the school taught him was the importance of strict accuracy in everything he attempted. Otherwise, according to Matthew, it made him proficient in Greek and Latin, competent in French, barely adequate in mathematics, and largely ignorant of the sciences. 'Yet,' he adds, 'his self-education in English literature, History and Theology was already considerable, and the school had achieved his father's objective of grafting him onto the metropolitan political elite.'[17]

In October 1828, aged nearly 19, Gladstone went up to Christ Church, Oxford, then – and for much of the nineteenth century – the most intellectually distinguished of Oxford colleges. Here, according to his first and most comprehensive biographer, John Morley, for the first year and a half he took things pretty easily, and constantly reproached himself for his 'natural indolence'. Then he changed, writing in his diary, 'The time for half-measures and trifling and pottering, in which I have so long indulged myself, is now gone by, and I must do or die.'[18]

He buckled down, and following in the footsteps of Sir Robert Peel, another middle-class boy whose self-made father had sent him to 'public' school and Oxford with the aim of integrating him into the aristocracy, finished up in 1831 with double firsts in *Literae Humaniores* and Mathematics. When Peel, who was to become Gladstone's mentor and political hero, achieved this feat 22 years earlier it was an unprecedented event. It had since been emulated several times, and in 1831 Gladstone shared the honour with George Anthony Denison, later to be a prominent churchman, who became a fierce opponent of Gladstone more than 30 years later when he attempted to reform Oxford University.

Yet studying was perhaps merely incidental to Gladstone's life at Oxford. It was a major formative influence both in his religious and political development. In religion, he drifted away somewhat from his Evangelical roots and associated more with High Church figures such as Edward Pusey, John Keble, F.D. Maurice and John Henry Newman, several of whom – to Gladstone's dismay – later joined the Roman Church, as did a future cardinal with whom he became acquainted, Henry Manning, who was at that time rather Low Church. At no time in his life was Gladstone tempted to follow suit. He was to his core an incorrigible Protestant, utterly convinced that each man or woman was personally responsible for his or her own salvation, and he wrestled uneasily with his own conscience on page after page of his diaries. He was especially perturbed by his inability to resist the temptations of masturbation, condemning himself as 'beast, fool, blackguard, puppy, reptile' on 17 November 1829, and pleading for 'God's help for Christ's sake in this besetting sin' in April 1831. He was devastated by the sudden death in February 1829 of his saintly elder sister Anne, writing that he immediately left for Seaforth in a state of 'abstracted shock, at first much dismayed, but afterwards unable to *persuade* myself of the truth of the news'.[19] 'This for Gladstone,' Shannon writes,

> was the first serious breakdown of a family link. He attempted to forge a replacement by making a solemn pact with his younger sister Helen that they should henceforth collaborate and monitor one another's religious and spiritual development in memory of their sister. This proved more troublesome than edifying. Helen, now a rather 'difficult' fifteen-year-old, was in no mood to submit to William's rather officious direction. Helen's distress upset her parents, who depended increasingly on her domestic presence. By October 1831 the situation reached the point where Tom [the eldest brother] had to be called in to write to William asking him politely to desist from 'religious speculations' with Helen.[20]

Despite such distractions, Gladstone led a very busy social life at Oxford, just as he had at Eton, attending wine and tea parties, going on long walks with friends, dining out, and going on outings such as the 'exceedingly pleasant' visit to Henley in June 1829 to watch the first Oxford and Cambridge boat race.[21] Some, at least, of Gladstone's fellow students found him an intolerable prig, however, and late one evening his rooms at Christ Church were invaded by a group of college 'hearties', who proceeded to beat him up. Gladstone recorded the occasion in his diary, in these words:

> Here I have great reason to be thankful to that God whose mercies fail not…
> 1). Because this incident must tend to the mortification of my pride, by God's grace…It is no disgrace to be beaten for Christ was buffeted and smitten…
> 2). Because here I have to some small extent an opportunity of exercising the duty of forgiveness.[22]

His favourite activity was listening to sermons, which he did several times a week, and he must have heard all the resident clergymen, and many visiting ones, eminent and less so, during his three years at the university. For some time, Gladstone thought seriously about offering himself for ordination as a priest, and wrote to his father asking permission to do so. The elder

Gladstone had much grander ambitions for his son, and wrote back gently discouraging him, and Gladstone – possibly secretly relieved – readily complied, and seems never to have had any regrets. Gladstone, who had already shone at Eton, was by a wide margin the best debater of his time at Oxford. He honed his skills in an essay club which he founded along with a group of Old Etonian friends. Intended as a counterpart to the Cambridge Apostles (of which Arthur Hallam was a member), it was known as the Weg (after Gladstone's initials). Unlike the Apostles, it did not survive the departure from the university of its founders. Yet Gladstone's finest performances were reserved for the Oxford Union, founded only five years earlier. Elected its President, his most notable speech, on 17 May 1831, was a vehement attack on the Reform Bill, then making its troubled way through Parliament. He spoke for 45 minutes, and carried the resolution against the bill by 94 votes to 38. Also speaking on the same side in the debate, though with far less impact, was his old Etonian friend the Earl of Lincoln, and he was deeply impressed by Gladstone's performance. Gladstone's opposition to the bill was no passing whim. He came to London and sat through the entire five-day debate in the House of Lords, at the end of which the upper house threw the bill out by 199 to 158 in a vote taken at six o'clock in the morning. Gladstone, who at that time held High Tory views, was ecstatic, and was disappointed when – a year later – the Lords reluctantly let the bill through, in the face of William IV's agreement to create a sufficient number of new Whig peers to vote them down.

Gladstone left Oxford at the end of 1831, exuberant in the wake of his outstanding examination results, and noting in his diary, 'It was an hour of thrilling happiness.' Nearly sixty years later, on 5 February 1890, he made almost the last of his many subsequent visits to the city, saying in a speech, 'There is not a man that has passed through that great and famous university that can say with more truth than I can say, I love her from the bottom of my heart.'[23]

On 7 January 1832, Gladstone settled down at Seaforth House, a country mansion just outside Liverpool to which the family had moved in 1815, to write a memorandum to his father, setting out his intentions for his future. He took immense trouble over the document, continuing and revising it on the eighth, fifteenth, sixteenth and seventeenth days of the month, before finally handing it over to his father. Having sensed that John

Gladstone's own quiet ambition was that his youngest and most brilliant son should enjoy the distinguished political career that he had himself been unable to achieve, he carefully sought arguments as to why he would be justified in following this course. He concluded that parliamentary reform was likely to be the prelude to an attack on the establishment of the Anglican Church. He therefore concluded that it was his duty to enter public life in order to resist that threat rather than follow 'the belief I formerly entertained' that he could more effectively perform this service by joining the priesthood. He now felt himself 'free and happy to own, that my own desires as to my future destination are exactly coincident with yours insofar as I am acquainted with them.'[24]

He resolved therefore to study the law, and in particular 'the constitutional branch of it', better to prepare himself. Gladstone recorded in his diary his gratification at learning from his father that his intentions met his wishes 'and my dear Mother's. God be praised.'[25] There can be no serious doubt that in attributing the decision both to his temporal and eternal fathers, he was, in fact, following his own desires. The bug of political ambition had already bitten the young Gladstone, however much he sought to dress it up.

It was decided that Gladstone should read for the bar at Lincoln's Inn, but before doing so he left, in February 1832, with his brother John for the 'Grand Tour', finishing up in Rome the following July. In the meantime, the Reform Bill was passed, and preparations were made for the general election of the reformed House. One of the strongest opponents of the bill had been the Duke of Newcastle, who was the proprietor of a series of 'rotten' or 'pocket' boroughs. Several of these had been eliminated by the bill, but he still had a predominant influence in the Nottinghamshire constituency of Newark. At the urging of his son, Lord Lincoln, the Duke wrote to John Gladstone asking whether William would be interested in being one of the two Tory candidates. John Gladstone thought the offer a bit premature, but wrote to his son in Rome, who accepted with enthusiasm. The following December he was duly elected, heading the poll with 887 votes, against 798 for his fellow Tory and 726 for the sole Whig candidate. Lord Lincoln was elected for the neighbouring seat of South Nottinghamshire. The overall result of the election, however, was a massive victory for the Whigs and their Radical allies, who won 479 seats, against 179 for their Tory opponents. It was an overwhelming endorsement of the Reform Bill, and a vote of confidence in Earl Grey's Whig government. Gladstone proved himself a strong and effective candidate, though he had to face incessant criticism from the Whigs over his father's ownership of slaves and recent publication of a pamphlet forcefully defending the rights of slave-owners. His election was undoubtedly aided by the widespread use of 'treating' and other corrupt practices by his supporters, of which the high-minded Gladstone was apparently largely unaware. He had expressed some qualms to his father about accepting the Duke's 'handsome contribution' to his expenses, fearing that this might compromise his independence. But he was reassured by his brother Tom, who was already an MP, that Newcastle 'had neither heretofore asked for pledges, nor now demanded them'.[26] Gladstone was just short of his twenty-third birthday, and it is instructive to compare the relative ease with which he was able to launch himself on a political career with the many obstacles (largely but not wholly of his own making) which confronted his future great competitor, Benjamin Disraeli. He had to fight no fewer than five contests, changing his party affiliation along the way, before entering the House of Commons in 1837, five years later than his younger rival, at the age of 32.

Gladstone's first months in Parliament were dominated by the slavery issue. Strongly pressed by the abolitionist lobby, of which the Prime Minister's eldest son Lord Howick MP (later the 3rd Earl Grey) was a leading advocate, the government agreed to bring in an Emancipation Bill. This included a subsidy of £15 million to compensate the slave-owners. Under the leadership of John Gladstone, whose West Indian estates were now valued by him at £336,000 – more than half his total worth – the plantation owners violently objected, asking instead for £20 million, plus a long-term loan of a further £10 million. John Gladstone expected both of his sons in the House of Commons to support his position, especially when he was personally attacked in the Commons by Lord Howick. Howick argued that the higher return that he enjoyed from his investment compared to other planters was because he worked his 'negroes' harder, and this was evidenced by their higher death rate. Both Tom and William vigorously defended their father, and William's first major speech as an MP was devoted to a reasoned appeal to improve the terms of the bill, which was later amended to increase the compensation to £20 million, but without any long-term loan. William agonised over 'this awful and solemn question' in his diary, but, as Checkland notes, he was acutely aware that

> his own comforts, his education and his father's ability to pay half the cost of his parliamentary seat were largely owed to the family income from slave labour…
>
> Certainly in after life William found it painful to look back on this part of his career.[27]

After the bill was passed, John Gladstone proved to be one of its main beneficiaries. He was compensated for 1609 slaves, and received over £75,000.[28]

It was not just his contributions to the debate on the Emancipation Bill which marked the early Gladstone out as an improbable future Liberal leader. In Checkland's words,

> Few of the shrunken band of Conservatives could have been as truly Tory as the young Member for Newark. The Irish Coercion Bill received his vote. He was against further concessions to Catholic claims in education or any other sphere in Ireland. He was adamant that Church and State should be inviolate: to this end he was against the admission of Jews to Parliament and against allowing dissenters to graduate from the universities unless they were prepared suitably to modify their views. He was in favour of flogging in the forces and of the award of commissions and of promotion in the army and navy on the basis of purchase and patronage. He was for the Corn Law and against the Property Tax. In sum, he was about as far to the right as the British political spectrum allowed.[29]

It was little wonder that the great historian Lord Macaulay, at that time a young Whig MP, writing in the *Edinburgh Review*, referred to Gladstone as 'the rising hope of those stern and unbending Tories'. The Tories, in a relatively small minority in the House of Commons, appeared to have little prospect of an early return to power, but sharp divisions soon began to emerge among the Whigs, who were deeply split over whether to introduce a wide range of further reforms, particularly concerning Ireland, where the Anglican Church of Ireland continued to enjoy a large income derived from tithes levied on the entire population, though 90 per cent or more were either Catholics or Presbyterians. Lord John Russell, one of the chief architects of the Reform Bill, led the faction wishing to end, or modify, the tithe system. He was fiercely opposed by Edward Stanley, the heir to the earldom of Derby, who was a former Irish Secretary and now

Minister for War and the Colonies. In June 1834, Stanley stormed out of the cabinet, and three other ministers resigned alongside him. Stanley hoped his little group would form the basis of a new 'centre' party, but they failed to gather a significant following, and eventually joined up with the Tories, Stanley (as the 14th Earl of Derby) becoming their leader for a period of 22 years, from 1846 to 1868. Lord Grey, ageing and dispirited by the lack of unity in his party, threw in his hand in July 1834. He was succeeded as Prime Minister by Lord Melbourne, who remained in office for a mere four months before being peremptorily dismissed by King William IV, who objected to his proposed appointment of Lord John Russell as Leader of the House of Commons. The King wished to appoint Sir Robert Peel, the Tory leader in the Commons, in Melbourne's place, but he was away on holiday in Italy, so he approached the Duke of Wellington instead. Wellington, who had not enjoyed his previous period as Prime Minister, between 1828 and 1830, declined to serve, but agreed to form a provisional government which would hold the fort until Peel's return some three weeks later, in December 1834.

Peel then took over the reins, keeping Wellington on as Foreign Secretary, while he himself combined the premiership with the role of Chancellor of the Exchequer. Among the junior ministers whom he appointed was the young William Gladstone, just three days short of his twenty-fifth birthday. He was appointed one of five Junior Lords of the Treasury, another being his friend Lord Lincoln. He held the post for exactly one month, being promoted to Under-secretary for the Colonies on 27 January 1835, serving under the Earl of Aberdeen, who was Minister for War and the Colonies. This was an excellent opportunity for Gladstone – as his chief was in the House of Lords, he became the chief spokesman for the whole department in the Commons. It also brought him into close contact with Aberdeen, one of the most senior and influential Tories, and a man known for his kindness and understanding. He was greatly impressed by Gladstone, and in the future became second only to Peel as his promoter and mentor. Nevertheless, Gladstone had some differences with Aberdeen over Colonial Office policies, notably over West Indian education, 'Gladstone wishing that any educational schemes for the ex-slaves there should be explicitly Anglican'.[30] Aberdeen, nominally an Anglican but effectively a Presbyterian, was unable to agree.

On accepting the premiership, Peel, not wishing to form a government based on a small minority of the House of Commons, successfully demanded a dissolution, and a general election was held in January 1835. Peel issued what became known as the Tamworth Manifesto (named after his constituency in Staffordshire), in which he presented his party, now known as the Conservative Party, as a progressive force, accepting both Catholic Emancipation and the Reform Bill, which Tories had fiercely resisted. He created a good impression, and the Conservatives gained more than 80 seats, but still finished up in a minority, with 275 MPs, against 383 for their Whig, Irish Nationalist and Radical opponents. It would only be a matter of time before the government was defeated on a confidence issue in a parliamentary vote. This duly occurred on 8 April 1835, and Peel promptly resigned after only 119 days in office. William IV was humiliatingly forced to re-appoint Melbourne, and after this no British monarch dared to dismiss a government which enjoyed a majority in the Commons.

Gladstone, who had been returned unopposed at Newark in the general election, now resumed his place on the opposition benches, his reputation suitably enhanced by his brief ministerial experience. He had long ceased eating dinners at Lincoln's Inn, and never qualified as a barrister. His main concern continued to be the protection of the Anglican Church against what he saw as Whig attempts to undermine its privileges, particularly in Ireland, where Lord John Russell, now Home Secretary, was still determined to divert part of its tithe income to secular purposes. At this time Gladstone held semi-theocratic views, believing that the state had a duty, through the established Church, to impose a Christian morality on its subjects. He argued the case for this in two books, *The State in its Relations with the Church* (1838) and *Church Principles Considered in their Results* (1840). He became closely involved with the Tractarian movement (also known as the Oxford Movement) of High Church Anglicans, attended church daily and, in 1838, drew up proposals for what he called a 'Third Order', a lay brotherhood of persons in public life. This was never formally established, but Gladstone with a number of like-minded friends later set up a small private all-male group which they called 'the Engagement'. They met regularly for prayer sessions and discussions on the religious life, committing themselves to devote a proportion of their incomes, and a great deal of their spare time, to charitable activities. The group adopted an austere set of 12 rules:

> 1 Some regular work of charity. 2 Attendance on the daily service. 3 Observance of the fasts of the church. 4 Observance of the hours of prayer (9, 12, 3). 5 Special prayers for the unity of the church and conversion of unbelievers at some hour: also for the other persons engaged. 6 Rule of number of hours to be spent in sleep and recreation. 7 Meditation with morning prayers – self-examination with evening. 8 To fix a portion of income for works of mercy and piety. 9 To consider with a practical view the direction of the church concerning confession and absolution. 10 Failing any spiritual director, to follow the judgement of one or more of those co-engaged in the case of breach of rule. 11 If unable to perform (1) contribute funds instead. 12 To meet, compare results, and consider amendments.[31]

On 20 June 1837 William IV died, and was succeeded by his niece Victoria, who had just passed her eighteenth birthday, thus avoiding the need for a regency. The change of reign necessitated an immediate general election, which took place in July 1837. It was again won by the Whigs and their allies, who accumulated 349 seats against 309 for the Conservatives. Gladstone came top of the poll at Newark. He had also contested the more prestigious seat of Manchester, which had a much larger electorate, but came third behind the two Whigs. He was joined on the Tory benches by Benjamin Disraeli, who was elected for Maidstone. The two men had little or no contact during the course of the new Parliament. Their political views diverged, with – in modern terms – Disraeli pretty far to the left wing of the party, Gladstone firmly on the right. Their religious and cultural interests were equally far apart, and they moved in different social circles, Gladstone confining himself largely to his fellow Etonians and Oxonians, while Disraeli mixed with a more heterodox, not to say more louche, set. He was ready enough to socialise with anybody, but many of his Tory colleagues avoided him because of his bohemian reputation, others through antisemitism.

During the late 1830s, Gladstone – seriously unsettled by the recent marriages of two of his elder brothers – made proposals to three aristocratic ladies. He proved himself an awkward and unpersuasive suitor, and was given short shrift by Caroline Farquhar, a society beauty, who according to a family tradition once said to her mother, on seeing her over-earnest wooer approaching, 'Mama, I cannot marry a man who carries his bag like that.'[32] Gladstone was very slow to take the hint, and shortly afterwards Caroline was married to a Whig MP, the Hon. Charles Grey, a younger son of the former Prime Minister and the victor over Disraeli in his first electoral contest, at Wycombe in 1832. Gladstone took his rejection hard, but after a while switched his attentions to Lady Frances Douglas, the eldest daughter of a Scottish peer, the Earl of Morton. As recounted by Richard Shannon,

> The pattern of the second suit was much like that of the first. A rather precipitate and alarming proposal to startled parents, flustered fending off what, from their exalted social station, would be a dubiously advantageous alliance, followed ultimately by a formal request to desist. To their infinite relief, the Mortons contrived to marry Lady Frances off to the heir of Earl FitzWilliam. Gladstone indulged in introspective reflections about his failures in love and the 'icy coldness' of his heart.[33]

He had more success with his third choice, Catherine Glynne, a sister of Sir Stephen Glynne, who had been with him both at Eton and Christ Church. A lifelong bachelor, he was the owner of the Hawarden castle and estate in North Wales. A largely inactive MP who represented Flintshire constituencies, first as a Whig and then as a Tory for 15 years, his main interest in life was the architecture of parish churches. He visited some 5500 of these during his life, and left detailed notes about all of them, which have proved an important source for modern architectural historians. In 1838, Gladstone met up with Glynne, who was on a continental tour, travelling with his mother and his two sisters, seemingly by chance, at Bad Ems, a spa in the Rhineland, to which he was escorting his own sister Helen, whose health had broken down. Leaving her there, he proceeded to Italy, where he had planned a tour with a fellow MP, Arthur Kinnaird. There he met up again with the Glynnes, and soon became enchanted with the elder of the two sisters. Flattered but somewhat baffled by his attentions, and disoriented by having recently been thrown over by a former fiancé, Catherine was hesitant, and it was only six months later that she accepted his highly convoluted proposal. Their engagement was announced on 8 June 1839, and they were quickly married on 25 July at Hawarden at a double ceremony in which Catherine's younger sister Mary was also married to George (later Lord) Lyttelton. The two couples then left on a joint honeymoon, which included a two-week stay at John Gladstone's Scottish estate at Fasque. Gladstone was 29, Catherine 27.

Catherine, who was related by birth to no fewer than four prime ministers (the Elder and Younger Pitt, Richard Grenville and William Grenville), might well have expected to make a rather grander alliance than with 'a young Tory MP of slightly eccentric reputation…She had many serious suitors (her husband made a list of nine such after their marriage) and was jilted by Colonel Francis Harcourt about 1835.'[34] Yet Stephen Glynne was delighted to accept Gladstone as his brother-in-law, while John Gladstone was enthralled that his youngest son had made such an aristocratic match. Catherine shared William's strong Christian beliefs, but their characters were very dissimilar, she being much more informal, vague and untidy, in contrast to her husband's methodical and meticulous ways. Gladstone proved himself an uxorious husband, and the marriage was largely successful, though they tended to drift apart in later years. In the first 12 years of their marriage, four sons and four daughters (one of whom died in infancy) were born. According to Matthew,

> The Gladstones were a comfortably-off couple, in every sense…Catherine Glynne brought with her, by her husband's calculation, £10,716.13s.4d. This roughly balanced what William Gladstone already had [from his father]… Apart from his salary during his brief period of office in 1834–5, Gladstone had not earned a penny of his wealth, which he valued in 1840 (including the mortgaged house and his wife's money) at £34,270.[35]

The house referred to was 13 Carlton House Terrace, a highly fashionable residence just across St James's Park from the Houses of Parliament and the principal government offices. As a bachelor, Gladstone had lived in the Albany, but on his marriage he had bought the lease of this house on a mortgage of £6500, charged at 6 per cent. He continued to live there until 1847, when his father made over to him his own nearby former London residence at 6 Carlton Gardens. In 1856 he moved back to an even grander house at 11 Carlton House Terrace, where he continued to live when he served as Prime Minister, between 1868–1874, using 10 Downing Street merely as an office.

# Three

# Peel and the great Tory split, 1841–7

One man – Sir Robert Peel – was to be a dominant influence in the careers of both Gladstone and Disraeli. Perhaps the outstanding British statesman of the nineteenth century, he acted as 'guide, philosopher and friend' to Gladstone, persisted in promoting him even when he proved himself contrary, and – if he did not turn him into the Liberal he eventually became – was instrumental in prodding him into becoming a fairly pragmatic 'centrist' politician rather than the rigidly reactionary Tory of his early years. For Disraeli, he did not perform a comparable function. Instead, he became the victim of the latter's fiery oratory, which destroyed his own career and opened the way to Disraeli's slow progression to the leadership of the Conservative Party.

What kind of man was Peel, and how did he come to play a key role in the destinies of both men? His background was similar to Gladstone's, though he was born 21 years earlier, in 1788. His father, the elder Sir Robert Peel, Bart, was a self-made man who had made an enormous fortune in the Lancashire cotton industry. It was not stained by slavery, but by the exploitation of child labour, for which he tried to make amends by bringing in the first factory legislation to protect the health of workers – much to the annoyance of his fellow mill-owners – after he was elected as an MP in 1790. Like John Gladstone, he aspired to bring up his children alongside the offspring of aristocratic families, and the young Robert (or Bob as he was known to his father) was educated at Harrow and Oxford, distinguishing himself intellectually at both places. A tall, well-built and physically imposing man, he did not – unlike Gladstone – succeed in overcoming an inbuilt sense of awe towards aristocrats, who shamelessly patronised him, not least because of the marked Lancashire accent which he retained all his life. Behind his bluff exterior he was a deeply sensitive man who felt it incumbent upon himself always to behave like a 'gentleman', a constraint which bothered few of his more high-born associates. A few weeks after his twenty-first birthday in 1809, as a reward for his 'double-first' degree at Oxford, his father bought him a 'pocket borough' in Ireland, and he became the Tory MP for Cashel, creating an immediate impact in the Commons by making what the Speaker described as 'the best maiden speech since the Younger Pitt's'. Within less than a year, Lord Liverpool, the Minister for War and Colonies, observing that Peel was much the most able of the newer pro-government MPs, snapped him up and made him one of the two under-secretaries in his department. At just 22, he started his ministerial career even younger than William Pitt, who became Chancellor of the Exchequer at 23.

Peel served for two years with great distinction, and when – on the assassination of Prime Minister Spencer Perceval in 1812 – Liverpool became Prime Minister it was no surprise that he rewarded Peel with a senior post. This was as Chief Secretary for Ireland. He remained in the job for six years, earning a reputation as a first-class administrator and universal praise for his energetic response to the failure of the Irish potato crop in 1817, when he exerted himself to obtain money and alternative supplies of food, which probably saved the country from widespread famine. The only black mark against him was that he fell out badly with the Irish Catholic leader Daniel O'Connell, who, with no great justification, regarded him as over-partial to the Protestant minority, dubbing him 'Orange' Peel. This label stuck, and led to an approach from the Anglican-dominated University of Oxford to accept nomination as one of their Members of Parliament, for which constituency he was elected unopposed in June 1817. When he finally returned from Ireland in 1818, still only 30 years old, he was already seen as a major political figure, and within three years became Home Secretary, and effectively number three in the government after the Prime Minister, Lord Liverpool, and George Canning, the Foreign Secretary. He remained Home Secretary until November 1830, with an interval of nine months during the very short premierships of Canning and Viscount Goderich. He resumed this post in the Duke of Wellington's government, from 1828 to 1830, doubling up with the leadership of the Commons. Described by a much later Prime Minister, Harold Wilson, as 'undoubtedly the greatest reforming Home Secretary of all time',[1] he had two great achievements to his credit – the complete re-codification of English criminal law, the first time this had been attempted since the thirteenth century, and the creation of the Metropolitan Police Force, which provided London for the first time with reliable and efficient policing. Its officers were known as 'Peelers', and later as 'Bobbies', after their founder.

Peel was also remembered for a third reform – Catholic emancipation – though, politically, this probably did him more harm than good. A highly controversial issue, the question of allowing Roman Catholics to sit in the House of Commons had bitterly divided the Tory Party for very many years. So much so that successive cabinets had agreed to differ on the issue, and to take no action, even though a growing majority of ministers was in favour of 'emancipation'. Peel was part of the pro-Protestant minority, though he did not feel strongly on the subject, and had growing doubts whether further resistance to Catholic demands was viable. Then, quite unexpectedly, in a by-election in County Clare in 1829, Daniel O'Connell decided to offer himself as a candidate, even though he was ineligible to be elected. He won by an overwhelming majority, and Wellington and Peel decided that immediate steps must be taken to enable him to take his seat if a civil war in Ireland was to be averted. They persuaded a reluctant George IV to allow them to introduce an Emancipation Bill, and Peel judged that, as he was widely seen as the voice of Ulster Protestants (or 'Orangemen'), it would be inappropriate for him to introduce the bill in the Commons, and determined to resign. Wellington, however, felt unable to carry the bill himself, and pleaded with Peel to stay on and take full responsibility for it. As Norman Gash, Peel's principal biographer, wrote, 'A more prudent, a more timid, a more selfish man would have left Wellington to deal with the situation as well as he could; Peel chose to remain.'[2]

The personal consequences for Peel were considerable. He was disowned by his Protestant supporters at Oxford, resigned his seat to seek a vote of confidence in a by-election, and lost to a fellow Tory in a poll in which it was reported by the diarist Charles Greville that 'an immense number of parsons' had taken part. He only got back into the House because an MP for a 'pocket' borough was persuaded to resign in his favour. Peel also incurred the lasting enmity of the 'ultra' or right-wing Tories, who freely castigated him as a 'traitor'. Twenty-nine of them voted with the opposition the following year to bring down the government, opening the way to the return of the Whigs under Earl Grey. Peel became the leader of the Tories in the House of Commons, was briefly Prime Minister of a minority government in 1834–5, and then set about reorganising the Tory Party, renaming it the Conservative Party. He became the dominant debater in the House of Commons during the period from 1835 to 1841, when he usually came off best in his confrontations with his Whig opposite number, Lord John Russell, who was the Leader of the House. The contrast between the two men could hardly have been greater. Peel measured 6 feet, 5 inches, whereas 'little Johnnie Russell', as he was known to his colleagues, was barely 5 feet, 4 inches tall. After the 1837 general election, the Conservatives were the largest party in the House of Commons, but the Whig government remained in office thanks to the votes of the followers of Daniel O'Connell, who now held the balance of power. But the government remained weak, due to the lacklustre leadership of Lord Melbourne, who spent a quite disproportionate amount of his time acting as Secretary to Queen Victoria, to the neglect of his prime ministerial duties. The diarist Charles Greville has left a graphic description of how Melbourne's daily routine was dominated by his attendance on the Queen:

> He is at her side for at least six hours every day – an hour in the morning, two on horseback, one at dinner, and two in the evening... Month after month he remains at [Windsor] Castle, submitting to this daily routine... he is always sitting bolt upright; his free and easy language interlarded with 'damns' is carefully guarded and regulated with the strictest propriety, and he has exchanged the good talk of Holland House for the trivial, laboured, and wearisome inanities of the Royal circle.[3]

Melbourne offered his resignation as Prime Minister in May 1839, after his Commons majority was reduced to five votes on a motion deploring the government's handling of the recent rebellion in Jamaica. A very reluctant Queen Victoria invited Peel to form a new government, but he declined to do so after she had made a series of difficulties, in particular by refusing his request that some of the Ladies of her Bedchamber, all of whom were

Whigs, should be replaced by Tories, as an indication of her confidence in the new government. This episode went down in history as 'the Queen's Bedchamber affair', and the delighted Queen was able to keep her beloved Melbourne as her chief minister for another two years. In 1841, however, after the economic situation of the country had sharply deteriorated, Melbourne's government went down to a heavy defeat in a general election. The Conservatives were returned, with 368 seats against a total of 290 for the Whigs, Radicals and Irish Nationalists. It was a truly historic victory: the first time in British history that 'a party in office enjoying a majority in the Commons had been defeated in the polling booths by an opposition previously in a minority'.[4] Among the 368 victorious Conservative candidates were Gladstone, who topped the poll at Newark, and Disraeli, who had abandoned his Maidstone constituency (where the greedy electors had become too demanding of cash hand-outs) but came comfortably second to his fellow Conservative candidate at Shrewsbury, another two-member seat. He had not, however, had an easy campaign. Supporters of his Whig opponents had plastered the walls of Shrewsbury listing court judgments against Disraeli for debts amounting to a total of £22,036.2s.11d, claiming that he was 'seeking a place in Parliament in order to avoid the debtors' prison'. Disraeli responded with a broadsheet, disingenuously claiming that the charges were 'utterly false'.[5] He also had to face, as he had several years earlier during the Taunton by-election, incessant antisemitic taunts.

There was now no question that Peel would become Prime Minister, and the way was smoothed for him by Prince Albert, who had married the Queen in February 1840, and who now exerted himself to ensure that there would be no repetition of the Queen's Bedchamber affair. He negotiated a compromise under which the three leading Whig ladies, and any others to whom Peel took objection, should be privately persuaded to resign, and the Queen herself would announce the appointment of their replacements, though Peel would communicate to her the actual names. On 10 December 1841 Peel commenced his second ministry, leading a cabinet of 14 members. The principal offices were assumed by Henry Goulburn as Chancellor of the Exchequer, the Earl of Aberdeen as Foreign Secretary and Sir James Graham as Home Secretary. The Lord Chancellor was Disraeli's former patron, Lord

Lyndhurst, while a notable recruit to the government was the former Whig Edward Stanley, who now finally threw in his lot with the Tories after having unsuccessfully attempted to form an independent 'centrist' grouping in the Commons. He became, for the second time, Secretary for War and the Colonies. The Duke of Wellington became Minister without Portfolio, and regained his former position as Commander-in-Chief.

Gladstone, despite having won Peel's warm favour, did not make the cabinet, but was awarded the senior post of Vice-President of the Board of Trade. This meant that he was the chief spokesman for the department in the House of Commons, given that the President was the Earl of Ripon. Ripon, a veteran politician, had first made his mark some twenty years earlier when, as John Robinson, he had been a successful Chancellor of the Exchequer and was dubbed 'Prosperity' Robinson. Later, in 1827–8, he had been a notably unsuccessful Prime Minister, as Viscount Goderich, and was dismissed by George IV after only four months in office, being subsequently compensated with an earldom. Now he was something of a 'burnt-out case', and the effective head of the department was Gladstone. Two years later, Ripon retired, and Gladstone took his place, joining the cabinet at the age of 33. In 1841 Gladstone had had some misgivings about entering the government, as he disagreed with British policy towards China, with whom the 'Opium War' (1839–42) was being waged. Gladstone regarded this as immoral, but salved his conscience by concluding that as he was not a member of the cabinet he had no responsibility for determining policy in this regard. Disraeli would have had no qualms whatsoever about becoming a minister, and was bitterly disappointed that no offer was made to him. This was in spite of his having written an obsequious letter to Peel, which concluded,

> I have tried to struggle against a storm of political hate and malice which few men ever experienced, from the moment, at the instigations of a member of your Cabinet [i.e. Lord Lyndhurst], I enrolled myself under your banner, and I have only been sustained under these trials by the conviction that the day would come when the foremost man in the country would publicly testify that he had some respect for my ability and my character ... I appeal to your own heart – to that justice and that magnanimity which I feel are your characteristics – to save me from an intolerable humiliation.[6]

Unknown to him, Mary Anne had written an equally sycophantic letter on his behalf, saying that she was 'overwhelmed by anxiety' that rejection would crush her husband's career. 'Literature,' she reminded Peel, 'he has abandoned for politics.'[7] Peel, who was besieged by similar importunities from many other MPs, wrote back civilly, saying he regretted he was not in a position to 'meet the wishes that are conveyed to me by men whose co-operation I should be proud to have, and whose qualifications and pretensions for office I do not contest'.[8]

There is some slight evidence, however, that Peel would have been ready to include Disraeli had it not been for the objections of his leading colleague, Edward Stanley. Stanley had a longstanding quarrel with Disraeli, concerning a scrape in which his brother had been involved, and which he – probably unjustly – blamed on Disraeli. Stanley is cited as having declared that 'If that scoundrel [were] taken in [he] would not remain [himself]'.[9]

Mortified by his rejection, Disraeli took himself and Mary Anne off to Paris, where (at least in his own account in a sheaf of letters to his sister), they were the stars of 'the season', being taken up by leading politicians such as Guizot and Thiers, writers such as de Tocqueville and Victor Hugo, and Count Walewski (Napoleon's illegitimate son, and a future Foreign Minister). Using introductions given to him by Ida, Duchesse de Gramont, the sister of Count d'Orsay, and by a banker friend of Lord Lyndhurst's, he managed to penetrate the highest levels of French society, and even contrived to meet King Louis Philippe, to whom he had addressed a lengthy memorandum, introducing himself as the leader of a group of influential British MPs anxious to forge a new alliance between France and Britain. The king took the bait, and spent long hours with Disraeli, regaling him with stories of what he called his 'life of great vicissitude'.[10] It cannot be doubted that Disraeli responded with the diet of treacly flattery which he later used with such effect on Queen Victoria. Yet any long-term benefit which Disraeli may have hoped to gain from his friendship with the French King was aborted by the February Revolution of 1848, which drove him into exile.

Back home, Disraeli applied himself with energy to rebuilding his political career. Hitherto he had been widely (and largely justifiably) seen as a brilliant but unprincipled opportunist, with no abiding political philosophy. He now set out to formulate one, based on a deeply romantic view of the historic role of the aristocracy, which he came to see as the receptacle of all that was noble and generous in British society. He combined this with a total disdain for the money-grubbing middle class and a sympathy for the poor and workers. He discerned a community of interest between the landed and labouring classes, and – by extension – between the Tories and the Radicals which justified his own peregrination between these two parties, which others saw as mutually exclusive. His elevated view of aristocrats was not just theoretical, but was based on actual models, in the shape of a small band of youthful MPs, all of whom had been educated together at Eton and Cambridge, known as Young England, which would – in modern terminology – be best described as a left-wing Tory pressure group. The three stalwarts of this group were Alexander Baillie-Cochrane (later Lord Lamington), MP for Bridport, the Hon. George Sydney Smythe, MP for Canterbury, and Lord John Manners, younger son of the Duke of Rutland, who represented Newark, where his fellow Tory MP was Gladstone. All three were extremely attractive and congenial young men. Initially, they may have looked upon Disraeli as a *parvenu*, but they were deeply impressed by his gifts, and he was welcomed into the group, and soon recognised as its effective leader. Among the supporters of the group was John Walter II, MP for Nottingham, and – more significantly – proprietor of *The Times*, which guaranteed them sympathetic press coverage, out of all proportion to their small numbers and limited parliamentary influence.

Disraeli now embarked on writing the trilogy of political and social novels – *Coningsby, Sybil or The Two Nations* and *Tancred* – which appeared between 1844 and 1847, and on which his reputation as a literary figure essentially rests. He is credited with having written the first political novels (preceding the more prolific Anthony Trollope by two decades). He sought to weave his own political ideas into the novels, in which the Young England trio and many other political figures appear in scarcely disguised forms. It is in *Sybil* that this famous passage occurs:

'Two nations between whom there is no intercourse and no sympathy; who are ignorant of each other's habits, thoughts, and feelings, as if they were dwellers in different zones or inhabitants of different planets; who are formed by a different breeding, are fed by different food, are ordered by different manners, and are not governed by the same laws'.

'You speak of –' said Egremont hesitatingly, 'THE RICH AND THE POOR.'[11]

On assuming office in 1841, Peel's main concern was with 'the Condition of England', as it was described in a famous pamphlet by Thomas Carlyle, published in 1840. This described the misery caused by one of the worst depressions of the nineteenth century, with widespread unemployment and poverty, particularly in towns such as Bolton and Paisley, where starvation was barely kept at bay. The nation was in tumult, with mass meetings by the Chartists and the Anti-Corn Law League constantly threatening public order, while the ten-hour day campaign by Lord Ashley (later the Earl of Shaftesbury) was infuriating industrialists. Meanwhile, the accumulated national debt had risen to £7.5 million, an unprecedented level in peacetime. Peel came to power with two clear objectives. One was to create a budget surplus. The other – closely allied – was to reorganise the taxation system so as to permit a progressive transition to free trade, lowering the price of food and raw materials, which would both ease poverty and stimulate demand, thus boosting an upward push to economic growth. To achieve a surplus, he suggested what no previous government had dared since 1816, when the temporary wartime income tax introduced by Pitt had been swept away by a backbench revolt in the Commons. He proposed a rate of 7d in the pound for incomes of over £150, to run for a three-year period. He probably had a shrewd idea that this period would be extended, and so it has proved, with income tax being the mainstay of government revenue ever since. Persuading the cabinet took some doing, with Stanley and Graham being particularly sceptical, but he gradually won them round, and the tax formed the central element in the budget which Peel personally introduced in March 1842, the Chancellor, Henry Goulburn, having deferred to him. Much of the surplus obtained through the tax was disbursed through a large range of tariff reductions, focussed on food and other essential items. Peel would have liked to remove all duty from corn, but fearful of the strong agricultural lobby, extremely well represented on the government benches, largely peopled by country squires, he proposed instead only a marginal liberalisation of the Corn Laws. These had been introduced in the aftermath of the Napoleonic Wars by Lord Liverpool's Tory government. They provided for a prohibitively high duty on foreign corn if the domestic price fell below £4 a quarter (eight bushels). This provided a high level of protection for the landed interest at the expense of consumers. In 1828 a sliding scale of duty had been introduced, replacing this sudden activation of full protection. Peel now proposed to reduce this sliding scale. Even this was too much for his Lord Privy Seal, the Duke of Buckingham, who was President of the Agricultural Protection Society. He resigned after only five months in office – a warning sign to Peel of possible future trouble from the bulk of his own party, which was strongly protectionist, but which he later ignored, to his cost.

No member of the government was more supportive of Peel, both in his determination to obtain a budget surplus and his introduction of free-trade measures, than Gladstone. He had initially had qualms about accepting a post in the Board of Trade, whose activities were far distant from his own prime concern of furthering the interests of the Church of England. Yet he buckled down to the minutiae of its work, showed himself to be a first-class administrator and a very able parliamentary spokesman on its behalf. In 1844 he carried a major piece of legislation – the Railways Act – through the Commons. Its provisions laid the basis for relations between the state and the railway companies for half a century or more. They included the option to purchase a line at the end of a certain term for 25 times the annual profit, the compulsory provision of accommodation on trains for 'poorer people', and that third-class fares should not exceed a penny a mile. His reputation as a hard-working, decisive and formidably well-informed minister soared, and he was tipped by John Stuart Mill to become Peel's successor as Tory leader. Publicly successful, he went through a deep religious and sexual crisis during these years. It began painfully to dawn upon him that his theocratic ideas were impracticable, and his attitude to the Conservative Party insensibly changed. Formerly, he had seen the party as the chosen instrument of God's will for the nation, but increasing familiarity with his fellow Tory MPs slowly disillusioned him.

Now he viewed the party more in terms of being marginally preferable to the Whigs and much more so to the Radicals, rather than a thing apart. He also suffered from acute sexual frustration. According to Matthew, he was almost certainly a virgin at the time of his marriage, but was highly sexed and found it difficult to abstain from sexual relations with Catherine during her repeated long periods of pregnancy when, according to Victorian custom, intercourse was strongly discouraged. He sought relief in furtive reading of pornography, but was driven more and more to his 'night-time work' of attempting to rescue 'fallen women'. This he had begun in 1840, as his chosen charitable work within the Engagement group, but despite the meagre success of his efforts – he estimated that only one of the first eighty or ninety women he took up with was 'redeemed' – he now stepped up his activities. They continued, including during his premierships, until his old age. He made little effort to conceal what he was doing, often taking the women he encountered back to his house for a meal with Catherine, who approved her husband's activities, though it is doubtful that she knew of their full extent. For Gladstone was physically attracted to many of them, and often succumbed to temptation, and then flagellated himself in atonement, signifying the occasions in his diary with a symbol resembling a whip. It is doubtful if he ever went 'the whole way', and indeed 17 months before his death he wrote a solemn declaration to his son, the Rev. Stephen Gladstone, now the Rector of Hawarden, assuring him that he had never 'been guilty of the act that is known as that of infidelity to the marriage bed' (see Chapter 10). Nevertheless, his diaries make it clear that he felt a very strong sense of having sinned on numerous occasions. Many of Gladstone's friends and colleagues became aware of his midnight prowls, and were concerned that they might cause a scandal, but scarcely the slightest innuendo appeared in the press until after his death. This side of Gladstone's life was virtually ignored in the monumental biography written by his friend and colleague John Morley, and it was only in 1927, during the course of a libel action between his son Herbert and a scurrilous author called Captain Peter Wright, that it became known to the general public. The jury in the trial, giving judgment in favour of Herbert Gladstone, added a note to the effect that the evidence had 'completely vindicated the high moral character of the late Mr. W.E. Gladstone'.[12] It was not until the publication of Gladstone's diaries in the final third of the twentieth century that the full extent of Gladstone's nocturnal activities and his own sense of shame became known to scholars.

Gladstone's acute conscience often put his continuance as a cabinet minister in doubt. In 1843 the government proposed to combine the two very small Welsh bishoprics of Bangor and St Asaph in order to provide emoluments for the newly established diocese of Manchester. Gladstone interpreted this as an attack on the Church in Wales, and proposed to resign in protest. He was only dissuaded from doing so by two of his most devout friends, James Hope Scott and Henry, later Cardinal, Manning.

They succeeded in convincing him that the Roman legal principle of *de minimis non curat lex* ('the law takes no account of trifles') was applicable in this case. In February 1845, however, he insisted on resigning over an affair which led many, apparently including Disraeli, to conclude that he was not a serious politician, and that his political career was effectively over. This was the question of increasing the annual public grant to Maynooth seminary in County Kildare, where a high proportion of Ireland's Catholic priests was educated. Founded in 1795, it had received a small subsidy, agreed by Parliament each year, since the Act of Union in 1800. Now Peel, in the interest of pacifying Irish discontents and in the hope of reconciling the Irish priesthood to the Union, proposed to make the grant permanent and to increase it considerably. Gladstone approved of Peel's policy, as a pragmatic necessity, but felt that as he had argued against any public support for the Catholic Church in his book on the Church and state, published seven years earlier, he could not now, as a minister, take a contrary view. He therefore determined to resign, even though he fully intended to vote in favour of the measure when it came before Parliament. In his resignation speech, which lasted more than an hour, he attempted to explain his position. The historian D.C. Somervell commented that 'Five minutes might have made the point clear, but excessive subtlety rendered the explanation itself inexplicable.'[13] He cited the speech which followed, of the famous Radical MP Richard Cobden: 'What a marvellous talent is this! Here have I been sitting listening with pleasure for an hour to his explanation, and yet I know no more why he left the Government than before he began.'[14]

Catholicism, and his attitude to it, proved a continuing thorn in Gladstone's side. As a fervent High Church Anglican, he was just about as close, liturgically, to the Catholic Church as it was possible for a Protestant to be, but he drew an absolute line against actual conversion to the Roman Church. It was greatly to pain him when one by one his closest associates, including several members of the Engagement, were to take this step, including both Hope Scott and Manning, who converted on the same day in 1851. But that was still some years ahead. In 1845, John Henry Newman, the most loved and admired of the High Church preachers to whom Gladstone had listened in his Oxford days, was received into the Roman Church. Gladstone was not personally close to the future Cardinal, but when he heard the stupendous news that Newman was contemplating this step, he wrote to Manning saying, 'I stagger to and fro like a drunken man. I am at my wit's end.' He later referred to Newman, in another letter to Manning, as 'a disgraced man'.[15] Even more distressing for Gladstone had been the conversion of his sister Helen three years earlier. He was closer to her than any other member of the family, and had always regarded himself as her mentor in religious matters. He now reacted explosively and, in what many would regard as a most 'unchristian' way, demanded that John Gladstone should expel her from his household, and refused her any contact with his own children. Fortunately, his father proved a great deal more tolerant, and not only allowed her to stay, but even permitted her to receive visits from her confessor. She, however, became addicted to opium, and, wishing to get away from any familial restraints, took herself off to Baden-Baden, where by 1845 both her situation and her health had sadly declined. The family decided to take the matter in hand, and though William was both the busiest and least diplomatic of her brothers, he took it upon himself to travel to Germany to bring her back home. When he arrived in Baden-Baden he found her in a terrible state, partly paralysed after taking an enormous dose of 300 drops of laudanum. She refused to return with him, but after receiving threats from the family to cut her off financially, reluctantly agreed to travel to Cologne with him, accompanied by a priest and a doctor. Gladstone returned disconsolately to London, and Helen followed him three weeks later, to live in her father's London house in Carlton Gardens.

One of the MPs to vote against the Maynooth grant was Disraeli, who, somewhat incongruously, was trying to set himself up as a standard-bearer for the Church of England, at a time when the Church was frequently referred to as 'the Tory Party at prayer'. This did not, however, prevent him from falling into difficulties with his party leadership. During the years between 1842 and 1845 he made a number of speeches which were increasingly critical of the government and of Peel himself. His motivation was almost certainly mixed. On the one hand, he was – perhaps subconsciously – giving vent to his disappointment that the Prime Minister had turned him down as a ministerial colleague. Yet there was also undoubtedly an element of calculation. Ambitious backbenchers seeking promotion have traditionally had two alternative strategies to pursue. One is that of extreme loyalty, acting as a lickspittle to ministers in the hope of being suitably rewarded in the course of time. The other is to act as a troublemaker, consistently speaking or even voting against the government in the expectation of being bought off by the offer of a job. Disraeli seems to have chosen the latter course. By now he was already building up a reputation as a highly effective parliamentary debater, who could be guaranteed to fill up the empty benches whenever he rose to speak. He had also long since abandoned his dandyesque attire, and clothed himself in a dull black coat, while trimming back, without altogether eliminating, his flowing black curls. In short, he was finally acquiring *gravitas*.

Disraeli attacked the government, and Peel personally, over several issues, but his main concern was that, having been elected on a protectionist platform, they had increasingly adopted free-trade measures, to the horror of their predominantly rural supporters and the relief of the largely Whig-supporting manufacturing interest. Disraeli did not mince his words, going so far as to say, in a debate on 17 March 1845, that a 'Conservative government is an organised hypocrisy.' If he had set out to be a 'candid' but reconcilable critic, he had clearly over-done it, and Peel had already responded, in 1844, by omitting Disraeli from the list of MPs sent a copy of the government whip at the beginning of the new parliamentary session. Disraeli was abashed, but now concluded that there was no longer any realistic prospect of reconciling Peel to him. If he were to have a decent future in the Tory Party it could only be through the destruction of its leader. He did not have to wait very long before the opportunity arose to bring this about.

In October 1845, a serious blight began among Irish potatoes, which formed the major element in the diet of some four million Irish. Three quarters of the crop was ruined, and Peel immediately realised that it would be necessary to suspend the Corn Laws in order that cheap grain, mainly from Canada, could be imported in large amounts. He also concluded that it would be politically impossible to re-impose the laws once they had been suspended, and decided that the only honest thing to do was to repeal them altogether. He found it impossible, however, to persuade his own cabinet, only three of whom, including the Home Secretary, Sir James Graham, initially supported him. In the meantime, the Leader of the Opposition, Lord John Russell, had launched a stirring appeal for abolition in an open letter issued in Edinburgh. Peel composed no less than five memoranda arguing the case to the cabinet in the period between 31 October and 4 December 1845. When the cabinet met on that date, two members, Stanley (who had now entered the House of Lords as Lord Stanley of Bickerstaffe) and the Duke of Buccleuch, declared that they would rather resign than back Peel's proposal, for which he received only lukewarm support from the majority of his other colleagues. Peel then decided to resign, recommending the Queen that Lord John Russell should be invited to form an administration to carry through the policy he had publicly recommended.

Queen Victoria promptly summoned Russell, who tried to form a government but failed, owing to the inability of his leading colleagues to agree on the allocation of ministerial posts. The stumbling block was Lord Palmerston, who had been Foreign Secretary in the previous Whig government led by Lord Melbourne and had made himself highly unpopular with his colleagues by his wilful refusal to submit his policies for cabinet approval. Several of them now refused to serve if Palmerston was again Foreign Secretary, but he refused point-blank to take any other post, and Russell felt he could not proceed without him. Peel would much have preferred Russell to have succeeded, so as to prevent a re-run of the events of 1829, when he had had to carry through, with Whig support, a measure (Catholic emancipation) of which the majority of his fellow Tories disapproved. Yet when the Queen appealed to him not to abandon her, he readily agreed to resume as Prime Minister. His decision was welcomed by his cabinet, with the exception of Stanley, who insisted on resigning, and Buccleuch, who asked for time to consider his position but eventually agreed to carry on. Peel was greatly encouraged by Wellington's strong support, given out of personal loyalty, though the General had previously been a supporter of the Corn Laws. He invited Gladstone to rejoin the government, taking Stanley's place as Secretary for War and the Colonies. He was happy to accept, being wholeheartedly in support of Peel's stand on the abolition of the Corn Laws, but was required to resign his seat and fight a by-election on his appointment to the cabinet. He then had a nasty shock, as the Duke of Newcastle, a fanatical supporter of the Corn Laws, refused to support his candidature at Newark, where he retained his influence as the virtual 'proprietor' of the seat. This put Gladstone in the anomalous and historically unique position of serving in the cabinet without being a member of either house.

Disraeli had left London in September 1845 for a lengthy visit to Belgium and France, reaching Paris in late November, so was absent as the crisis developed. He had long conversations with both François Guizot, the King's Chief Minister, and Louis Philippe himself. He rejoiced when Peel resigned in early December, and told the King he did not expect him to return. Anticipating that Palmerston would again become Foreign Secretary in the government which Lord John Russell was attempting to form, he wrote him a long letter recounting the conversations which he had had, doubtless in the hope of making a mark with him as someone of great influence with the rulers of France. He returned to London on 16 January, for the Queen's opening of Parliament six days later. There was no mention of the Corn Laws in the Queen's Speech, but Peel intervened in the subsequent debate, on 22 January, to explain the circumstances in which he had resumed office. He embarked upon a magisterial explanation of the necessity of abolition in the face of the Irish famine, which was already claiming hundreds of thousands of lives. (It was eventually estimated, by the Census Commissioners that 'nearly a million' perished, and over two million emigrated to the United States or Canada.) Peel's speech was heard in stony silence by the great mass of Tory squires sitting on the benches behind him. He was followed in the debate by the Leader of the Opposition, Lord John Russell, who gave an account of his own role, and the reasons why he had eventually concluded that he was unable to accept the Queen's invitation to form a government. He praised Peel for the way he had conducted himself during this period, and pledged that he and his party would support the passage of a bill to provide for the immediate abolition of the Corn Laws.

When Russell sat down there was only one MP who wished to continue the debate. It was the Member for Shrewsbury, Benjamin Disraeli. He had not originally intended to speak, having meant to wait until such time as the abolition bill was tabled, but felt provoked by the tone and content of Peel's intervention. He now extemporised a speech of great power and penetration. He made no reference at all to the Irish famine, but embarked on a direct attack on the Prime Minister for his perfidy in having fought the election five years previously on a platform of protectionism, and was now proposing the opposite. This was a betrayal, he argued, of the Conservative Party, which Peel had done so much to build up, and which had entrusted him with its confidence. He likened Peel's conduct to the actions of a Turkish admiral who had been entrusted with the command of the Ottoman fleet 'in the late war in the Levant':

> The Sultan personally witnessed the departure of the fleet; all the muftis prayed for the success of the expedition, as all the muftis prayed for the success of the last general election. Away went the fleet; but what was the Sultan's consternation, when the lord high admiral steered at once into the enemy's port.[16]

The House collapsed in raucous laughter, as it did again when Disraeli went on to say that the Tory Party had accepted Peel as 'a leader to accomplish the triumph of protectionism; and now we are to attend the catastrophe of protectionism ... Ours was a fine child,' he said.

> Who can forget how its nurse dandled it, fondled it? What a charming babe! Delicious little thing! Did you ever see such a beauty for its years? This was the tone, the innocent prattle. And then the nurse in a fit of patriotic frenzy, dashes its brains out, and comes down to give master and mistress an account of this terrible murder.[17]

The whole speech was one prolonged philippic against Peel, and an exhortation to Tory MPs to cleave to their traditional views rather than succumb to the arguments now advanced by their leader. He concluded,

> Let men stand by the principle by which they rise, right or wrong. I make no exception. If they be wrong, they must retire to that shade of private life with which our present rulers have so often threatened us ... Do not then because you see a great personage giving up his opinions, do not cheer him on – do not yield so ready a reward to political tergiversation. Above all, maintain the lines of demarcation between parties; for it is only by maintaining the independence of party that you can maintain the integrity of public men, and the power of influence of Parliament itself.[18]

When Disraeli sat down he was the recipient of several minutes' applause from serried ranks of Tory backbenchers, while Peel and his front-bench colleagues seemed stunned. Among the more enthusiastic back-bench MPs was Lord George Bentinck, who had sat in the House for 18 years, but had hitherto been a largely silent member, devoting the greater part of his time and energies to horseracing. He kept racing stables in three counties, was the owner of a horse called Crucifix – which in a single season (1840) won the Two Thousand Guineas, the One Thousand Guineas and the Oaks – and took the leading part in exposing the most notorious racing fraud of the nineteenth century, when in 1844 a four-year-old horse called Running Rein was passed off as a three-year-old and won the Derby. He was not previously acquainted with Disraeli, but he now approached him and proposed joining forces with him in an all-out attempt to defeat the Corn Law Abolition Bill, which Peel was about to table. They made a formidable team. Disraeli was by now regarded as the most accomplished orator in the Commons, while Bentinck, a leading figure in the Jockey Club, in the words of Peel's biographer, Norman Gash, 'now brought to the Protectionist cause the ruthless determination and singlemindedness which he had formerly shown in hunting down dishonest trainers and crooked jockeys on the Turf. Violent and unscrupulous by temperament he made up for his political inexperience by tenacity and force.'[19]

Known colloquially as 'the jockey and the Jew', they now set about marshalling the mass of Tory MPs into a distinct 'Protectionist party', with its own whips and office-holders, while backing extra-parliamentary groups, such as the Agricultural Protection Society and a new campaigning body known as the Anti-league (in opposition to the much longer-standing Anti-Corn Law League). Although Bentinck's own contributions to parliamentary debates were at times counter-productive because of the uncontrolled vehemence of his rhetoric, his organisational talents were an undoubted asset. His impeccable background as a leading aristocrat, the younger son of a duke, and close relative of two former prime ministers (his grandfather the 3rd Duke of Portland, and his uncle George Canning), also helped to set off remaining suspicions of Disraeli as a flashy upstart. Disraeli and Bentinck, who in the process became great friends, now carefully planned the protectionist strategy, designed to slow parliamentary progress on the Abolition Bill and to muster maximum opposition to it at every stage, while also aiming to ensure that if Peel succeeded in carrying the bill it would be a pyrrhic victory, with his own eviction from power following soon after. The debate on the second reading of the bill began on 9 February 1846, and continued for no less than 12 parliamentary days, much of it devoted to discussing a 'wrecking amendment' moved by two Protectionist MPs. The division finally took place on 27 February, when the bill was referred to a committee of the whole House. The government won the vote, by a majority of 97 in a House of 581 members present. But they won only with the support of 227 Whigs and Radicals. Of the Tories voting, only 112 supported Peel, while 242 followed Bentinck and Disraeli. These two continued to play a major role in the committee stage, in which Peel himself was the main spokesman for the government, and faced a continual onslaught from Disraeli in a series of venomous speeches, to which he had no ready response.

Nor was any other minister in a position to lend him support. The majority of the cabinet's 'big hitters' were in the Lords, and Gladstone – still without a parliamentary seat – was forced to watch impotently from the Strangers' Gallery while the leader he adored was pitilessly mauled. The experience left an enduring mark on him. Many years later, after Disraeli's death, John Morley, later Gladstone's biographer, asked him 'whether Disraeli's philippics were really as effective as people said. "Mr. G," he recorded, "said Disraeli's performances against Peel were quite as wonderful as report makes them. Peel altogether helpless in reply." Robert Blake quotes this in a lecture he gave at Cambridge in 1969, in which he asked, 'Is it possible that Gladstone's real hostility to Disraeli first stemmed from a sense of frustration at his own forced inability to answer on behalf of a chief to whom he was devoted?'[20]

Eventually, on 15 May 1846, the bill reached its third reading in the Commons. The debate was totally dominated by a three-hour speech by Disraeli, as full of wit as invective, which was long remembered as one of the finest of his career, and was received with rapture by a large majority of the occupants of the Tory benches. Yet he came within an ace of totally discrediting himself. Not confining himself to Peel's promotion of the Corn Bill, he launched a withering attack on the whole of the Prime Minister's political career, accusing him of never having any ideas of his own, but of consistently filching them from others: 'His life has been a great appropriation clause. He is a burglar of others' intellect ... there is no statesman who has committed petty larceny on so great a scale.'[21]

For once, Peel was ready with a potentially devastating reply. After referring to 'the continued venomous attacks of the Member for Shrewsbury', he continued,

> Sir, I will only say of that hon. Gentleman, that if he, after reviewing the whole of my public life – a life extending over thirty years previously to my accession to office in 1841 – if he then entertained the opinion of me which he now professes…it is a little surprising that in the spring of 1841, after his long experience of my public career, he should have been prepared to give me his confidence. It is still more surprising that he should have been ready – as I think he was – to unite his feelings with me in office, thus implying the strongest proof which any public man can give of confidence in the honour and integrity of a Minister of the Crown.[22]

Disraeli was stunned by Peel's *riposte*, but instead of ignoring Peel's words, and implicitly recognising that he had scored a rare debating point, he leapt to his feet and told a blatant lie. 'I can assure the House,' he said,

> that nothing of the kind ever occurred; I never shall – it is totally foreign to my nature – make an application for any place…I never asked a favour of the government, not even one of those mechanical things which persons are obliged to ask…and as regards myself I never directly or indirectly solicited office… It is very possible that if, in 1841, I had been offered office, I dare say it would have been a very slight office, but I dare say I would have accepted it… But with respect to my being a solicitor for office it is entirely unfounded…[23]

He was skating on extremely thin ice in making such a comprehensive denial, for not only had he implored Peel to give him office in 1841, but two years later had solicited a sinecure post for his brother Ralph, again unsuccessfully. Yet he got away with it, presumably gambling on the likelihood that Peel had not kept the incriminating letter. In fact he had, and his friend and colleague Lord Lincoln, who had walked to the House with Peel the same morning, claimed that he had actually seen the letter in the Prime Minister's dispatch case.[24] Peel, however, refrained from producing the letter and reading it out to the House, which would have destroyed Disraeli's credibility. Why he did so, we shall never know. Perhaps this proud but highly sensitive man concluded that it would be ungentlemanly to reveal the contents of what was intended as a private letter. Disraeli did not escape some damage to his reputation, at least in the short term. There was much muttering in the Carlton Club and in the parliamentary lobbies about Disraeli's conduct, and 'the general impression seems to have been adverse'.[25]

At the end of the debate, at 4 a.m. on 16 May, the bill received its third reading, with a majority of 98, more than two-thirds of the Tory MPs again voting against. The measure went up to the House of Lords, where it enjoyed a relatively easy passage, despite a rumbustious speech against by Lord Stanley. He otherwise refrained from making any very strenuous efforts to organise against the bill, and the Duke of Wellington succeeded in persuading a majority of Tory peers to vote in favour, or at least abstain. On 25 June 1846 the bill received its third reading, and became law. On the very same day, the government was defeated in the Commons on the second reading of the Irish Crimes Bill, a coercive measure firmly opposed by the Whigs and Radicals, but one which would in normal circumstances have been supported by the vast majority of Tories. In fact, 79 of them, vigorously urged on by Bentinck and Disraeli, voted against, in a clear act of 'revenge' against Peel's alleged 'treason'. Four days later he resigned, and went down to the House of Commons to deliver what was probably his greatest ever speech. His peroration was long remembered, and acted as his political epitaph:

> I shall leave a name execrated by every monopolist who...clamours for protection because it accrues to his individual benefit; but it may be that I shall leave a name sometimes remembered with expressions of goodwill in the abodes of those whose lot it is to labour, and to earn their daily bread in the sweat of their brow, when they shall recruit their exhausted strength with abundant and untaxed food, the sweeter because it is no longer leavened by a sense of injustice.[26]

Peel's hope was handsomely fulfilled: he remains the only Conservative peacetime leader to be widely revered by the working class. By contrast, the Conservative Party, of which he was the founder, has largely airbrushed him out of its history, blaming him rather than Bentinck or Disraeli for the 1846 split in the party which condemned it to spending the best part of a generation in opposition. Without Disraeli's and Bentinck's efforts, it is possible, even probable, that Peel might have been able to bludgeon the sullen majority of his party into accepting the repeal of the Corn Laws, and it is sometimes suggested that a less arrogant, less prickly, more clubbable man might have pulled it off, even in the face of their determined campaign. This seems highly unlikely. Yes, he might have been able to win round a few more of his opponents if he had shown more tact and made a personal effort, but the size of the majority against him strongly suggests that any such effect would have been marginal. Peel's intensely unflattering assessment of the mass of his fellow Tory MPs is a sufficient explanation of why he disdained to make a more serious attempt to woo them:

> How can those who spend their time in hunting and shooting and eating and drinking know what were the motives of those who are responsible for the public security, who have the best information, and have no other object under Heaven but to provide against danger, and consult the general interests of all classes![27]

On Peel's resignation, Lord John Russell was appointed Prime Minister, as leader of a minority Whig government. Peel and his followers were effectively excluded from the Conservative Party, which chose Lord George Bentinck as its leader in the Commons, while Lord Stanley eventually succeeded Wellington as leader in the Lords, and from 1848 was recognised as being the overall party leader. In the general election of 1847, Russell's Whigs, and their Radical and Irish allies, won 323 seats against 321 for the Conservatives, though the latter were divided between around 225 Protectionists and just under 100 Peelites. The Whig government remained in power, and had little difficulty in securing comfortable majorities in parliamentary votes, due to the deep split among their opponents. The Peelites included virtually all the most able Tory MPs, with the exception of Disraeli, which opened the way to his rapid promotion within what was left of the Conservative Party. Peel made no attempt to organise his followers into an effective opposition party, and conducted himself more as an elder-statesman figure, making very occasional parliamentary speeches, mostly on foreign affairs, where he was a severe critic of Palmerston, who was once again Foreign Secretary. On 29 June 1850, the day after he had excoriated Palmerston in one of his finest speeches, he went riding on Constitution Hill, between London's Green Park and Buckingham Palace. His horse suddenly stumbled, threw its rider and then fell heavily on top of him. Peel suffered injuries from which he died four days later, aged 62. Gladstone's hero, and Disraeli's victim, was no more…

# *Four*

# Party realignment, 1847–52

The general election of 1847 marked the beginning of a period of instability in British parliamentary politics. For more than a decade there was no overall one-party majority in the House of Commons, and each general election produced what would now be known as a 'hung Parliament', with minority governments or coalitions becoming the norm, a virtual three-party system having replaced the former Tory–Whig duopoly. There were henceforth three distinct party groupings in the Commons – the Whigs (with their Radical and Irish Nationalist allies), the Conservatives and the Peelites. The latter still considered themselves Conservatives, but were divided from their former associates both by their belief in free trade and, even more, by their repulsion at the treatment that Peel had received at the hands of Disraeli. Periodically, there were attempts to reunite the Tory Party, but they came to nothing, and eventually, before the 1857 general election, the surviving Peelites, of whom by then Gladstone was the leading figure, merged with the Whigs and Radicals to form the Liberal Party. The two-party system was effectively restored, and was to be reinforced by the 1867 Reform Act, which greatly enlarged the electorate and opened the way to more disciplined and more representative party formations.

Both Gladstone and Disraeli fought new seats in the 1847 election. Gladstone had been out of Parliament since December 1845, when he had resigned his Newark seat on appointment to the cabinet. After the Duke of Newcastle had blocked his return, he put out feelers to no fewer than ten other constituencies where he might fight a by-election, but to no avail. Finally he received an invitation to run in the general election from supporters at Oxford University, which – for nearly 350 years, between 1604 and 1950 – had the right to elect two members to represent it in the House of Commons. This distinction – which it shared with Cambridge University – made it one of the most unusual and prestigious of constituencies, and there was usually strong competition to represent it. As a distinguished scholar of the university, and given his great interest in and commitment to religion, Gladstone may have seemed a most likely candidate for the university, which was a stronghold of the Church of England, with a high proportion of the voters being clergymen. The franchise covered all graduates of the university. Eventually, three candidates were nominated for the two seats, all of them designated as Conservatives, as Whiggism received very little support at Oxford. The candidates were divided more on religious than political grounds, however. The most senior of them, Sir Robert Inglis, had represented the university since 1827, when he had defeated Sir Robert Peel, who was repudiated by the strongly Anglican electors for his about-turn on Catholic emancipation. Inglis was described by Roy Jenkins as 'a genial man of reactionary views ... he was impregnable in his seat'.[1] Gladstone was seen essentially as a High Church candidate, though he was also generally backed by the more 'liberal' voters. He was opposed by Professor Charles Round, a strong Evangelical, who was backed, among others, by Lord Ashley, later the 7th Earl of Shaftesbury, the famous Tory factory reformer, who described Gladstone as 'a mystified, slippery, uncertain, politico Churchman, a non-Romanist Jesuit'.[2] The 'scandal' of Helen Gladstone's conversion to Catholicism was also brought up against him, but he managed to hold off Round, and secure a reasonably comfortable second place:

| | |
|---|---|
| Sir R.H. Inglis (Conservative) | 1700 |
| W.E. Gladstone (Conservative) | 997 |
| C.G. Round (Conservative) | 824 |

One advantage of fighting a university constituency was that it was relatively cheap, the highly educated and generally affluent electorate being beyond the reach of bribery. Gladstone's expenses during the 1847 campaign, met exclusively by his father, amounted to £1350.[3] One vote which Gladstone found particularly difficult to attract was that of his eldest brother Tom, like himself a graduate of the university. Tom had remained a strong Evangelical, and disapproving of William's High Church views announced that he was proposing to vote for Professor Round. This provoked a ferocious reaction from John Gladstone, who insisted that Tom, who like William was entirely dependent financially on his father, should put family solidarity before religious principle. He meekly conformed. John Gladstone's ambition had been that all his four sons should become Tory MPs, and sit with him simultaneously in the Commons. It was only partially fulfilled. Both Tom and his third son, John Nielson, secured election on several occasions, but for insecure seats, and neither made much of a mark in the House. The much abler second son, Robertson, a more independent character, resisted his father's pressure to fight a number of promising constituencies, pleading ill health, though he did serve as Mayor of Liverpool in 1842. Robertson took over much of his father's business interests as the patriarch grew older, but he progressively liberated himself from his stern Tory principles, becoming a Liberal long before William took the same course.

As for Disraeli, he was able to abandon his Shrewsbury seat and seek election as one of the three county MPs for Buckinghamshire. This was a direct result of his newly won popularity among the large number of country gentleman on the Tory benches, which prompted this quintessentially urban figure to seek to emulate them. He acquired a small country house and estate at Hughenden near his father's (rented) home at Bradenham, and was elected unopposed, along with two other Tories, for the Buckinghamshire constituency. This provided him, for the first time, with a secure political base, and he continued to represent the seat, usually unopposed, for almost 30 years, until his elevation to the House of Lords, in August 1876. Disraeli began negotiations to buy Hughenden in March 1846, and agreed a price of £34,950 the following year, but the deal was not completed until 1848. It was way beyond his means, and even Mary Anne's, who was stretching herself to help repay his debts. Nor was his legacy from his father, who died in 1848, sufficient to make up the difference. Lord George Bentinck and his two brothers came to his help by advancing him a loan of £25,000, which Disraeli never expected to have to repay.

Hughenden Manor, which today belongs to the National Trust, was, according to its official guide book, originally 'a plain, white-painted Georgian house', which was transformed by Mary Anne Disraeli 'into the neo-Gothic building of brick finials, vaulted ceilings and plush furniture we know today'.[4] Here Disraeli used to refresh himself during the long parliamentary recesses, strolling in the woods, planting trees and admiring the proud peacocks which strutted on the terraces. He loved to play the country squire, and became a local magistrate and a regular worshipper at the parish church, of which he was the patron, but declined to take his aping of aristocratic ways to ridiculous lengths, and refrained from adopting their traditional pastimes of hunting, shooting or fishing (unlike Gladstone, who recorded in his diaries having blown off the top of his left forefinger in a shooting accident in 1842).

Disraeli remained on the closest of terms with Bentinck, and effectively acted under him as deputy Tory leader in the House of Commons. Yet Bentinck's own leadership was shortlived. Although he was a fanatical protectionist, he otherwise held quite liberal views, notably on religious toleration, which did not endear him to many of his followers. An early cause of dissension was a move by the new Prime Minister, Lord John Russell, to permit Jews to sit in the House of Commons. Russell was elected as an MP for the City of London, his fellow Whig, Baron Lionel de Rothschild, winning the other seat. Russell moved a bill to allow Rothschild to take a Jewish oath, rather than the prescribed 'Church and State oath', to enable him to take his seat. A large majority of the Whigs voted for the measure, but very few Tories, though these included both Bentinck and Disraeli. To the general surprise, Gladstone also spoke and voted in favour, which got him into severe trouble with his university electors. Gladstone was to recall, many years later, how impressed Russell had been by Disraeli on that occasion – 'I remember once sitting next to John Russell when D. was making a speech on Jewish emancipation. "Look at him," said J.R., "how manfully he sticks to it, tho' he knows that every word he is saying is gall and wormwood to every man who sits around and behind him."'[5] Nor did the reason Disraeli advanced for his action do anything to endear him to his fellow Tories. He concluded his speech by saying,

I cannot sit in this House with any misconception of my opinion on this subject. Whatever may be the consequences on the seat I hold…I cannot, for one, give a vote which is not in deference to what I believe to be the true principles of religion. Yet, it is as a Christian that I will not take upon me the awful responsibility of excluding from the legislature those who are from the religion in the bosom of which my Lord and Saviour was born.[6]

The bill was passed, but was thrown out by the Lords, and Rothschild and his co-religionists had to wait until 1858 before they could take their seats in the Commons. Bentinck was so disgusted by the small-mindedness of his fellow Tories, which he described to Disraeli as 'the tea table twaddling of a pack of Old Maids…when the greatest Commercial Empire of the world is engaged in a life and death struggle for existence', that he resigned the party leadership six days after the vote, on 23 December 1847. He told J.W. Croker, a leading Tory politician and essayist, that he preferred not to wait until he was 'cashiered'.[7] After his resignation, Bentinck's health quickly deteriorated, and within a year he died from a heart attack while walking near his Welbeck Abbey home, on 11 September 1848. He was only 46 years old. Disraeli was greatly affected by his death, and embarked upon writing a long, lively but laudatory biography, published in 1852 under the title *Lord George Bentinck: A political biography*.

When Bentinck resigned the Tory leadership in the Commons, Disraeli might reasonably have expected to be chosen as his successor, as he was head and shoulders above any other Tory MP, both as a speaker and as a parliamentary tactician. But the overall party leader, Lord Stanley, exerted himself to prevent this. He wanted to be fully consulted by the Tory leader in the Commons, and he disapproved of Disraeli on social grounds, regarding him as an opportunistic *parvenu*. He also feared that Disraeli's leadership would forestall any possibility of reunion with the Peelites, who had been appalled by the vehemence of his attacks on Peel. He therefore agreed with Bentinck that the new leader should be the Marquess of Granby, an unexceptionable Tory aristocrat, and he was duly elected by the protectionist MPs. Granby, the elder brother of Disraeli's friend Lord John Manners and heir to the Duke of Rutland, was lacking in self-confidence, and refused to serve, which meant that for the whole of the 1848–9 session the party was leaderless in the Commons. Yet Stanley continued to look elsewhere, and proposed John Herries, a veteran ex-civil servant who had served in Peel's 1834–5 government. But Herries, too, was diffident, and Stanley eventually acquiesced in an agreement that the party should be led in the Commons by a triumvirate of Granby, Herries and Disraeli. This arrangement was contemptuously described by the editor of the *Morning Post* as an attempt 'to place the leader of the Conservative party like a sandwich between two pieces of bread (very stale bread – Herries and Granby), in order that he might be made fit for squeamish throats to swallow'.[8] Disraeli, however, comported himself as if he were the sole leader, and the other two quietly effaced themselves, but it was only in 1851 that Stanley was prepared to accept him as leader, and another two years before he brought himself to invite him to a house party at his seat at Knowsley Hall, where other leading protectionists had been regular visitors over a long period. Despite this unpromising beginning, Stanley (who in 1851 became the 14th Earl of Derby, on the death of his father) and Disraeli were to work together, as respective party leaders in the two houses, with surprising harmony for the best part of two decades.

In May 1848, Disraeli met the great Austrian former Foreign Minister and Chancellor Prince Klemens von Metternich, in temporary exile following the wave of revolutions which shook Austria and many other European states. The two men held lengthy discussions, and Disraeli was greatly influenced by the cynical and worldly views of the man who had dominated European politics for forty years. He told the Earl of Stanhope that had Metternich 'not been a Prince and a Prime Minister, he would have been a great professor', and he ever after described himself as Metternich's 'faithful scholar'.[9]

Meanwhile Gladstone, now an ex-cabinet minister, was going through a period of great stress and instability. He had not particularly distinguished himself, as Roy Jenkins, citing John Morley's comprehensive biography, makes clear, saying that he was 'at best an indifferent Colonial Secretary'.[10] He mentions his 'unfortunate advocacy of the resumption of convict dispatch to Australia', and his 'clumsy sacking of the Governor of Tasmania'.[11] More generally, his effectiveness was greatly reduced by his not being in a position to defend his policies in the House of Commons. Colin Matthew, however, credits him with speeding the pace towards self-government of colonial territories, especially in the case of New Zealand.[12]

On his return to the Commons in July 1847, Gladstone did not initially play a very active role. For several years his life was dominated by personal and family problems which took a heavy toll on his time and attention. Some of these were caused by the improvidence and lethargy of his brother-in-law, Sir Stephen Glynne. He was the part-owner of the Oak Farm brick and iron works near Stourbridge, which went bankrupt in 1847. This had a devastating effect on the family finances, and even put in jeopardy his continued ownership of the Hawarden estate. Gladstone, who on his marriage had taken up residence there with Catherine, now moved sharply to take over control of Glynne's affairs. Over a period of years, he managed to re-establish them with financial help from his own father, now known as Sir John Gladstone, having been created a baronet by Peel in his resignation honours in 1846, more a tribute to his son than to himself. Glynne continued to live at Hawarden, nominally as head of the household, but he was gradually superseded by Gladstone as the chatelain of Hawarden, and after Sir Stephen's death in 1874 bought out the remaining members of the family. The estate is owned today by Sir William Gladstone, Bart., a descendant of Gladstone's eldest brother Tom. Sir William also owns Sir John Gladstone's Scottish estate, at Fasque.

Gladstone's own family increased rapidly during the first 15 years of his marriage, with Catherine undergoing nine pregnancies, one of which resulted in a miscarriage. Their first child was William Henry, born in 1840, followed by Agnes (1842), Stephen Edward (1844), Catherine Jessy (1845), Mary (1847), Helen (1849), Henry Neville (1852) and Herbert John (1854). Gladstone was an affectionate father who took his parental duties very seriously. He was greatly affected by the death of Jessy, aged five, in April 1850, and in October of the same year, much concerned by the poor health of Mary, he and Catherine, several months pregnant, took her on a visit to Naples which lasted four months. Mary's health responded well, though Catherine suffered a miscarriage during what proved to be a somewhat hectic visit. While in Naples, Gladstone attended the trial of a leading liberal opponent of the Bourbon régime and visited a notorious prison where prisoners were kept in appalling conditions. On his return to London, he published two indignant *Letters to Lord Aberdeen*,[13] a former Foreign Secretary who, since the death of Peel in July 1850, was the recognised leader of the Peelites. In these, Gladstone condemned the

69

Kingdom of the Two Sicilies as 'the negation of God erected into a system of government'. Gladstone's published letters deeply embarrassed Aberdeen, who had no wish to be involved in the controversy, but they gave Gladstone an overnight international reputation. He was seen by conservatives throughout Europe as a dangerous supporter of revolutionaries, but was heroised by liberals. It was the first of many passionate pronouncements by Gladstone on foreign affairs, which sat ill with his domestic reputation as a cautious politician who still considered himself a Conservative. One of Gladstone's less admiring biographers, Professor Richard Shannon, criticised him for his 'absurd' and disproportionate response, noting that Naples was a good deal less oppressive than other European regimes, such as Austria, which, with the aid of Russian troops, had brutally suppressed the Hungarian revolution in 1848.[14]

During this period Gladstone continued to be anguished over his attitude to religion and its interaction with politics. By 1845, his family biographer, Professor Checkland, noted, 'William had entirely abandoned the basic position of his book [*The State in its Relations with the Church*] and had become an advocate of a liberal view of religion.'[15] In 1850 an event occurred which even led him to question whether the Church of England should remain the 'established church', or if it would not be better for it to sever its links with, and dependence on, the Queen and Parliament. This was the so-called 'Gorham judgment' by the Judicial Committee of the Privy Council. The Rev. G.C. Gorham, a Low Church clergyman, had been nominated to the living of Brampford Speke in Devon by the Lord Chancellor, who was the patron of the parish. Yet the Bishop of Exeter, Henry Phillpotts, refused to install him, on the grounds that his views on baptism were heretical. Gorham appealed against the Bishop's decision through a series of ecclesiastical courts, which finally ruled in favour of the Bishop. Gorham then took the matter to a lay court, the Judicial Committee of the Privy Council, which overruled the Church authorities and insisted that Gorham should be duly installed. Gladstone was appalled that the Church was unable to make its own decision on a matter of religious doctrine, and together with a number of other prominent Anglo–Catholic laymen helped to prepare a rousing declaration of protest to be submitted to the entire bench of bishops. It was not long, however, before he began to get cold feet, and he eventually withheld his own signature from the declaration. Perhaps it was because he had doubts as to whether it was appropriate for him, as a Privy Councillor, to sign a denunciation of the Council's Judicial Committee. However, Roy Jenkins, who discussed the issue at some length in his biography, thought his refusal owed more to 'a more general and uncharacteristic sense of caution and tactics'.[16] Whatever his motive, many of his close associates in High Church circles felt badly let down by him. These included his closest friend, James Hope Scott, and Henry Manning. Some 13 months later, both defected to the Roman Catholic Church on the same day, which had a devastating effect on Gladstone. Like John Henry Newman, who had preceded him by six years, Manning was subsequently made a cardinal. For the last 27 years of his life, he served as a highly influential and controversial Archbishop of Westminster, combining the most extreme ultramontane doctrinal views with liberal attitudes on social issues. He and Gladstone had no personal contact whatever for ten years after his defection, but later resumed a somewhat forced, wary and very spasmodic acquaintance. Gladstone remained in the Church of England, but his turmoil over the Gorham affair undoubtedly made it easier for him to contemplate disestablishment of the Anglican Church of Ireland. He carried this out through the Irish Church Act of 1869, during his first government.

In 1848, the 'year of revolutions' in Europe, Gladstone served as a special constable during the giant Chartist demonstration in London. Many respectable citizens feared the European revolutions would spark off similar violent disturbances in Britain, but the demonstration in London passed off peacefully, and proved to be the 'swansong' of the Chartist movement, which petered out shortly after. The following year he embarked on a highly quixotic mission, travelling some 3010 miles over 27 days to Paris, Marseilles, Naples, Rome, Milan, Geneva, Lake Como and back in pursuit of Lady 'Suzie' Lincoln. She was the errant wife of his friend and political colleague the Earl of Lincoln, who, after 17 years of marriage, had abandoned her husband and five children and eloped to Italy with her lover, Lord Walpole, a descendant of the first Prime Minister, by whom she had become pregnant. Gladstone's objective was to persuade 'Suzie' to renounce her sin and return to her family, but – failing that – to collect sufficient evidence to enable Lincoln to promote a private parliamentary bill to dissolve the marriage, the only legal way in which, at that time, he could obtain a divorce. At each stage of the journey, Lady Lincoln refused to see him, and after she had given birth to a baby boy Gladstone abandoned the chase and busied himself with collecting evidence, for which he 'enlisted the services of the governor of the province, the chief of police, the landlord of his hotel, the midwife'.[17] In his diary, Gladstone mused,

> Oh that poor miserable Lady L. – once the dream of dreams, the image that to my young age combined everything the earth could offer of beauty and joy. What is she now! But may that Spotless Sacrifice whereof I partook, unworthy as I am, today avail for her, to the washing away of sin and to the renewal of the image of God.[18]

Gladstone gave evidence to the House of Lords committee examining the bill, and the divorce was finally granted on 14 August 1850. Lady Lincoln was soon abandoned by Walpole, a notorious rake, became an opium addict, and gave up her baby to the care of Italian nuns. On 5 October 1855 Gladstone wrote to his brother Robertson that she had died.[19] He was misinformed: she subsequently married a Belgian farmer, and in 1881, now known as Lady Susan Opdebeck, she turned up at 10 Downing Street and demanded to see the Prime Minister. An astonished Gladstone recorded in his diary that 'after some 32 or 33 years I felt something and could say much.'[20] He entered into a correspondence with her and exerted himself to ensure that the 7th Duke of Newcastle, her grandson, should pay her an allowance of £400 a year, on which she lived with her husband at Burgess Hill, Sussex until her death, aged 75, in 1889.

Lady Lincoln was not the only 'fallen woman' that Gladstone endeavoured to redeem during this period of his life. During the months of May, June and August 1850 he recorded in his diary 16 occasions on which he had accosted prostitutes on London streets and attempted to persuade them to give up their way of life.[21] Shannon notes that one such encounter was 'after the occasion of the Royal Academy dinner, where Gladstone sat next to Disraeli, who was "very easy and agreeable". Doubtless Disraeli would have been intrigued had he known of his prim neighbour's post-prandial plans.'[22]

On two of the 16 occasions Gladstone annotated his diary entries with a symbolic representation of a whip, which indicated he had flagellated himself in an attempt to purge any carnal thoughts or actions to which he may have succumbed. In general, his night-time activities tended to increase both in number and fervour during periods of stress in his life, resulting from religious or family problems.

Despite many personal distractions, Gladstone gradually resumed his role as a leading front-bench politician. After the death of Peel, in July 1850, the Earl of Aberdeen became the acknowledged leader of the Peelites, while Sir James Graham, the former Home Secretary, took the leading role in the Commons. Gladstone, Sidney Herbert, the former War Secretary, and the ageing former Chancellor of the Exchequer, Henry Goulburn, were his most senior colleagues. Lord John Russell's minority Whig government was dependent on the Peelites' support to get its legislation through Parliament, and Russell made spasmodic attempts to lure them into his team. Yet they still regarded themselves as Conservatives, and most of them remained aloof, with the exception of Peel's second son, Frederick, who accepted a junior ministerial appointment. In December 1851, John Gladstone died at his Scottish home, four days short of his eighty-seventh birthday. William was at the bedside of his formidable father, and recorded in his diary that 'I thrice kissed my Father's cheek and forehead before and after his death: the only kisses I can remember.'[23] His mother had died 16 years earlier at the age of 64. Henceforth Gladstone regarded himself as the head of the family, though he was the youngest of four brothers. The second brother, Robertson, continued to manage the family businesses on behalf of his siblings.

Disraeli was at this time far more singlemindedly committed to his political career than Gladstone. He worked very hard as Tory leader in the Commons, spending long hours every day in the chamber, and voraciously consuming government blue books and other official documents in order to inform himself on virtually any issue which might emerge in parliamentary debates. Given the paucity of talent on the Tory benches, it was necessary for him to intervene much more frequently in debates than would be normal for a party leader. He was a highly resourceful parliamentary tactician, but was severely restrained by Stanley, who would seldom countenance opportunist deals with Radicals and Irish MPs in attempts to detach them from their support of the Whigs. His long relationship with Stanley, which Robert Blake describes as 'an incongruous partnership',[24] is a fascinating story. Stanley was only five years his senior, but appeared to be much older. Born in 1799, he was very much an eighteenth-century-style politician, born into a grand

and immensely wealthy Whig family. He was a leading figure in Earl Grey's Whig government, in 1830–4, and was widely expected to be his successor. He dashed his chances, however, by resigning from the cabinet in protest against moves to abolish the compulsory payment of tithes to the Anglican Church in Ireland, and subsequently joined the Tories. He entered Sir Robert Peel's government as Secretary for War and Colonies in 1841, effectively becoming Peel's closest associate before disagreeing with him over the abolition of the Corn Laws. Perhaps the finest debater in the House of Commons, his influence was somewhat reduced when – on account of ill health (he was a persistent sufferer from gout) – he accepted a peerage in 1844, as Lord Stanley of Bickerstaffe. Nevertheless, when the party split in 1846, with the virtual expulsion of the Peelites, there was no other conceivable candidate for the Tory leadership, which he was to hold for 22 years. Despite his great abilities, he was by no means ideally fitted for the role. A man of strong convictions, he was, at best, only semi-committed to front-line politics. He had too many other interests – horseracing (the Derby was named after his family and it was his life-long ambition, never fulfilled, that one of his many horses should win the race), classics (he wrote an admired translation of *The Iliad*), the Church of England, country pursuits (hunting and shooting), card-playing and visiting the grand houses of fellow aristocrats, to name a few. The novelist and Tory MP Sir Edward Bulwer-Lytton, later a minister in his third government, summed up Derby (he became the Earl of Derby after his father's death in 1852) in his political poem *The New Timon*: 'The brilliant chief, irregularly great, Frank, haughty, rash, the Rupert of debate.'[25]

The reference was to the dashing Cavalier commander in the Civil War, Prince Rupert of the Rhine, and to a speech Disraeli had made in 1844, replying to one by Stanley. 'The noble lord,' he said, 'in this case, as in so many others, is the Prince Rupert of parliamentary discussion; his charge is resistless; but when he returns from pursuit he always finds his camp in the possession of the enemy.'[26]

Despite Derby's initial reservations, he and Disraeli gradually came to respect and even like each other, but they never became at all close. Even after 20 years, according to Robert Blake, Derby still began his letters 'My dear Disraeli', who replied at first to 'dear Lord Stanley', then to 'my dear Lord', but did not go beyond that. It was not until the end of 1853 that he was invited to Knowsley. Stanley, though pressed from time to time with suitable deference, never visited Hughenden.[27]

They often disagreed, but would discuss their differences with candour, and in the end Disraeli almost always deferred, with more or less good grace. He would grumble at times to his intimates, but was never disloyal to his chief. On a number of occasions, Derby prevented him from taking potentially fruitful initiatives, but at least equally often he dissuaded him from foolish ones. As an experienced former senior minister, he had a much better sense than Disraeli of the practical difficulties of introducing new policies, and as he grew older became progressively more cautious, leaving far behind the impetuosity of his youth. For most of the two decades of their partnership, Derby's relations with Disraeli could fairly be described as correct but distant. It was a different matter with his son and heir, Edward Henry Stanley, who, at the age of 22, had succeeded Lord George Bentinck as Tory MP for King's Lynn. Less gifted than his father, but more level-headed and much more liberal, he was enchanted by Disraeli, and became one of his most devoted and admiring supporters. In January 1851 he visited Disraeli at Hughenden, taking long country walks with him, talking politics nearly all the time, though he discovered – he reported in a long letter to his father – that Disraeli's other main preoccupation was religion. 'I mean by this,' he wrote,

> 'the origin of the various beliefs which have governed mankind, their changes at different epochs, and those still to come.' On the historical aspects he had no disagreement, but Disraeli 'seemed to think that the sentiment, or instinct of religion, would, by degrees … vanish as knowledge becomes more widely spread'. [Edward] Stanley hoped that the anticipation was 'unfounded'.[28]

Disraeli went on to reveal himself as a Zionist ahead of his time. According to young Stanley, he spoke 'with great apparent earnestness' about 'restoring the Jews to their own land'. The Holy Land, he explained,

> might be bought from Turkey: money would be forthcoming; the Rothschilds and leading Hebrew capitalists would all help: the Turkish empire was falling into ruin: the Turkish Govt would do anything for money: all that was necessary was to establish colonies, with rights over the soil and security from ill treatment. The question of nationality might wait until these had taken hold. He added that these ideas were extensively entertained among the [Jewish] nation. A man who should carry them out would be the next Messiah, the true Saviour of his people.[29]

75

The Russell government was weak and quarrelsome, and was not generally expected to last long. Disraeli, however, thought it would be difficult to dislodge, saying in an aphorism, which like many of his quips prefigured the paradoxical wit of Oscar Wilde, 'It might last as long as it liked. It was a weak government, and therefore durable. Strong governments always fell to pieces.'[30]

Disraeli's prediction might well have proved true, but for a major misjudgement by the Prime Minister. He reacted with unaccustomed fury to a move by Pope Pius IX, in the autumn of 1850, to re-establish the Catholic hierarchy in England. The Pope issued a papal bull dividing the country into 12 territorial bishoprics, and appointed Nicholas Wiseman as the Cardinal Archbishop of Westminster and Primate of the Church in Great Britain. There was an immediate outcry by leading Protestants, and Lord John sought to put himself at the head of the protests, writing an open letter to the Bishop of Durham, denouncing what he called an 'act of aggression by the Pope'. He then introduced a bill, entitled the Ecclesiastical Titles Bill, making it a criminal offence for Catholic priests to accept geographical titles. The motion introducing the bill was carried overwhelmingly by the House of Commons, by a margin of 438 to 95. However, the minority was made up of the very groups on which Russell depended to keep his government in power – the Peelites, the Irish and many of the Radicals. The Irish were opposed because they were overwhelmingly Roman Catholic, the Peelites and the Radicals because they believed in religious toleration. Russell was soon to pay dearly for alienating them: on 20 February 1851, the government was defeated on a motion to equalise the voting franchise in borough and county constituencies, in a vote in which the Conservatives abstained. He immediately submitted his resignation to the Queen, who sent for Lord Stanley. Stanley, painfully aware of the paucity of talent on the Tory benches, initially declined her invitation to form a government, and advised her to 'induce the Peelites to coalesce with Russell'.[31] Nothing came of this suggestion, and Stanley eventually agreed to have a try. He then made strenuous attempts to recruit the Peelites himself, especially Gladstone, to whom he offered any post in the government except the Foreign Secretaryship, but they declined to serve unless he was willing specifically to abandon protectionism. This he was unwilling to do, and after five days of fruitless negotiations, during which he discovered that even several of the abler Tories were unwilling to serve, he threw in his hand, and the Queen then successfully pressed Russell to resume office. This he did, but the whole episode had grievously undermined his own authority. Disraeli was bitterly disappointed, and took the failure to form a Tory government much harder than Stanley. The latter had been half-hearted in his endeavours, and was only too pleased to get back to his country pleasures. For Disraeli, trying to replace the Russell government was his daily preoccupation, and he was now greatly disheartened, and for a brief while contemplated throwing up politics altogether and pursuing a full-time literary career. This mood did not last long, at least partly because he feared the consequences of giving up his parliamentary seat, and thus again exposing himself to the risk of imprisonment for debt. At this time he was also suffering from marital difficulties with Mary Anne, who suspected him, probably justifiably, of infidelity. In July 1849, Disraeli wrote to his sister Sarah that he had moved temporarily into a hotel to escape Mary Anne's wrath. When he returned home, he had 'found all of my private locks forced — but instead of love letters, there were only lawyers' bills and pecuniary documents. [These] may yet produce some mischief – but I hope not... Still there had been violent temper and scenes.'[32]

The trouble with Mary Anne blew over, but Disraeli continued to have a hard time fending off his creditors. Then, in early 1851, a letter arrived out of the blue which gave a faint glimmer of hope that his difficulties might eventually be resolved. It came from a wealthy widow, Mrs Brydges Willyams, living in Torquay, whose maiden name had been da Costa, and was the last living descendant of a famous family of Sephardic Jews. She had long been an admirer of Disraeli's, and had previously written to him several times expressing support for his political views. Disraeli had never bothered to reply. But this letter was altogether a different matter: it was, she wrote, about a 'private subject':

> I am about to make my Will, and I have to ask, as a great favour, that you will oblige me by being one of the executors ... I think it right to add that whoever are my executors will also be my residuary legatees, and that the interest they will take under my will, although not a considerable one, will at all events be substantial.[33]

Intrigued, Disraeli consulted the recently republished volume of his father's *Curiosities of Literature*, to which he had contributed a preface in which he had quite fortuitously made a favourable reference to the da Costa family. He hastened to send her a copy, together with one of his own novel *Tancred*, which had glorified the Jewish race. He described this as 'a vindication, and I hope, a complete one, of the race from which we alike spring'.[34] This was the first of more than 250 letters which he wrote to her over the next dozen years, supplemented by annual visits, accompanied by Mary Anne, to Torquay. He readily agreed to the only condition she had set, which was that she should be buried in a vault at his home at Hughenden. His diligence was eventually rewarded: when she died in 1863, he inherited around £40,000. This was not enough totally to clear his debts, but it eased his situation significantly, and thereafter he was free of pressing financial worries.

One of Russell's major problems was the insubordination of his Foreign Minister, Lord Palmerston MP. Palmerston had grown used to running the Foreign Office, with virtually no control by the Prime Minister, in his earlier stint under Lord Melbourne, and he continued to do so under Russell. An imperious character, he treated foreign governments, and even monarchs, with little concern for diplomatic niceties, which Russell deprecated but caused concern to Queen Victoria and Prince Albert. Russell attempted to shuffle him out of the Foreign Office by offering to go up to the Lords himself and making Palmerston Leader of the Commons. This he flatly refused to discuss, his public and parliamentary reputation having been greatly boosted by the Don Pacifico affair in 1850.

Don Pacifico, a Portuguese Jew who claimed to be British (as he was born in Gibraltar), had made a largely fraudulent claim against the Greek government for damage to his property during a riot in Athens. When the Greeks refused to pay, Palmerston had sent a fleet to blockade Piraeus, which forced the hand of Greek government but also provoked an international crisis. Palmerston was censured by the House of Lords, but when a similar motion was tabled in the Commons, and was widely supported across the House, Palmerston routed his critics with a powerful speech, concluding with the words, 'As the Roman, in days of old, held himself free of indignity, when he could say "Civis romanus sum" ["I am a Roman"]; so also a British subject, in whatever land he may be, shall feel confident that the watchful eye and the strong arm of England will protect him against injustice and wrong.'[35]

Palmerston's speech provoked a strong jingoistic backlash, and he became something of a national hero overnight. He now regarded himself as untouchable, but he reluctantly agreed to the Queen's demand that he should in future submit all proposed actions and dispatches for her approval before implementing them. Then, in December 1851, he went too far, publicly endorsing Louis-Napoleon Bonaparte's coup d'état, overthrowing the Second Republic in France after the cabinet had agreed to take a neutral stance. Russell's patience finally snapped, and he peremptorily dismissed Palmerston, replacing him with Earl Granville, the Whig leader in the Lords. Two months later, in February 1852, Palmerston got his 'tit-for-tat', in his own words, when he moved a hostile amendment to the government's Militia Bill, securing its defeat in a parliamentary vote. Russell immediately resigned, and the Queen called upon Stanley (who had recently succeeded his father to become the 14th Earl of Derby) to form a new government.

This time Derby acted with much greater determination. Realising from his earlier attempt that there was little chance of attracting Peelite support – unless he was ready to renounce protectionism – he set his cap instead at Palmerston, whom he correctly identified as the most conservative of the Whigs. He offered him any post in the projected government apart from the Foreign Secretaryship, to which Queen Victoria would not agree. As an added inducement, he offered also the leadership of the House of Commons, which Disraeli helpfully volunteered to cede to him. 'Palmerston would not like to serve under me, who[m] he looks upon as a whipper-snapper,' he wrote to Derby, who replied that he would 'never forget the self sacrifice'.[36] Palmerston was tempted by the offer, and went to Derby's house in St James's Square to discuss it with him. In the end, however, he politely declined, for reasons described by his modern biographer James Chambers.[37] He had reluctantly concluded that his reputation, particularly among his many Radical supporters, would be gravely damaged if he was seen to cross the floor of the Commons purely in order to achieve office, without being accompanied by any other Whigs and without achieving any reversal of Tory policies. He implied to Derby that he would reconsider

79

the offer if the Tories were prepared to abandon protectionism and if other Whigs were also invited.

These were steps that Derby was not – *yet* – willing to take, so he was forced to form a wholly Tory government, which would be heavily outnumbered in the House of Commons. Disraeli was confirmed as Leader of the House, and would have much preferred to combine this with either the Foreign or the Home Secretaryship. Derby, however, had other ideas, and pressed him to become Chancellor of the Exchequer. When Disraeli demurred, claiming that he had 'no knowledge' of Treasury affairs, Derby retorted, 'You know as much as Mr. Canning did. They give you the figures.' (George Canning, better known as a longstanding Foreign Secretary, combined the post of Chancellor with the Prime Ministership in the last four months of his life.) If Disraeli had misgivings about becoming Chancellor, they were not shared by his wife, still besotted by him despite her recent suspicions. Addressing the envelope proudly to 'The Right Honourable the Chancellor of the Exchequer,' she sent a note to 11 Downing Street: 'Bless you, my darling, your own devoted wife wishes you joy. I hope you will make as good a Chancellor of the Exchequer as you have been a husband to your affectionate MARY ANNE.'[38]

Apart from Disraeli, Derby had very little talent to draw upon for other ministerial posts. The Foreign Secretary was the Earl of Malmesbury, best known as Derby's favourite shooting companion on his Knowsley estate, and most of the other appointees were virtually unknown. Indeed, the government became known as the Who? Who? government, after the hard-of-hearing Duke of Wellington had repeatedly queried the unfamiliar names when a list of the cabinet members was read out to him. Derby had to put up with a great deal of ridicule about some of the more obscure choices. Lady Clanricarde, the wife of a rather raffish Whig peer, asked him at a dinner party, 'are you sure, Lord Derby, that Sir John Pakington (the new Colonial Secretary) is a *real* man?' and was disconcerted when he coolly replied, 'Well I think so – he has been married three times.' Apart from Disraeli, the ablest member of the cabinet was probably Spencer Walpole, the Home Secretary, a collateral descendant of Sir Robert Walpole and nephew of the assassinated Prime Minister Spencer Perceval, after whom he had been named. The cabinet also included Disraeli's friend from Young England days, Lord John

Manners, while Derby's son Edward, now known by the courtesy title of Lord Stanley, became Under-secretary for Foreign Affairs. The government took office on 23 February 1852. Derby's objective was to govern calmly in a non-controversial manner in the hope of building up confidence with the electorate and winning a majority at the subsequent general election, to which he was committed in the summer of 1852. In the meantime, he eschewed introducing any protectionist measures. Disraeli, however, wanted to go much further than this, and urged Derby formally to repudiate protectionism, which he was sure would prove an electoral handicap to his party, as well as acting as a major barrier to reunion with the Peelites. Though he had been happy to use protectionism as the means to destroy Peel, he had never – unlike both Bentinck and Derby – believed in it as a matter of faith. Derby had no illusions about this, telling Prince Albert that 'He did not think that Mr. Disraeli had ever had a strong feeling, one way or the other, about Protection or Free Trade, and that he would make a very good Free Trade Minister.'[39]

Derby refused to take Disraeli's advice, and was determined to stick with his party's traditional policies at least until they had been decisively repudiated by the voters. The election was duly held in July 1852, and the Conservatives made numerous gains, largely at the expense of the Peelites, but remained in a minority. Both Disraeli and Gladstone were re-elected in their constituencies, each of them coming second. The new membership of the House of Commons was analysed by Derby in a memorandum which he sent to Prince Albert, as follows: '286 Conservatives, 150 Radicals, 120 Whigs, 50 in the Irish Brigade and 30 Peelites'. Derby then made a major pitch to the Peelites, concentrating in particular on Lord Aberdeen and on Gladstone, who had pursued a policy of benevolent neutrality towards the government prior to the election. Derby now made the grand gesture of renouncing protectionism. Speaking in the House of Lords in November 1852, he admitted that 'a very large majority of the British people…no longer sought a reimposition of the Corn Laws…On the part, then, of myself and my colleagues, I bow to the decision of the country.'[40]

His concession came too late. The Peelites – or most of them – were no longer interested in reuniting the Conservative Party. They were looking instead to co-operate more closely with the Whigs. Derby discussed the situation with the Queen and, in more detail, with Prince Albert, who discouraged any further dealings with Palmerston, whom he bracketed with Disraeli for the 'laxity of his political conscience'. But he strongly recommended a further approach to Gladstone, of whom he said, 'whatever his political crochets may be, he is a man of the strictest feelings of honour and the purest mind.'[41]

Albert suggested that he should be made Leader of the Commons in place of Disraeli, but Derby demurred, saying that he was 'quite unfit' for the post, and had none of that 'decision, boldness, readiness and clearness necessary'. He added that he 'could not in honour sacrifice Mr. Disraeli, who had acted very straightforwardly to him as long as they had anything to do with each other, and who possessed the confidence of his followers. Mr. Disraeli had no idea of giving up the lead.'[42]

In the autumn of 1852, Disraeli committed an unfortunate *gaffe*, which revived much of the distrust which he had done so much to live down. The Duke of Wellington died at 83, and of the many tributes paid to him, Disraeli's – delivered in the House of Commons on behalf of the government – was widely hailed as the most eloquent. To his great embarrassment, it later transpired that a key paragraph in his speech had been taken, virtually word for word, from an oration made some 19 years earlier by the French politician Adolph Thiers at the funeral of Marshal Gouvion Saint-Cyr. He was immediately accused of plagiarism, but was stoutly defended by *The Times*, which described his accusers as a 'whole pack of jealous littérateurs…flinging as much dirt as they can at the only littérateur who has ever yet succeeded in breaking that solid aristocratic phalanx which has hitherto monopolised the high offices of state'.[43]

Disraeli was, nevertheless, very upset by the affair, and it somewhat distracted him from his main activity at this time, preparing the budget, which he was due to present on 3 December 1852. His task was not an easy one. His followers eagerly expected him to make major concessions to the three interests – land, sugar and shipping – which had suffered as a consequence of the repeal of the Corn Laws and the other free-trade measures introduced by the Peel and Russell governments. (In fact, their suffering was greatly exaggerated – the introduction of free trade had led to a general rise in prosperity, from which even the countryside had benefited.) The trouble was that to pay for these concessions, other tax increases were necessary, as it was regarded as politically impossible to run a deficit, and there was very little scope for cuts in expenditure.

Disraeli decided that the most practical way of appeasing the landed interest was to halve the malt tax, currently levied at a rate of 2s.7d per bushel. He coupled this with halving the duty on hops, which would reduce the price of beer, a popular measure in towns as well as the countryside. Shipping was to be appeased by reducing or scrapping various minor duties, while sugar importers were granted the privilege of being able to refine sugar kept in bond. He also sought wider popularity by reducing the heavy tax on tea, and sought to pay for most of his concessions by changes to income tax, which had been reintroduced by Peel, and was currently levied at 7d in the pound on all incomes over £150. In a bid to win the support of Radical MPs, he proposed to distinguish between earned and unearned income, reducing the rate for the former to 5¼d., while retaining the latter at 7d. He also decided that profits of farmers in England should be assessed only on one-third instead of one-half of their rental. These concessions should be paid for by lowering the exemption level to £100 for earned and £50 for unearned income, while extending income tax to Ireland, where it had not previously been levied. He also reintroduced a house tax, which had been abolished several years earlier. The net effect of these and of other more minor changes would have been to produce a reasonable surplus of half a million pounds or more. But a few days before he was due to present the budget, Disraeli was presented with demands for a major increase in defence expenditure. This was in response to the referendum called by Louis-Napoleon Bonaparte to approve his proclamation as Emperor Napoleon III. This provoked wild fears that, like his more famous and much more formidable uncle, he would attempt an invasion of Britain, and an immediate demand from the service ministries (backed by the Queen) to increase their estimates. Derby queried some of their requests, but insisted that a deeply unhappy Disraeli should adjust his budget to meet several of them. This he unwillingly did, but left himself with a projected surplus of no more than £100,000, which Derby judged insufficient, and insisted that he should make still further changes, to increase this amount to more than £400,000. These late changes were ill-considered and undermined the whole coherence of the budget, which appeared more as a series of desperate expedients rather than a well-thought-out plan.

Nevertheless, on 3 December Disraeli, though suffering from the after-effects of 'flu, presented his budget with apparent confidence, and in a five-hour speech did his level best to win over the dozen or more votes which he needed to attract from the opposition benches if his measure were to survive. A full-scale debate, scheduled to continue over four days, began on 10 December, and it did not go well for Disraeli. He was particularly strongly attacked by two former chancellors of the exchequer, Henry Goulburn and Sir Charles Wood, and by the former Home Secretary, Sir James Graham, all three highly respected members of the House. Sensing the likelihood of defeat, Disraeli invited the leading Radical MP, John Bright, to his house late on the evening of 15 December, the eve of the final day of the debate. Although their views differed widely on most political issues, the two men enjoyed friendly relations, and Disraeli talked very frankly to his visitor in an effort to see whether there was any chance of winning over Radical votes, even at this late stage. He even offered, according to a written record of their talk kept by Bright, to give up his proposals both for a house tax and for reducing the malt tax if the Radicals would abstain. It was to no avail, as Robert Blake records in his biography:

> Half amused, half shocked, Bright declared that he could not entertain any sort of bargain and privately noted, 'He seems unable to comprehend the morality of our political course'...Even if Bright had been prepared to play, the game would have been effectively ended by Derby, who seems to have known what Disraeli was up to.[44]

Blake records that the following morning Disraeli received a blunt letter from Derby, saying, 'We have staked our existence on our Budget *as a whole*...How can we declare by concession on the house tax that we will deprive ourselves of doing *anything* for that interest, to which, after all, we owe our position?'[45]

So when Disraeli rose the following evening to reply to the debate, he already knew that defeat was probable. He decided, however, to go down fighting, and made a rumbustious speech which provoked great enthusiasm on the Tory benches, and laid into his critics – Wood, Goulburn and Graham in particular – with great ferocity, and not refraining from the use of 'unparliamentary language'. He concluded by declaring that if he were to lose the vote, it would be because all the diverse elements of the opposition had combined against him: 'Yes! I know what I have to face. I have to face a coalition. The combination may be successful. A Coalition has before this been successful. But Coalitions though successful have always found this, that their triumph has been brief. This, too, I know, that England does not love Coalitions.'[46]

He sat down at 1 a.m., expecting the House to proceed to a vote, but Gladstone rose from his seat and demanded the floor. The Deputy Speaker, who was in the chair, ruled him out of order, but Gladstone, speaking with great passion, ignored him, and pressed on. He began by rebuking Disraeli for flouting 'the laws of decency and propriety' of the House by the tone and manner in which he had attacked his critics. He then proceeded to a forensic dissection of Disraeli's entire budget, considering each item in turn, demonstrating that they were ill-thought-out and unlikely to produce the effects which the Chancellor foresaw. He concluded by casting severe doubt on Disraeli's claim to have secured a surplus of £400,000, saying that there was a 'palpable hiatus' in his figures for the income tax, and that in reality the budget would result in a deficit. The House was gripped by Gladstone's bravura performance, the dramatic effect of which was heightened by a raging thunderstorm outside, which periodically lit up the gloomy chamber with lightning flashes. By the time he sat down, at 3.15 on the morning of 17 December, there was not a single non-Tory MP who was prepared to support Disraeli's proposals. The House divided, and the government was defeated by 305 votes to 286, a majority of 19. Derby, who had glumly watched the debate from the public gallery, lost no time in drawing the obvious conclusion. Within a few hours he was on the train to the Isle of Wight to submit his resignation to Queen Victoria, who was relaxing at her country residence, Osborne House. The government had lasted a mere 292 days.

# Five

## The Palmerston era begins, 1853–8

Disraeli did not enjoy the pounding he received from Gladstone, but took his defeat, and that of the government, philosophically enough, unlike Derby, who made a petulant statement in the House of Lords the following Monday, 20 December, announcing the government's resignation. Disraeli's parallel statement in the House of Commons was much more good natured, and he even went so far, in response to a private request from the Leader of the Opposition, Lord John Russell, to make a handsome apology to the three former ministers – Henry Goulburn, Sir James Graham and Sir Charles Wood – whom he had attacked so fiercely in his winding up speech in the budget debate. In fact, Disraeli had benefited greatly from his short period in high office. He was now a much more famous public figure, and was, for the first time, widely seen as a likely future Prime Minister. His waxwork figure now appeared in Madame Tussaud's, and he was familiarly known to almost the entire nation as 'Dizzy'. He had vastly enjoyed being a minister, and – not least – it had had the effect of greatly improving his standing with the royal family, which previously could hardly have been lower. Queen Victoria, appalled by his attacks on Sir Robert Peel, had described him as 'detestable, unprincipled, reckless and not respectable',[1] while Prince Albert had dismissed him as having 'not one single element of the gentleman in his composition'.[2] The Queen, however, was agreeably surprised by the great trouble which Disraeli took in writing his daily reports to her on proceedings in Parliament. Previous prime ministers, or leaders of the

House of Commons, had apparently regarded this duty as an awful bore, and had confined themselves to the briefest and driest of summaries. Disraeli's reports, however, she wrote to her uncle, King Leopold of the Belgians, 'are just like his novels.'[3] As well as being much more lively, Disraeli's reports were scrupulously fair to the opposition; he described a speech by Sir James Graham as 'great ... elaborate, malignant, mischievous,'[4] and one by Russell as 'one of his ablest – statesmanlike, argumentative, terse, and playful; and the effect he produced was considerable.'[5] On one occasion he apologised to the Queen, writing that 'such bulletins are often written in tumult, and sometimes in perplexity and ... he is under the impression that your Majesty would prefer a genuine report of the feeling of the moment, however miniature, to a more artificial and prepared statement.'[6] He need not have worried; Victoria's reaction was exactly what he had hoped. Prince Albert, too, had reason to revise his previously unfavourable assessment, though he was still wary of him, as was evident from a private conversation which he had with Lord Derby, following his resignation at Osborne House. Derby wrote to his eldest son, Edward, now Lord Stanley, reporting the conversation, which the latter recorded in his diary:

> He spoke often of Disraeli, extolled his talent, his energy, but expressed a fear that he was not in his heart favourable to the existing order of things. My Father defended his colleague: said he had been unnaturally held down for several years, and then suddenly raised to the highest position. 'He has better reason than anyone to be attached to our constitutional system since he has experienced how easily under it a man may rise.' The Prince was glad to hear it, but still thought Disraeli had democratic tendencies 'and if that is the case he may become one of the most dangerous men in Europe.' My Father, with his accustomed frankness, related the substance of this conversation to Disraeli.[7]

On giving up his post, Disraeli wrote to the Queen and the Prince, thanking them for their kindness. He did not fail to pile on the flattery, saying of Albert that he 'would ever remember with interest and admiration the princely mind in the princely person.'[8] Disraeli was acutely aware that though the influence of the monarchy was declining, the Queen still possessed, and was willing to use, the power to veto the appointments of those she considered unsuitable for the senior offices of state.

As for Gladstone, he was in a mood of high excitement and nervous tension at this time. He had represented his speech at the end of the budget debate as a spontaneous reaction to what he felt was Disraeli's unwarranted attack on his critics. In reality, it was a carefully prepared oration, the objective of which, whether consciously or not, was to advertise his own superior qualifications for the post of Chancellor. Two days before, he had written to his wife, Catherine, that 'I am sorry to say that I have a long speech fomenting in me, and I feel as a loaf might in the oven.'[9] He had recently stepped up his 'rescue work', seeking out 'the same woman, Elizabeth Collins, 25 times, finding her on twenty occasions, then scourging himself'.[10] The most recent occasion was on 9 December, the evening before the debate began, and Gladstone recorded in his diary having scourged himself after 'a conversation not as it should have been'.[11] After delivering his speech, he had dropped into the Carlton Club before going home, but had then slept very fitfully, for less than two hours. He noted in his diary that 'My nervous system was too powerfully acted on by the scene of last night. A recollection of having mismanaged a material point (by omission) came into my head when I was half awake between 7 and 8, and utterly prevented my getting more rest.'[12]

Gladstone was still a member of the Carlton Club (then as now the centre of High Toryism), and remained so until 1860, by which time he had already been a Liberal cabinet minister for a year. It was just round the corner from his home in Carlton House Terrace, and therefore highly convenient. He visited the club again on 20 December, the day the government's resignation was announced, and was immediately set upon by a group of half-drunk, younger members who threatened to throw him across the road into the Reform Club, where, they insisted, he properly belonged. The young Tories were right: Gladstone still called himself a Conservative, but in reality he had by now become a Liberal, in all but name. Matthew, the principal editor of the *Gladstone Diaries*, argues that by the early 1850s Gladstone had, in place of his earlier views,

> developed a number of interests, which were not necessarily coherently interlocked but which, taken as a whole, made it increasingly difficult for him to co-operate with the Tory rump ... [They] placed him with the political economists on fiscal policy (Liberals to a man) – with the Whigs on civil liberties – with the Radicals Molesworth and Roebuck on colonial affairs, and – whether he liked it or not – with the moderates of European Liberalism on the Italian question.[13]

It was immediately evident when Derby resigned that his government would be replaced by a coalition of Whigs, Radicals and Peelites. As leader of the Whigs, Russell assumed that he would be Prime Minister, but it soon became clear that he would be unacceptable because of his action in introducing the (unworkable) Ecclesiastical Titles Bill, which had alienated the Peelites, the Irish and many Radical MPs, and even some of the Whigs. So the Queen approached the 3rd Marquess of Lansdowne, the Whig leader in the Lords, who declined the honour. The choice then fell on George Hamilton-Gordon, 4th Earl of Aberdeen, the former Foreign Secretary who had been the acknowledged leader of the Peelites since Peel's death in 1850. Although the Peelites made up not much more than 10 per cent of the Coalition MPs, they contributed almost half the cabinet, partly due to the undoubted fact they included a high proportion of the most talented members of the House. Among these, Gladstone was confident that he would be appointed Chancellor of the Exchequer, but he almost didn't get the post. Although Aberdeen was favourably disposed to Gladstone, who had served under him as Under-secretary for Foreign Affairs in Peel's first government, in 1835, his preference was for Sir James Graham, who, however, preferred the Admiralty. Sir Charles Wood, who had been Chancellor from 1846 to 1851, was also seriously considered, but Queen Victoria and Prince Albert strongly pressed Gladstone's claims, and Aberdeen acceded to their wishes. The 15-member cabinet, made up, Gladstone noted, entirely of noblemen, himself only excepted, was – on paper at least – one of the most distinguished in the entire nineteenth century, including four past, present or future prime ministers. These included Lord Palmerston MP, as Home Secretary, the Queen having refused to accept him as Foreign Secretary. This post went instead to a deeply disappointed Lord John Russell, who, however, decided after only two months that he preferred to be Leader of the Commons, and made way for the Earl of Clarendon. The Secretary for War and Colonies was Gladstone's old friend the former Earl of Lincoln, who had now succeeded to the title of Duke of Newcastle, Sidney Herbert was Secretary for War, and Sir Charles Wood was President of the Board of Control (responsible for India).

Gladstone's first period as Chancellor of the Exchequer (a post he was to hold four times, including twice as Prime Minister) opened with an unedifying quarrel with his predecessor, Disraeli, which brought out the worst in both men. The Chancellor's official robes, first worn by the Younger Pitt, had been passed on to each of his successors, who bought them from their own predecessors, but Disraeli insisted on keeping them. They are still on display at his home at Hughenden Manor, and a disgruntled Gladstone was forced to have a new set made at his own expense. This dispute, and a parallel one about paying for furniture at the Chancellor's official Downing Street residence, only served to confirm the low opinion each of them had formed of the other. Eventually Gladstone, under protest, sent Disraeli a cheque for £307.16s.6d for the furniture, equivalent to perhaps £20,000 today. In the meantime, he was forced to fight a by-election in his Oxford University constituency before he could move into 11 Downing Street. This proved to be more than a formality, and he was strongly challenged by Spencer Perceval Jnr, the son of the assassinated Prime Minister, who was a fanatical Evangelical and ultra-orthodox Tory. He ran Gladstone quite close, polling 892 votes to the Chancellor's 1022.

Gladstone's joining the Aberdeen coalition proved to be the turning point of his career. Hitherto, he had often been seen as something of a maverick whose heart was not really in the political game. From now on he was viewed as a serious contender for power with a strong political commitment. This was because he had, at last, apparently put behind him the uncertainty which had gripped him following his abandonment in the mid-1840s of the quasi-theocratic views he had advanced in his book *The State in its Relations with the Church* (1838). After much heart-searching, he had now found a new purpose to his life, which was to carry on and complete the great mission that Sir Robert Peel, his mentor and promoter, had set himself. This was to complete the transition from protection to free trade, and to transform the British fiscal system. His appointment as Chancellor promised to provide him with the necessary springboard, and he had little difficulty in persuading himself that this was God's will for himself and for the nation.

Gladstone's first task as Chancellor was to produce a budget which would replace Disraeli's, which had been rejected by the Commons in December 1852. He had under four months in which to prepare proposals, which he was to present to the House on 18 April 1853. Normally a prodigiously hard worker, he spent, according to his first biographer, John Morley, up to 15 hours a day working on the details at his Treasury desk. He set his sights high: according to Roy Jenkins, himself the author of three difficult budgets, he was aiming at 'not so much a budget for a year as a system of finance for the third quarter of the century'.[14] It was not easy going: he had great difficulty getting his proposals past the cabinet, which fiercely debated the draft budget for 15 and a half hours, over five sessions. Apart from Russell, all the leading members were unhappy about one or more of his proposals, with Wood, Graham, and even the 73-year-old Lord Lansdowne, who had been Chancellor of the Exchequer almost half a century earlier, being especially obstreperous. But Gladstone, who had done his homework well, and was infinitely better informed than any of his critics, managed to divide and rule over them on each particular contested point, and finally emerged with his proposals intact. It remained to get them through the Commons.

The centrepiece of Gladstone's budget was his proposal for extending income tax. First introduced by the Younger Pitt in 1798 as a temporary measure to help pay for the war with revolutionary France, this highly unpopular tax was abandoned very soon after Napoleon's final defeat at Waterloo, following a parliamentary revolt against the proposal of Lord Liverpool's government to continue it in peacetime. Reconstituted, again as a temporary measure, by Sir Robert Peel in 1842, it had since then been continued only on a yearly basis, with a general understanding that it would soon again be phased out. It was currently levied at a rate of 7d in the pound, or just under 3 per cent, on incomes exceeding £150. Now Gladstone boldly proposed extending the tax for a period of seven years while reducing the threshold to £100, and extending it (as Disraeli had earlier proposed) to Ireland. Gladstone, who was to describe it in his budget speech as 'an engine of gigantic power for great national purposes' proposed to use the revenue raised for a further great leap forward in progress towards free trade. Customs duties on 123 articles were removed completely, and were significantly reduced on another 135, while the excise duty on soap was completely removed. Gladstone made out a powerful case for what he was proposing, but sought to gild the lily by promising the eventual abolition of the tax. His proposal envisaged that it would be reduced to sixpence in the pound in 1855, and to five in 1857. 'On the 5th of April, 1860,' he was to announce, 'the income tax will by law expire.'[15] It was not to be: the outbreak of the Crimean War in 1854 put paid to any idea of reducing national revenues in the medium term, and income tax has remained ever since as the major source of public funds.

On 18 April 1853, Gladstone rose to introduce his budget at 5 p.m., and did not resume his seat until four and three-quarter hours later, the longest speech in his entire career. It was an astonishing performance, which kept the attention of the House throughout its entire length. Long before he sat down it was evident that he had achieved an oratorical triumph. It was described by the Foreign Secretary, Lord Clarendon, as 'the most perfect financial statement ever heard within the walls of Parlt for such it is allowed to be by friend and foe'.[16] Russell reported to Queen Victoria that it was one of the most powerful financial speeches ever made in the House of Commons. 'Mr. Pitt,' he wrote, 'in his days of glory might have been more imposing, but he could not have been more persuasive.'[17] The Prime Minister, Lord Aberdeen, passed on to his Chancellor the Queen's delight 'at the great success of Mr. Gladstone's speech last night', and assured him that 'if the existence of my government shall be prolonged, it will be your work.'[18] Disraeli, understandably, refrained from joining in the chorus of praise, maintaining that Gladstone had largely followed his own financial projects, 'though in a caricatured and exaggerated form'.[19]

The diarist Charles Greville, who at the time was a Clerk to the Privy Council, shrewdly noted that the budget 'had raised Gladstone to a great political elevation, and what is of far greater consequence than the measure itself, has given the country assurance of a *man* equal to great political necessities, and fit to lead parties and direct governments'.[20]

Shortly after his budgetary triumph, Gladstone reacted vigorously to a blackmail attempt by a young unemployed Scottish commercial traveller named William Wilson. He observed Gladstone talking to a woman who had accosted him in Leicester Square, and threatened to expose Gladstone as 'an immoral frequenter of prostitutes' by reporting the incident to the *Morning Herald*, unless the Chancellor of the Exchequer found him a public post, either in the Inland Revenue or elsewhere. Gladstone angrily refused and, summoning a policeman, brought charges of extortion against the young man, who was subsequently sentenced to 12 months' hard labour. Taking pity on his pathetic accuser, Gladstone then intervened with the Home Secretary, Lord Palmerston, and ensured that he was released after serving only two months of his sentence. He confided to his diary that 'these talkings of mine are certainly not within the rules of worldly prudence',[21] and the publicity which followed made him 'the butt of many a sly witticism, such as Clarendon's comment to the Duchess of Manchester on "our Jesuit", with his "benevolent nocturnal rambles".[22] Nevertheless, he continued his activities unabated, in the hope – which largely proved justified – that his high moral reputation would be unimpaired.

Although as Chancellor Gladstone was formally junior to several other cabinet ministers – at that time the chancellorship was not seen as the natural stepping stone to the premiership – he was now widely regarded as the 'strong man' in the government, and he and Disraeli were perceived as the heirs apparent of their respective leaders. In 1853 it must have seemed very likely that one or other of them would accede to the premiership within the next few years. In fact, it was to be 15 years before either of them reached this eminence. This was because they were held up by more elderly figures who remained centre-stage for much longer than had seemed likely. In the case of Disraeli, only Derby was blocking his way. In 1853 he was only 54 – a mere five years older than Disraeli – but his health was poor, his commitment to politics was only spasmodic, and he was ill-suited to carrying out the more routine duties of a party leader. It must have seemed improbable that he would cling to the Tory leadership for another decade and a half. Gladstone, aged 44, had several senior figures potentially blocking his way, but they were all considerably older than himself. Aberdeen, already 69 and a compromise choice as Prime Minister, was not expected to linger very long in that office. Both Russell and Sir James Graham were 61, and their careers already seemed in steep decline. Neither of them seemed at all likely to hold up his progress for more than a few years. What nobody foresaw in 1853 was that a much older figure – the 69-year-old Lord Palmerston, after a ministerial career that began as long before as 1807, was about to take off and become the dominating figure in British politics over the next dozen years, becoming Prime Minister at the age of 71 and dying in office ten years later.

Henry John Temple, the 3rd Viscount Palmerston, was an Irish peer and major landowner in both Ireland and England whose entire political career, which lasted 58 years, was spent in the House of Commons. His first ministerial appointment, aged 22, was in the Tory government of the 3rd Duke of Portland (1807–9), and he continued in office under each of his five successors – Spencer Perceval, the Earl of Liverpool, George Canning, Viscount Goderich and the Duke of Wellington. He was regarded as a liberal Tory, and follower of George Canning, and when Wellington purged the leading Canningites from his government, in 1828, Palmerston resigned in sympathy. He subsequently joined the Whigs and resumed his ministerial career, as Foreign Secretary, in Earl Grey's government (1830–4), filling the same post in the subsequent Whig ministries of Lord Melbourne and Lord John Russell. Having been the most liberal of the Tories, he now became the most conservative of the Whigs, at least concerning domestic politics. In Foreign Affairs, however, he had much sympathy with liberal and nationalist opponents of the three great authoritarian powers, Russia, Austria and Prussia. Over and above that, however, he was a great British nationalist and imperialist, blending subtle diplomatic moves with bombastic outbursts. He readily resorted to gunboat diplomacy, precipitating wars with both China (the first Opium War) and Afghanistan in the late 1830s, and dangerously risking conflicts with both France and the United States. That, and his habit of not consulting his cabinet colleagues, made him highly unpopular with his fellow ministers, but – particularly after the Don Pacifico affair (see page 78 above) – won him much acclaim with the increasingly jingoistic British public, and he was dubbed 'the people's darling' (the subtitle of his biography by James Chambers).[23] Extraordinarily hard-working, he was a man of gargantuan sexual and gastronomic appetites, and was a notorious libertine, with numerous mistresses, the most longstanding of whom was Lord Melbourne's married sister Emily, Countess Cowper. He was the undoubted father of two of her three children, and when her boring, drunken and neglectful husband finally died in 1837, he immediately proposed to her, and they were married two years later. This was to the distress of the snobbish Melbourne, who thought she was lowering herself, as the widow of an earl, by marrying a mere viscount, and an Irish one at that. Palmerston had, in the meantime, incurred the enduring enmity of the young Queen Victoria, who suspected him of attempting to rape one of her ladies-in-waiting while staying overnight, as a house guest, at Windsor Castle. The affair was hushed up, and he narrowly avoided having to resign, but it was only with extreme reluctance that she was willing to contemplate accepting him as a minister in later governments. As we have seen, she vetoed his appointment as Foreign Secretary in Aberdeen's government, and he had to satisfy himself with the Home Secretaryship, a post in which he was not particularly interested. It was expected that he would be little more than a passenger in the government, and that he would soon retire to the wide acres of his Hampshire estate at Broadlands, later renowned as the country seat of the Mountbatten family. If it had not been for the onset of the Crimean War, which broke up the Aberdeen government, this might well have been the outcome.

Gladstone's budget set the tone for a reforming government, and measures for overhauling the Indian administration, penal reform and the admission of Jews to the House of Commons were soon passed, though the last measure was overthrown by the Lords. Gladstone himself took the lead in framing a bill, technically introduced by Russell as Leader of the House, to reform and modernise the University of Oxford. As MP for the university, Gladstone had vigorously resisted the appointment of a royal commission to investigate its shortcomings several years earlier, but when its report was issued he found himself in agreement with many of its recommendations. He embarked upon a vast consultation exercise, involving a voluminous correspondence all in his own handwriting, before drafting the bill, which provided for a continuation of the university's collegiate structure while somewhat diminishing the almost unlimited powers of the college heads, removing the Anglican monopoly, widening the entry requirements and facilitating the creation of new colleges or private halls, which eventually led to the creation of five colleges for women. Gladstone showed great courage in championing changes which were opposed by many of his more conservative voters. They did not immediately repudiate him, but he was never able to build up a solid majority, and he was ultimately to lose his seat in 1865, when he was forced to find another constituency. Following his university reforms, Gladstone next aimed to reform the civil service, then recruited on the basis of patronage, by opening it up to meritocratic competition. He appointed his private secretary, Sir Stafford Northcote (later Earl Iddesleigh), together with Sir Charles Trevelyan, a distinguished former administrator in India (and Lord Macaulay's brother-in-law), to prepare a report which advocated that entry into the service should henceforth be by competitive examinations. Gladstone enthusiastically accepted the Northcote–Trevelyan Report, but was unable to persuade his cabinet colleagues to implement it. It was not until he became Prime Minister for the first time, in 1868, that he was able to put into effect proposals which implemented the report. This effectively ensured that in future virtually all the top civil-service posts would be monopolised by the most able graduates of Oxford and Cambridge.

At Russell's instigation, a thoroughgoing overhaul of the educational system was now projected, and Russell himself drew up a Reform Bill, but these proposals were pre-empted by the outbreak of the Crimean War, which shortly brought Aberdeen's administration to a humiliating end. The war was originally provoked by the desire of the newly crowned French Emperor Napoleon III to enhance French influence in the Near East. He strongly backed the claims of Catholic monks to extend their control of 'holy places' in Turkish-controlled Palestine, which led the Russian Tsar, Nicholas I, to intervene on behalf of their Orthodox rivals, and indeed to insist that he should be recognised as the guarantor of the rights of Orthodox Christians throughout the Ottoman Empire. To reinforce his claim, he sent his troops into the two principalities of Wallachia and Moldavia (essentially modern Romania), which were under Turkish suzerainty, and refused to withdraw them until his claims were met. The British reaction to the clear threat of war between Russia and Turkey was bedevilled by sharp disagreements within the cabinet. The peace-loving Aberdeen strongly favoured efforts to seek a diplomatic solution to the crisis, but was highly critical of the Turks and believed, in the last resort, that they should be pressured to concede to Nicholas's demands. Palmerston, however, despite having no formal responsibility for foreign policy, vigorously asserted his own view that the Russians must be resisted at all costs, and believed that they could be forced to back down by making clear that Britain, along with France, would join in on Turkey's side if war broke out. As Muriel Chamberlain argues in her biography of Aberdeen, 'Either policy, carried through consistently, might have brought success. What was to prove fatal was the mixing of the two.'[24]

Public opinion, still inflamed against Russia by its role in suppressing the Hungarian revolution of 1848, was largely on Palmerston's side, and Aberdeen's position in the cabinet was a weak one. The Turks, confident that Britain and France would come to their aid, declared war on Russia in October 1853 after it refused to withdraw from the two principalities. Aberdeen still hoped to keep Britain out of the war, but his position became untenable when a Turkish naval squadron was sunk by a Russian fleet at Sinope, in the Black Sea. He was forced to agree to the dispatch of a British fleet, and the sending of an ultimatum to the Russians to withdraw to their base at Sebastopol in the Crimea. When the Russians declined to do so, Britain and France declared war on 28 March 1854. Aberdeen, who had neither the appetite nor the aptitude to be a war leader, would have been well advised to resign at this stage, but he agreed to carry on in the – vain – hope of limiting the scale of the hostilities. Gladstone took little part in the cabinet discussions on the issue, but was unenthusiastically resigned to the necessity for war, which was strongly backed by the opposition, including by Disraeli, who had been a warm admirer of the Ottoman regime ever since his voyage to Turkey and the Levant as a young man. As Chancellor, Gladstone's main concern was that – unlike in previous major conflicts – the war effort should not be financed on borrowed money, pushing the country into debts which would take many years to pay off. He also wanted the public to be aware of the cost of the war, which the government had so lightheartedly stumbled into, and to attend, as he put it in his budget speech, 'not only to the necessity of war', but to 'the first and earliest prospects of concluding an honourable peace'.[25] In his 1854 budget, therefore, he temporarily increased income tax from 7d to 10½d in the pound, expressing deep disappointment that this would play havoc with his plans, announced only the previous year, for a gradual phasing out of the tax. Nor was his hope to be realised that the national debt would not be sharply increased by the costs of the war, which proved far higher than the original estimates.

In September 1854, some 64,000 allied troops landed in the northern Crimea, in the confident expectation that a quick march on Sebastopol would settle the issue. Three bloody battles were fought – at Alma, Balaclava and Inkerman – over the next two months, and the allied troops then became bogged down outside the fortified city as the Russian winter set in. Meanwhile, the invention of the telegraph and the presence in the war zone of newspaper correspondents, notably W.H. Russell of *The Times*, enabled the British public to read – as they never had before – first-hand accounts of the horrors of war. The effect was comparable to that on US viewers of the television coverage of the Vietnam War a century later. They learned of appalling administrative confusion, the absence of effective equipment, winter clothing and adequate medical attention for the wounded troops, and serious strategic and tactical errors by the British and French commanders. The government was subjected to a barrage of criticism, in which Derby played a leading role, making a series of effective speeches in the House of Lords. Aberdeen, always a poor speaker in the upper house, was pathetically incapable of mounting an effective defence. The Radicals joined with the Tories in attacking the government, and one of their number – John Arthur Roebuck, the MP for Sheffield – tabled a motion calling for a parliamentary committee of enquiry into the state of the army before Sebastopol. At this point Lord John Russell, who had retained the post of Leader of the Commons, decided to abandon ship, and resigned from the government rather than defend its position in the ensuing debate, in which it was left to Gladstone, at best a halfhearted supporter of the war effort, to oppose the motion. He made a spirited speech, but it was coldly received by the House, and the government lost the division by 304 votes to 148.

The following day, 30 January 1855, Aberdeen went to Windsor to submit his resignation to the Queen. There were widely seen to be four possible candidates to form a new government – Derby, Lansdowne, Russell and Palmerston, and it was perhaps Derby's (and Disraeli's) misfortune that the Queen sent for him first. Ignoring the earnest plea of his colleague, Lord Ellenborough ('Don't leave the room without kissing hands'), Derby temporised, and said that because of the strong public support for Palmerston it would be necessary to include him in the government. He declined to accept office until he had discussed the situation with Palmerston and the leading Peelites. He then approached Palmerston, Gladstone and Sidney Herbert and invited them to serve. Palmerston declined, Gladstone made difficulties, insisting that other Peelites, notably Graham, should also be invited, while Herbert eagerly accepted. Discouraged, Derby returned to the Queen the following day to tell her that he could not proceed. Disraeli was appalled, but Gladstone, who was highly confused about his own objectives at this stage, except that he wanted to exclude Palmerston from the premiership at almost any cost, was delighted, unrealistically believing that it would be possible for Aberdeen to be recalled. When Lansdowne attempted to form what would otherwise be an entirely Whig government, with him continuing as Chancellor, Gladstone turned the offer down – a decision he later described as 'one of the most important as well as least pardonable errors of my political life'.[26] When Lansdowne failed, the Queen, remarking that it 'would have to be one of those terrible old men', sent for Russell, who quickly discovered that he could not muster sufficient support. So then the unthinkable – both for her and Gladstone, who heartily detested Palmerston – happened. Not only was she constrained to approach the 71-year-old Irish peer, but he unexpectedly succeeded in forming a government with no apparent difficulty. This he accomplished by reconstituting the Aberdeen coalition, excluding only Aberdeen himself and the Duke of Newcastle, who – as War Secretary – was a ready scapegoat for the apparent fiasco in the Crimea.

Gladstone was highly reluctant to join a government led by Palmerston, whom he described as 'in no way equal to the duties which fall upon a Prime Minister'.[27] Yet he was persuaded by fellow Peelites that it was his patriotic duty to do so, and so – when the new cabinet was announced on 6 February 1855 – he was again listed as Chancellor of the Exchequer. Yet three weeks later he abruptly resigned, taking with him Sir James Graham and Sidney Herbert. The stated reason for Gladstone's resignation was the decision of the cabinet to respect the will of the House of Commons and agree to the appointment of the Roebuck enquiry. Gladstone strongly objected to this, he told the House of Commons, on the grounds that this would place 'in the hands of a small number of Members of Parliament duties which appertain essentially to the executive government', and that no government which did so 'ever can and ever ought to enjoy the respect of Parliament'.[28] There is no doubt that this was Gladstone's honest opinion, but it is only a partial explanation of his decision to quit. There were at least three other motivations: his distaste for serving under Palmerston, his distress at the scapegoating of Aberdeen and Newcastle, and the collapse of his fiscal strategy, as it was clear that indirect taxes would now have to be restored and government borrowing increased to pay for the escalating costs of the war. Moreover, Gladstone fully expected that Palmerston's premiership would be shortlived. When he went to Buckingham Palace on 28 February 1855 to surrender his seals of office, he assured Prince Albert that 'it would not last a twelvemonth'.[29] He was not the only person greatly to underestimate Palmerston's capacity. Disraeli, writing to Lady Londonderry complaining that Derby had 'for the third time…in the space of six years' thrown away an opportunity to form a government, said of Palmerston that 'he is really an imposter, utterly exhausted, and, at the best, only ginger beer and not champaign, and now an old painted Pantaloon, very deaf, very blind and with false teeth, which would fall out of his mouth when speaking, if he did not hesitate and halt so much in his talk.'[30]

Yet this 'old Pantaloon' was able, within 12 months, successfully to wind up the Crimean War, amidst much public acclaim, and, with one short interval, continued to govern Britain for over nine years, till his death on 18 October 1865. In different ways, the ensuing decade was to be one of acute frustration, for Disraeli in particular, but also for Gladstone, at least until he again became Chancellor, in 1859.

During the period of Palmerston's first government, from 1855 to 1858, Gladstone and Disraeli were both in opposition, and often found themselves voting in the same lobby. They were both in favour of adopting the terms accepted by the Russians midway through the siege of Sebastopol, which would have meant the abandonment of Palmerston's attempt to exclude the Russian navy from the Black Sea, and two years later – in 1857 – they combined to help defeat Palmerston in a vote against his provocation of the so-called second Opium War against China. Gladstone led the charge: in a speech described by a colleague as 'the finest delivered in the memory of man in the House of Commons,'[31] he supported a censure motion tabled by the Radical MP Richard Cobden, which was carried by 263 votes to 247. To no avail: Palmerston called a general election – which he easily won – gaining numerous seats from both Tories and Peelites. The war, during which both Canton and Tientsin were briefly occupied, continued until the Treaty of Peking brought it to a temporary end in October 1858. There was, however, no question of any close co-operation between Disraeli and Gladstone. They were wary of each other, and while Disraeli loyally supported Derby's periodic attempts to lure Gladstone back to the

Tory ranks, Gladstone refused to contemplate this, largely because of his dislike for the Tory leader in the Commons and his bitter memories of how he had destroyed his own hero, Peel. He wrote a letter to Derby on 14 February 1857 explaining that he and Disraeli could not co-exist in the same party. He noted in his diary that he had told Derby that 'from motives which I could neither describe nor conquer I was quite unable to enter into any squabble or competition with him for the possession of a post of prominence ... He understood besides that Disraeli "could not be thrown away like a sucked orange".[32]

Gladstone was at a loss to decide, at this stage, where his true political home was. He was suspended almost equally between the Whigs and the Tories (who had now definitively abandoned protectionism), while his own Peelite group was rapidly declining through defections, election losses and the ageing and death of several of its leading members, including Goulburn, Graham, Herbert and Aberdeen, all of whom were to die between 1856 and 1861. In 1861, also, Prince Albert was to die – from typhoid fever – at the age of 42. This was to remove one of Gladstone's strongest admirers, who had used his influence over the Queen to ensure his appointment as Chancellor in 1852. Henceforth Victoria became progressively more hostile to Gladstone, while taking an increasingly benign view of Disraeli, who had endeared himself to her by contributing perhaps the most eloquent of the many tributes paid following her husband's untimely death.

In July 1855, Gladstone turned away from his political concerns to embark on a large-scale study of the works of Homer. Published in three volumes in 1858, under the title *Homer and the Homeric Age*, it was not regarded as a serious academic work, but as a quixotic, and thoroughly unsuccessful, attempt to demonstrate that these pagan works, dating from the ninth or eighth century BC, prefigured Christian teaching, and were divinely inspired. Despite the enormous effort which – as in all his undertakings – he devoted to this bizarre enterprise, he had few illusions about the quality of his end product, advising a friend, 'to start with the third volume because it was probably the least unreadable'.[33] He was brought back to the political fight by the introduction by Palmerston's newly re-elected government of a bill providing for the establishment of civil divorce courts. Previously, divorce had been possible only through the passage of a private act of parliament, which was ruinously expensive, and effectively meant that it was open only to the upper classes. The new bill was backed by the Archbishop of Canterbury and by nine bishops, but was fiercely opposed by Gladstone, as an attack on the powers of the Church of England. One of only a small minority of opponents to the bill, he fought it tooth and nail, making no fewer than 73 interventions during debates on the different parliamentary stages, 29 of them in the course of a single protracted sitting. Gladstone appeared to be setting himself up against any possibility of divorce for the middle and lower classes, and laid himself open to charges of hypocrisy because of his very active role in collecting evidence for Lord Lincoln's divorce seven years earlier. Despite his efforts to filibuster the bill, it was duly passed, and came into effect on 1 January 1858, as the Matrimonial Causes Act.

Lord Derby was slowly warming to Disraeli, and – in his best *de haut en bas* manner – made him a number of complimentary gestures, from time to time. As Chancellor of Oxford University, it was his prerogative to bestow honorary doctorates, and in June 1853 Disraeli received an Honorary D.C.L., 20 years after his father Isaac, who also had not attended a university, had been awarded the same honour. Disraeli was grateful enough, but his pleasure was perhaps somewhat mitigated by the fact that Gladstone (as well as Lord Macaulay, Bishop Samuel Wilberforce and Edward Bulwer-Lytton) was also honoured at the same occasion. Nor was he over-impressed when he belatedly received an invitation to a house party at Derby's Lancashire seat Knowsley Hall. Expecting to find a house of great luxury, he wrote disappointedly to Mary Anne, who had been unable to accompany him because of an attack of influenza, that it was

> a wretched house, yet very vast: an irregular pile of many ages: half of it like St. James's Palace, low, red, with turrets, set in grounds almost as large as Windsor … Despite Derby's wealth it was furnished like a second-rate lodging house … not from stinginess, but from sheer want of taste, although the stables were beautifully kept. No one has more splendid horses and equipages than Lord Derby.[34]

Disraeli was much more taken with Hatfield House, the Hertfordshire seat of the 2nd Marquess of Salisbury, which he visited two years later, writing to Mary Anne, that 'we dined every day in a baronial hall in the midst of a real old English park at the time of Queen Elizabeth, interminable avenues of lime and chestnut and oceans of fern, six feet high; golden yew trees and glancing deer.'[35]

Nor was he discomfited by the unexpected arrival of the Marquess's son, Lord Robert Cecil, a recently elected Tory MP and one of his strongest critics, who habitually referred to him as 'a political charlatan'. He warmly embraced his young parliamentary colleague, saying, 'Ah, Robert, Robert, how glad I am to see you.' It was to be many years before young Robert (the future 3rd Marquess and three times Tory Prime Minister) felt able to reciprocate. He kept his distance from his parliamentary leader, even though Disraeli was consistently encouraging to him, and did everything to help facilitate his political career.

Disraeli, chafing at Derby's failure to lead the Tories in a consistently combative manner, did what he could to sharpen up the party's act, replacing the ineffective and corrupt Chief Whip William Beresford and his equally corrupt successor Forbes Robertson, who was actually unseated from his Liverpool constituency for bribery, with the more dynamic and undoubtedly more honest Sir William Joliffe, later Lord Hylton. Beresford had also been responsible for the party organisation outside Parliament, and Disraeli removed this from his control, and put it under his own solicitor, Philip Rose. Disraeli was also unhappily aware that the press, at this time, was largely pro-Whig (or, at least, pro-Palmerston), and sought to create a publication which was firmly on the Tories' side. Backed by Lord (Edward) Stanley, and financed by several of Disraeli's richer friends, *The Press* started life as a weekly, its first number appearing on 7 May 1853. Robert Blake commented that 'It can at least be said that Disraeli's second venture as a newspaper proprietor was more successful than his first,'[36] referring to his experience with *The Representative*, in 1825. Its contributors, apart from Disraeli himself, who anonymously wrote most of the leading articles, included Stanley, Bulwer-Lytton and George Smythe, his old colleague from Young England days. Disraeli described the paper as 'though Tory…of a very progressive and enlightened design', and it had little appeal to more orthodox Tories. Although Disraeli took pains not to be publicly associated with the paper, he was, argued Blake, in 'an essentially false position' to be both a leader of the party 'and at the same time not only proprietor of, but anonymous contributor to, a polemical organ well to the left of party centre'.[37] Disraeli eventually recognised this, and sold the paper after five years. When Palmerston became Prime Minister for the first time, in 1855, Disraeli almost lost one of his closest supporters, Edward Stanley. Palmerston invited him to join the government, and Stanley, who was one of the most 'liberal' Tories, was tempted to accept. He travelled up to Knowsley Hall to consult his father, who – disturbed in the middle of a game of billiards – enquired, 'What brings you here, Edward? Are you going to be married or has Disraeli cut his throat?'[38] Derby quickly talked his son out of accepting Palmerston's offer, and Edward privately resolved that he would never contemplate leaving the Tories during his father's lifetime. (Much later – after serving as Foreign Secretary, both under his father and Disraeli – he switched to the Liberals, in 1880, later becoming Colonial Secretary under Gladstone, as the 15th Earl of Derby.)

The loss of his £5000 salary as Chancellor of the Exchequer was a serious setback for Disraeli, but the republication in 1853 of several of his novels, in a one-shilling edition, produced sales of 300,000 copies in the first year. This eased his financial position substantially, but he suffered a heavy blow in 1857 when Lord George Bentinck's eldest brother, who had by then become the 5th Duke of Portland, suddenly called in the loan which had been made Disraeli to allow him to purchase Hughenden Manor. Never having expected to repay this, he now had to resort to usurious moneylenders. The precariousness of his position can be judged from a letter which he had recently written to his accountant, Henry Padwick, concerning his income-tax liability. He estimated that his total income for the year, including that of Mary Anne, was £4798.11s.10d; his debts, excluding what he owed for Hughenden, amounted to £27,750.[39] After repaying Portland, he was almost £60,000 in the red, and over the next five years he once again suffered acute money worries, until a rich Conservative landowner, Andrew Montagu, of Melton in Yorkshire, offered to buy up his debts, 'charging him a very low rate of interest instead of the heavy exactions of the moneylenders to whom he had previously had recourse'.[40] His friend Baron Lionel de Rothschild also made a generous contribution, as he had on a number of previous occasions. Two years after that, in 1863, Mrs Brydges Willyams died, and the promised legacy, amounting to more than £40,000, duly arrived. This enabled him finally – at the age of 59 – to pay off the debts which he had first begun incurring as a 20-year-old.

In 1857 Disraeli had acquired a new young admirer and supporter, Ralph Earle, who was working as an unpaid attaché at the British Embassy in Paris. Young (20 years old), clever, good-looking and utterly unscrupulous, Earle immediately appealed to Disraeli, who was perhaps reminded of his own young self, and his relationship to the publisher John Murray. Earle began to feed Disraeli – in almost daily letters – with leaked information about secret British diplomatic initiatives, and – in particular – concerning Palmerston's dealings with Napoleon III, which Disraeli used in attempts to undermine Palmerston, and to provoke a breach between him and the French Emperor. In 1858, Disraeli appointed Earle as his private secretary, writing to Mrs Brydges Willyams that he was 'only 23, but a man in matured thought and power of observation,'[41] and subsequently arranged for his election as a Tory MP. Earle's apparent intimacy with Disraeli angered another of his young favourites, Lord Henry Lennox, who felt that he was being displaced as Disraeli's *confidant*. Lennox, a born intriguer, was doing his best to undermine Derby's position as leader, in the hope that he would at last stand down and leave Disraeli a free hand. Invited to a house party at Lady Jersey's, also attended by Derby, he complained in a letter to Disraeli that the Earl was:

> completely absorbed in his pleasures, absolutely refusing to talk about politics. As a Leader of a Party he is more hopeless than ever! Devoted to Whist, Billiards, Racing, Betting and making a fool of himself with either Ladies Emily Peel or Mary Yorke. Bulwer-Lytton came … for three days and was in despair. Not one word could he [Lennox] extract from Derby about Public Affairs; nothing but the Odds and Tricks.[42]

Disraeli himself was beginning to weary of his life as an understudy to Derby, and, as he advanced through his sixth decade, must have wondered whether time was passing him by, and if he would ever reach the summit of his ambitions. A graphic description of how he appeared on an April day in 1856 has been left by the American novelist Nathaniel Hawthorne, who observed him crossing the Central Lobby of the House of Commons, and who recorded in his diary,

> By and by there came a rather tall, slender person in a black frock [coat], buttoned up, and black pantaloons, taking long steps but I thought rather feebly or listlessly. His shoulders were round; or else he had a habitual stoop in them. He had a prominent nose, a thin face, and a sallow, very sallow complexion, and was a very unhealthy looking person; and had I seen him in America, I should have taken him for a hard-worked editor of a newspaper, weary and worn with night-work and want of exercise, shrivelled and withered, before his time. It was Disraeli, and I never saw any other Englishman look in the least like him.[43]

Two years later, the prospects for Disraeli must have looked even bleaker: Palmerston was still in power, vastly popular and with a recently enhanced majority, and fresh from having successfully suppressed the Indian Mutiny (now known as the Indian Rebellion). There seemed no reason to believe that he could be shifted in the foreseeable future. Then, suddenly, Palmerston appeared to lose his grip, and resigned in a huff. Two unrelated events contributed to his downfall. One was the appointment of the Marquess of Clanricarde as Lord Privy Seal when the office became vacant late in 1857. Palmerston had overruled the recommendation made by Lord Lansdowne, as Leader of the House of Lords, and insisted on appointing Clanricarde, a protégé of Lady Palmerston. Clanricarde, a former minister in Lord John Russell's government, had excellent political credentials, but was a well-known rake who had very recently been involved in a scandalous court case involving one of his 'apparently unlimited number of illegitimate children'.[44] Virtuous opinion was outraged, as Victorian respectability was now well on the way to replacing the loose Regency morals of Palmerston's youth, and a substantial body of MPs, particularly on the Radical benches, was deeply offended. Then, on 14 January 1858, a group of Italian nationalists, led by Count Felice Orsini, launched three bombs against a coach conveying the Emperor Napoleon III and his wife Eugénie to the Paris Opera. They were unhurt, but eight people were killed and 142 injured. It turned out that the plot had been hatched in England, and the bombs manufactured in Birmingham. French public opinion was enraged, and Napoleon's Foreign Minister, Count Walewski, sent a note, in very moderate tones, to Palmerston containing a simple request:

> Her Britannic Majesty's Government can assist us in averting a repetition of such guilty enterprises by affording us a guarantee which no state can refuse a neighbouring state, and which we are authorised to expect from an ally. Fully relying, moreover, on the high sense of the English cabinet, we refrain from indicating in any way the measures which it may see fit to take in order to comply with this wish.[45]

Palmerston enquired, and discovered that the manufacture of 'infernal machines' was defined in English law only as a 'misdemeanour' rather than a 'felony', and introduced a bill, the Conspiracy to Murder Bill, to make it clear that it was a serious offence. When presented for a formal first reading, on 7 February, it was easily carried, with a majority of 200, with

Disraeli adding his support. Over the next ten days, however, there was a strong reaction, both in Parliament and the press, with Palmerston, to his anger and astonishment, finding himself accused of supine surrender to French threats. Disraeli, sensing that the government might be defeated on the second reading of the bill, reversed his position (against the cautious advice of Derby), and it was rejected by 234 votes to 215, in a relatively poorly attended House. Palmerston could easily have rectified the situation by calling for a vote of confidence the following day, but he hot-headedly set off for the Palace and submitted his resignation, which Queen Victoria had no hesitation in accepting. She sent for Lord Derby, who – this time – agreed, without demur, to try to form a government.

# Six

## Derby again, but then 'Pam' goes on and on…, 1858–65

In forming his second government, Derby decided that if necessary he would again lead a minority Tory government, but once again approached Gladstone, as well as the 3rd Earl Grey, son of the former Whig Prime Minister, with offers to participate. Both declined, so Derby, who had told the Queen that 'if he refused the Conservative Party would be broken up for ever',[1] once again had to make do with the limited talents to be found on the Conservative benches. His team was, however, adjudged to be somewhat superior to the feeble cabinet he had led in 1852. It included three new cabinet ministers – his son, Edward Stanley, as Colonial Secretary, General Jonathan Peel, a son of the former Prime Minister who had recently left the Peelites to rejoin his old party, as War Secretary, and Lord Ellenborough as President of the Board of Control (responsible for India). Disraeli was again Chancellor of the Exchequer and Leader of the House of Commons, while Spencer Walpole and the Earl of Malmesbury resumed their former posts, respectively as Home and Foreign Secretary. The government took office on 23 February 1858; within little more than three months it was reshuffled following the resignation of Ellenborough, who had proved a disastrous failure in handling the aftermath of the Indian Mutiny. Derby was anxious to replace him with a firm and decisive minister capable of holding his own in the House of Commons, and both he and Disraeli agreed that Gladstone would be the ideal choice. Disraeli, sensing that his great rival would not be willing to serve under him in the Commons, offered to give up the leadership in favour of the Peelite Sir

James Graham, but Graham declined. Disraeli then took it upon himself to make a direct appeal to Gladstone, sending him a remarkable letter:

*Confidential.* GROSVENOR GATE, May 28, 1858. – I think it of such paramount importance to the public interests that you assume at this time a commanding position in the administration of affairs that I felt it a solemn duty to lay before you some facts, that you may not decide under a misapprehension.

Our mutual relations have caused the great difficulty in accomplishing a result which I have always desired. Listen without prejudice to this brief narrative …

Disraeli then listed a whole series of occasions, over eight years, when he had offered to efface himself in order to facilitate Gladstone's joining a government led by Derby. He continued,

Don't you think the time has come when you might deign to be magnanimous?

Mr. Canning was superior to Lord Castlereagh in capacity, in acquirements, in eloquence, but he joined Lord C., when Lord C. was Lord Liverpool's deputy [in 1812–22], when the state of the Tory party rendered it necessary. That was an enduring and, on the whole, not an unsatisfactory connection, and it certainly terminated very gloriously for Mr. Canning.

I may be removed from the scene, or I may wish to be removed from the scene. Every man performs his office, and there is a Power, greater than ourselves, that disposes of all this. The conjuncture is very critical, and, if prudently yet boldly managed, may rally the country … To be inactive now is, on your part, a great responsibility. If you join Lord Derby's Cabinet, you will meet there some warm personal friends; all its members are your admirers. You may place me in neither category, but in that, I assure you, you have ever been sadly mistaken … Think of all this in a kindly spirit. These are hurried lines but they are heartfelt … – B. Disraeli.[2]

He might just as well have saved himself the trouble of writing. Gladstone replied on the same day in a letter, described by one of his biographers, Sir Philip Magnus, as 'polished but cold as ice':[3]

11, CARLTON HOUSE TERRACE, May 25, 1858

MY DEAR SIR, – The letter you have been kind enough to address to me will enable me, I trust, to remove from your mind some impressions with which you will not be sorry to part.

You have given me a narrative of your conduct since 1850 with reference to your position as leader of your party. But I have never thought your retention of that office [a] matter of reproach to you, and on Saturday last acknowledged to Mr. Walpole the handsomeness of your conduct in offering to resign it to Sir James Graham.

You consider that the relations between yourself and me have proved the main difficulty in the way of certain arrangements. Will you allow me to say that I have never in my life taken a decision which turned on them ...

At the present moment I am awaiting counsel which at Lord Derby's wish I have sought. But the difficulties which he wishes me to find ways of overcoming are broader than you may have supposed ...

I state these points fearlessly and without reserve, for you have yourself well reminded me that there is a Power beyond us that disposes of what we are and what we do, and I find the limits of choice in public life to be very narrow.

I remain, my dear sir, very faithfully yours, W.E. Gladstone.[4]

Before replying to Derby's invitation, in a letter which made no mention of Disraeli, Gladstone sought advice from both Graham and Lord Aberdeen. The former, who explained that his own refusal of the leadership of the House was purely due to his feeling that he was now too old to assume a senior post, strongly recommended Gladstone to accept. It would be wrong, Graham argued, for Gladstone to stand aloof on the basis of solidarity with the other Peelites. 'The little group is broken up,' he asserted. Newcastle was biding his time, Sidney Herbert and Edward Cardwell would go with the Liberals, Aberdeen, like himself, would henceforth be a political bystander rather than a participant. 'The result is you are on your own'; he could, 'with perfect honour', join Derby.[5] Aberdeen, however, told Gladstone that it was impossible for him, 'acting alone, to join Lord Derby's administration under the present circumstances',[6] expressing the view that public opinion was moving strongly in a Liberal direction, and that Gladstone would damage his own future prospects by defying it. Gladstone was less sure than Aberdeen on the latter point, but in general the former Prime Minister's views coincided pretty well with his own. Despite his disclaimer in his letter to Disraeli, it seems certain that his unwillingness to be associated with him was Gladstone's prime motivation in turning down what was a remarkably candid and generous offer. Never again was either man to make any gesture towards the other, and their rivalry now seemed set in stone. There was, however, a certain asymmetry about their attitudes to each other. Gladstone heartily disapproved of Disraeli on moral grounds, over and above his continued wrath at his treatment of Peel. He admired Disraeli's talents as a speaker and parliamentary tactician, and his consistently unfavourable judgements on his conduct were – very occasionally – modified by notions of 'fair play' or Christian charity. But Gladstone never rated Disraeli very highly. It was different with Disraeli, who was never known to express moral disapproval of anybody. Indeed, he reputedly once described Gladstone as 'a man without a single redeeming defect', and was annoyed by his unremitting high-mindedness. Eventually, he came to regard his rival as a charlatan, though he had a high regard for his abilities, and – despite the possible threat to his own position – was sincere in his desire to reintegrate him into the Conservative Party. Over the years, however, his dislike for Gladstone gradually grew, and by the end of his life something approaching cool hatred was their mutual attitude.

When Gladstone declined to take the India post, Derby appointed Edward Stanley instead, and persuaded Edward Bulwer-Lytton to replace him as Colonial Secretary. Lytton was not a success as a minister, but it caused much interest, and no little amusement, that – for the one and only time in British history – two romantic novelists were serving together in the cabinet. It was Lytton who was responsible for one of the most bizarre episodes in Gladstone's life. At a loss to know what to do about the future of the Ionian islands, a former Venetian colony which had been a British protectorate since 1815, Lytton proposed that Gladstone should be sent there as Commissioner Extraordinary to sound out the views of the inhabitants. Disraeli strongly backed the proposal, though it is not clear whether he viewed it as an indirect way of attaching Gladstone to the Tory government or as a ruse to get him away from Westminster so that his formidable debating power should not be available to the opposition. Virtually all of Gladstone's political associates advised him not to accept, but – mesmerised by the prospect of walking in the footsteps of the ancient Greeks, whom he admired so much – and being bored by his current inactivity, he agreed to go, and set off for Corfu with great enthusiasm on 8 November 1858.

But the mission, which lasted less than four months, was not a success and bordered on being a fiasco. He undertook his duties with his customary diligence, but he did not endear himself to the overwhelmingly Greek population by addressing them either in Italian or in ancient Greek, which was unintelligible to them. Gladstone discovered that the predominant feeling on the islands was in favour of *Enosis* (union with Greece). He was not unsympathetic, but he felt it premature, and recommended instead progress towards home rule. He also fell out with the High Commissioner, Sir John Young, who was promptly dismissed by Lytton, Gladstone being appointed in his place. To his great distress, he then learned that the High Commissionership – unlike his original appointment – was ruled by the government law officers to be incompatible with membership of the House of Commons, and his Oxford University seat was declared vacant. A horrified Gladstone promptly resigned the appointment within three weeks, and prepared to return home. Two weeks later, however, he was returned unopposed in a by-election, and he remained in Corfu until his hastily appointed successor arrived on 16 February 1859. In the meantime he presented his constitutional proposals to a specially summoned representative assembly of the islands, which rejected them almost unanimously. Derby's government took no action on Gladstone's recommendations, but four years later Palmerston's second government agreed that the islands should be coded to Greece. Gladstone returned home overland via Venice, taking in a lot of sightseeing on the way, and stopping off in Turin to dine with Count Cavour, the Prime Minister of Piedmont–Sardinia. In alliance with Napoleon III, Cavour was in the final stages of preparation for war with Austria, which was intended to deliver the whole of Northern Italy into Piedmontese hands. This journey served to reignite Gladstone's enthusiasm for Italian unity, which had first been sparked by his earlier visit to Naples in 1850–1.

Although Disraeli's official post was Chancellor of the Exchequer, for which he was very glad to receive the large salary of £5000 a year, he was much more deeply involved as Leader of the Commons. As Chancellor, he introduced only one budget – shortly after taking office – and it was, for all practical purposes, that which had already been prepared by his predecessor in Palmerston's government, Sir George Cornwall Lewis. A major piece of legislation which he piloted through the Commons was the India Bill, which, in the aftermath of the Mutiny, wound up the East India Company, transferring control of the administration to a viceroy and abolishing the post of President of the Board of Control, substituting that of Secretary of State for India. He also oversaw a compromise agreement which finally led to Jews being able to take their place in the House of

Commons. The House had on several occasions passed bills enabling its members to take a non-Christian oath, but each time it had been over-ruled by the House of Lords. Yet at each election for the past 11 years Disraeli's friend Lionel de Rothschild had been elected as one of the MPs for the City of London and had been unable to take his seat. In 1858 yet another Oaths Bill was passed by the Commons, but was overthrown by the Lords. On this occasion, the Commons did not meekly accept the rebuff, but established a committee to resolve the problem, and included the still unsworn de Rothschild among its membership. Eventually, and against the wishes of Derby, who was resolutely opposed to Jewish MPs, an agreement was reached that each House should henceforth be responsible for determining its own membership. Very few Tory MPs apart from Disraeli backed this agreement, and it was carried only because of overwhelming support from the opposition. On 26 July 1858, de Rothschild was 'quietly sworn in, shaking hands with Disraeli on his way to his seat'.[7] He was to be followed by half a dozen other Jewish MPs over the next eight years. None represented Disraeli's own party, which would not elect a Jew until Saul Isaac was elected for Nottingham in 1874.

Yet the most controversial piece of legislation introduced during the session was a new Reform Bill. For many years after the passage of the 'Great' Reform Bill in 1832, 'reform' had been a dead issue, at least in Parliament, and – in 1839 – Lord John Russell, the 1832 act's chief architect, had declared that no further measures were necessary, and was dubbed 'Finality Jack' for his pains. Outside Parliament, the Chartist movement had continued to campaign for universal male suffrage and other reform measures, but after the failure of its last major demonstration in 1848, the movement disintegrated. In the 1850s, however, a number of Radical and Whig politicians, including Russell, began to agitate for at least a moderate enlargement of the suffrage, but Palmerston was adamantly opposed to any reform measures. Disraeli, however, managed to persuade Derby that – in order to pre-empt the possibility of a more radical measure being introduced by a future Whig government – it would be preferable to introduce their own bill carefully designed to favour the Tories in its overall effect. After much haggling in the cabinet, Disraeli produced a bill whose main provisions were the equalising of the franchise between borough and county constituencies at male householders with an income of £10, together with a new £20 lodger franchise, and the redistribution of 70 seats from smaller to larger boroughs (18) and the counties (52). In addition, Disraeli proposed plural voting for a number of favoured groups (described by John Bright as 'fancy franchises') – these included men whose income included £10 a year from Consols (undated British government fixed-interest bonds), those with £60 in the Savings Bank, university graduates, ministers of religion, lawyers, doctors and certified schoolmasters. When the bill came before the House, Lord John Russell submitted a hostile amendment, carefully drafted to appeal both to those who felt the bill went too far and those who thought it did not go far enough. His amendment was carried by 330 votes to 291. Gladstone, still highly confused as to whether he was really a Conservative or a Liberal, made 'a vigorous if irrelevant defence of rotten boroughs and voted for the Bill',[8] but this was insufficient to save a measure hand-made by his great rival. Instead of resigning after his government's defeat, Derby asked the Queen for a dissolution, which she granted. A general election ensued in April–May 1859, in which the Tories made net gains of 26 seats – not enough to secure a majority. In a desperate attempt to remedy this deficiency, Disraeli wrote a letter to Palmerston, proposing that if he, 'together with a following of about 20 or 30 gentlemen', were to come over to the government 'it would have more than an absolute majority of the House'.[9] Disraeli strongly implied that not only himself but also Lord Derby would efface themselves, allowing Palmerston to resume the premiership. Palmerston replied immediately declining the offer, adding that 'no want of personal good feeling towards Lord Derby or yourself'[10] had contributed to his decision. In fact, he and Russell were about to patch up their longstanding quarrel in a move to unite the opposition parties, in order to eject Derby's government. On 6 June 1859, an historic meeting took place at Willis's rooms (the former Almack's club) in King Street, St James's, attended by 274 MPs – Whigs, Radicals and Peelites. At this meeting (which was not attended by Gladstone), both Palmerston and Russell declared that they were prepared to serve under each other's leadership, according to whoever was invited by the Queen to be Prime Minister. The meeting agreed to seek the first parliamentary opportunity to bring the government down, and voted unanimously to merge their forces in a new party – the Liberal Party. They did not have long to wait: the following day, Spencer Cavendish MP,

Marquess of Hartington and heir to the dukedom of Devonshire, moved a motion of no confidence in the government, opening a three-day debate in which all the leading parliamentarians, with the conspicuous exception of Gladstone, participated. Despite a superbly defiant speech by Disraeli, the newly united opposition held together, and the government was defeated by 323 votes to 310. Gladstone, possibly because he was appalled by the prospect of Palmerston again becoming Prime Minister, voted – for the last time in his life – with the Tories. The second Derby government came to an end after one year and 111 days, a modest improvement on the 292 days achieved by his first administration.

In a forlorn attempt to avoid reverting again to one of the two 'terrible old men', Victoria invited Earl Granville, the Liberal leader in the Lords, to form a government. Granville asked Palmerston to serve as Leader of the House of Commons, which he accepted, confident in the belief that Russell would refuse to become the third person in the government, and that without his support Granville would be unable to proceed. So it turned out, and the Queen then approached the now nearly 75-year-old Palmerston. He immediately accepted, and Russell readily agreed to serve under him as Foreign Secretary. 'Pam', as he was now familiarly known, proceeded to fill all the other government posts from within the ranks of the newly constituted Liberal Party, while also putting out feelers to Gladstone. The latter, given his longstanding disapproval of Palmerston, his unsatisfactory experience of serving under him for three weeks at the beginning of his 1855–8 administration, and his very recent vote in support of Derby's government, might well have been expected to decline. Virtually all his instincts told him to do so, but these were outweighed by his renewed passion for Italian unification. The war between Piedmont and France, on the one hand, and Austria on the other, had just broken out. Palmerston had, in a recent speech, come down firmly on the Italian side, while Derby and Disraeli's sympathies were clearly with the Austrians. Metaphorically holding his nose, Gladstone responded positively to Palmerston, but insisted that the only post he could accept was that of Chancellor of the Exchequer. Palmerston, who had already offered the post to his previous Chancellor, Sir George Cornwall Lewis, reluctantly agreed. This was to the chagrin of at least one of the most prominent Whigs, the former Foreign Secretary the Earl of Clarendon, who consequently found himself excluded from the top ministerial posts, declining to take anything more junior. His wife complained bitterly,

> Why he who voted in the last division with the Derby ministry should not only be asked to join this one, *but be allowed to choose his office*, I cannot conceive, or rather, I *can* conceive, for I know that it is for his power of speaking. They want his tongue and they dread it in opposition. And so, tho' G. Lewis had accepted the office ... he has been requested to make way for Gladstone, which accordingly he has done and accepts the Home Office instead.[11]

Gladstone's acceptance of office under Palmerston was also compared unfavourably in some Radical circles with the stout refusal of Richard Cobden, who at Gladstone's suggestion had been proposed as President of the Board of Trade. Having previously been at least as critical of the Prime Minister as Gladstone, he now declared that he would feel 'a ... sense of a loss of personal dignity and self-respect that would follow official subordination to a Minister of whom he had thought and spoken so ill as he had thought and spoken of Lord Palmerston'.[12]

The Conservatives, too, having tried so long and so hard to lure Gladstone back into their own ranks, now reacted with some indignation. They put up a heavyweight candidate – the Marquess of Chandos (later the 3rd Duke of Buckingham) – to oppose him in the by-election which followed his appointment, a move which disconcerted Gladstone, who had expected to be returned unopposed. He was re-elected by 1050 votes to 859, but the margin was narrow enough to suggest that his days as a member for the Oxford University seat might well be numbered. Given his propensity to resign, or to threaten to do so, on the slightest pretext, and his known antipathy to Palmerston, there were many who predicted that their new partnership would not last for long. Gladstone, however, remained on board for the whole of Palmerston's second premiership, which lasted for six years and 128 days, until his death in office in October 1865. He found that he and Palmerston had more in common than he had suspected, including a marked aversion – at that time – to parliamentary reform, with both men restraining the ambition of Lord John Russell to introduce a new bill extending the franchise to some, at least, working-class men. It also helped that Palmerston left him a relatively free hand in his role as Chancellor of the Exchequer, except that Gladstone had periodically to fend off prime ministerial pressure for military expenditure which he regarded as excessive.

There are many who consider Gladstone to be the greatest man ever to have held the premiership, a view held by Roy Jenkins in concluding his biography in 1995, though he later changed his mind and awarded the palm to Churchill.[13] Few, however, would challenge his pre-eminence as Chancellor of the Exchequer. He held the post for far longer than any of his successors, serving four times, twice in conjunction with the premiership, for a total of 12 and a half years. He effectively created the post as it exists in modern times, and none of his successors has rivalled the impact which he made. Before his time, the Prime Minister still wielded substantial financial powers in his function as First Lord of the Treasury, and the Chancellor played only a secondary role, comparable to that of the Chief Secretary to the Treasury today. Gladstone subsumed to his office all the financial powers formerly wielded by the Prime Minister, and clearly established that the Chancellor should normally be seen as the second person in the government, even though the office remained – in formal terms – junior to those of the secretaries of state. In the words of Jenkins, one of his most successful followers in the office, he gave his annual budgets 'such a sweep and force that their presentation became a fixture of the national life comparable to Derby Day or the State Opening of Parliament'.[14]

Gladstone found that the nation's finances had deteriorated sharply since his previous spell as Chancellor, in 1852–5, and he inherited a deficit of over £5 million. He attributed this to the laxness of his recent predecessors – Disraeli and George Lewis – and in his July 1859 budget, presented within four weeks of his assuming office, he proposed a sharp increase in income tax from five pence to nine pence in the pound, the highest-ever peacetime rate. The budget went through without great difficulty, with only a two-hour discussion in the cabinet, where the only dissenter was Lewis, who, as Roy Jenkins comments, 'had as Chancellor in 1855–8 been largely responsible for the build-up of the deficit, and was also manifestly sour at not himself being in that office'.[15] In the House of Commons there was also little opposition, with Disraeli mounting no great challenge, and the budget was approved without a division. In all his budgets, one of Gladstone's main aims, as he made very clear, was 'retrenchment'. He had a horror of what he regarded as unnecessary public expenditure, and once famously said that 'No Chancellor of the Exchequer is worth his salt who is not ready to save what are meant by candle-ends and cheese-paring in the cause of his country.'[16]

In the following year, 1860, he raised income tax by a further penny, but his budget was most notable for marking a further massive step towards free trade, reducing the total number of items on which customs duties were levied from 419 to 48, of which only 15 produced any significant revenue. This budget had been preceded by the negotiation of the Anglo–French Commercial Treaty by the former Radical MP Richard Cobden, whom Gladstone had authorised to act on behalf of the British government. This historic measure, agreed at a time when tension was rising sharply between the two countries following widespread fears, expressed notably by Palmerston, that the adventurous foreign policy of Napoleon III might lead to war, had an immediate calming effect. It also did much to boost trade with Britain's closest neighbour, which previously had been almost insignificant, with barely half of one per cent of British exports going to France. A major concession to France in the treaty was a heavy cut in wine duties, which was extended in Gladstone's budget to all other countries. Gladstone also proposed the total abolition of the heavy duties levied on paper, the effect of which would be a very substantial fall in the price of books and newspapers, leading, in particular, to a large rise in newspaper circulations. The Tory-dominated House of Lords, however, voted down the bill implementing this measure, believing that it would encourage the publication of dangerous or subversive material which would fall into the hands of a mass public, a view also held by Palmerston. Gladstone fumed against what he described as a *coup d'état* by the Lords, but in the following year he reintroduced the measure, and ensured that all the budget proposals would henceforth be incorporated into a single consolidated Finance Bill, judging that the Lords would not dare to defy a convention – dating back to the seventeenth century – that the Commons alone should decide financial policy. They did not, and it was another half century before they nerved themselves to do so, in rejecting Lloyd George's 'People's budget' of 1909. Thus was the last 'tax on knowledge' repealed. Several newspaper proprietors, grateful for the boost in sales which ensued, responded by giving Gladstone a consistently 'good press', which meant that his fame and reputation spread widely across the country, rather than being restricted to a narrow metropolitan elite.

Consequently, Gladstone began to receive a flood of invitations to speak at meetings in all parts of the country, many but by no means all of which were sponsored by local Liberals. He was, in fact, the first politician to take advantage of the extensive railway network built over the three preceding decades to operate on a national level. He was particularly fond of speaking in two great halls, St George's Hall in his native Liverpool and the Free Trade Hall in Manchester. He built up a large following in Lancashire, and received an invitation from Liberals in the newly created South Lancashire constituency (a three-member seat) to be one of their candidates. Sensing that his Oxford University seat might be difficult to defend following his adhesion to the Liberals, Gladstone accepted, and – as the law then allowed – prepared to stand in both constituencies in the ensuing election, which was to take place in 1865. Wherever he spoke, Gladstone attracted large crowds, particularly of working-class men, many of whom were not qualified to vote. Most of them were skilled workers, and keen chapel-goers, and Gladstone's earnest manner and high moral tone held an instant appeal for them. Gradually, too, he radicalised his message, and before long he was christened 'the People's William' by the *Daily Telegraph*, then a pro-Liberal newspaper. Other leading politicians belatedly tried to emulate Gladstone by speaking around the country, but none of them were able to draw such large crowds or to establish such a rapport with their auditors. Disraeli was more successful than most, but was unable to match Gladstone as a platform orator. In the more intimate atmosphere of the House of Commons, it was a different matter. Though their styles of speaking were quite different, and each of them had their triumphs and (rare) disasters, they were more evenly matched.

The outbreak of the US Civil War, in 1861, had a number of effects in Britain, particularly in Lancashire, where the cotton industry was grievously affected by the success of the Northerners in cutting off supplies from the Southern states. The British government affected a neutral stance, though most Liberals were sympathetic to the North. Gladstone, however, committed a grievous mistake in a speech he made in Newcastle-upon-Tyne on 7 October 1862, at a time when the war was going badly for the North. He was reported as saying,

We know quite well that the people of the Northern states have not yet drunk of the cup and they are still trying to hold it far from their lips – which all the rest of the world see that they must drink of. We may have our own opinion about slavery; we may be for or against the South, but there is no doubt that Jefferson Davis and other leaders of the South have made an army; they are making a navy; and they have made what is more difficult than either, they have made a nation.[17]

Gladstone's words almost caused an international incident, with the American Ambassador, Charles Adams, preparing to pack his bags until he was dissuaded with great difficulty by Foreign Secretary Russell, who wrote an angry letter to Gladstone, saying, 'I think you went beyond the latitude which all speakers must be allowed.'[18] John Bright, an admirer of Gladstone, nevertheless wrote that 'He is as unstable as water in some things; he is for union and freedom in Italy and for dissension and bondage in America.'[19] He wrote to Cobden that Gladstone 'was born of a great slave-owning family and I suppose the taint is ineradicable.'[20] Much later, only two years before his death in 1898, Gladstone was to admit that he had made a 'mistake, but one of incredible grossness, and with such consequences of offence and alarm attached to it, that my failing to perceive them justly exposed me to very severe blame.'[21]

The long years of Palmerston's second premiership proved a dismal time for Disraeli, who was virtually forbidden to mount any forceful opposition by Derby, who despaired of besting the Liberal leader and was reassured by his deeply conservative views on domestic political issues. Writing to Disraeli on 12 January 1860, he instructed him to 'keep the present men in and resist all temptations to avail ourselves of a casual majority.' Disraeli protested that 'you cannot keep a large army in order without letting them sometimes smell gunpowder.'[22] He had recently been stricken by the death, at the age of just under 57, of his unmarried sister Sarah. Ever since the death of her fiancé, William Meredith, in 1831, she had devoted herself entirely to her brother, entering into a prolonged and intimate correspondence with him, in which he opened up to her in a way which he did with nobody else. Replying to a letter of condolence from Lord John Manners, he described her as his 'First and ever faithful friend.'[23] Writing reproachfully to his brother Ralph, Disraeli complained that 'We have never had a line from you since your last visit here – and of course, we never hear from James. This is not the way to keep the family together – poor darling Sa's last hope and prayer.'[24]

In fact, Disraeli seldom encountered either of his brothers, except when they pestered him for patronage on their behalf. He felt very much a man alone, less and less appreciated by the bulk of Tory MPs under his charge. Lord Robert Cecil openly criticised him in a series of articles in the *Quarterly Review*, while the large number of country squires on the Tory benches showed their lack of enthusiasm by staying away from the Commons. Edward Stanley noted that the opposition benches were 'completely bare, except for the front bench, from 7 to 10 every night, unless an important party division is likely'.[25] The only Conservative without a party position who attended regularly, he said, was Richard Spooner, 'now 80 years of age: and he is a banker, not a squire'.[26] Deeply discouraged, Disraeli momentarily contemplated giving up politics altogether, and resuming his career as a novelist. He was soon dissuaded by Derby, who could discern nobody on the Conservative benches in the Commons who could adequately replace him. The only possible candidate was Stanley, whose views were so far to the left that his father could not contemplate passing the leadership to him.

While still a young man, Disraeli had enjoyed close friendship with two men who were his rough contemporaries – Count d'Orsay and Edward Bulwer-Lytton. D'Orsay returned to live in Paris in 1849, and died there in 1852, while he and Bulwer-Lytton drifted apart, and were never close again, although they were cabinet colleagues in the mid-1850s. Never again did Disraeli enjoy easy relations on a basis of equality with men his own age, though he collected a band of much younger followers, of whom Lennox and Ralph Earle were leading examples. Throughout his life, he felt more comfortable in the company of women than of men, and it is understandable that at times when his morale was low he turned to them for solace. One such person may well have been Dolly Nevill, who lived diagonally across the road from the Disraelis in Upper Grosvenor Street, and was a close and longstanding friend both of Disraeli and of Mary Anne. Lady Dorothy Walpole Nevill, a descendant of the first British Prime Minister, Sir Robert Walpole, is described by the American historian Stanley Weintraub as 'vivacious and youthful, with three children and a largely absent husband, and a reputation for flouting convention that had followed her from girlhood'.[27]

Disraeli, who was 22 years her senior, is quoted by Weintraub as describing her as 'without absolute beauty', but 'wild and bewitching'.[28] On 4 March 1865, aged 38, she gave birth to a third son, Ralph Nevill, 'almost certainly conceived in London in June 1864'[29] when Mary Anne was already ensconced for the summer at Hughenden while Disraeli was detained in London by his parliamentary duties, and the baby's putative father, Reggie Nevill, was far away at his country seat. Young Ralph grew up to live the 'unstrenuous life of an unattached gentleman of leisure',[30] and died in June 1930 at the age of 65, having written nearly thirty books, none of them of any great distinction. At no time in Disraeli's lifetime was it suggested that he was Ralph's father, but Weintraub devotes half a chapter to presenting the (circumstantial) evidence that he was, and this certainly appears a probability. The other half of the same chapter[31] concerns a young woman, Kate Donovan, who was conceived by an unknown mother in the same year as Ralph Nevill's birth. A surviving photograph of her, when she came of age in the later 1880s, and after she had married and emigrated to Australia, shows her to be 'strikingly like Disraeli'. The evidence linking her to him is flimsy, except that when making his will Disraeli was known to have made separate provision, through his solicitor, Sir Philip Rose, for a 'minor child'. Weintraub concludes,

> The evidence for Disraeli's paternity is plausible without being conclusive. By Victorian standards his behaviour would have been acceptable for a gentleman of rank. His society was one in which women were often left to bear both the children and the burden. In the case of Ralph and Kate one child had a legal father and inheritance; the other was apparently provided for.[32]

# Seven

# The struggle for reform, 1865–8

Palmerston's second government was by no means a reforming administration; indeed it produced very little significant legislation of any kind. Palmerston had set his face against any measure of parliamentary reform, and had concentrated almost entirely on foreign policy. Apart from yet another war with China, in which an Anglo-French force had burned down the Emperor's summer palace, the main issues of contention concerned the struggle for Italian unification, the US Civil War and the Schleswig–Holstein dispute. The last of these resulted in humiliation for both Palmerston and Russell, the Foreign Secretary, who had publicly encouraged the Danish government to absorb the two duchies, which had a predominantly German-speaking population, into the Kingdom of Denmark, despite threats from both Austria and Prussia, and then left the Danes to their own devices when the two powerful German states launched an invasion in 1864. Palmerston cheerfully brushed his embarrassment aside by claiming that the Schleswig–Holstein question was so complex that 'only three men in Europe had ever understood it, and of these the Prince Consort was dead, a Danish statesman (unnamed) was in an asylum and he himself had forgotten it.'[1] For the rest, his bluster and noisy and belligerent defence of supposed British interests in international disputes ensured his lasting popularity among an increasingly jingoistic populace. Moreover, he benefited from exceptionally favourable press coverage. He and Lady Palmerston were famous for giving lavish parties at their home at 94 Piccadilly, to which virtually the whole of 'society' was invited. They were not unique in doing this among leading aristocratic politicians, but they – to the horror of their stuffier rivals – also extended invitations to the 'gentlemen of the press'. Newspaper proprietors and editors, hitherto being regarded as being distinctly 'below the salt', were highly flattered, and rewarded their hosts with unswerving support in their publications. When Palmerston was cited as co-respondent in a divorce case, at the age of 79, this only added to his popularity, as he was widely admired for being up to such activities at his advanced age. In fact, the case was dismissed by the judge, and the lady involved denied that she had had sexual relations with the Prime Minister.

For whatever reason, Palmerston, then aged 80, had no difficulty in winning the general election which ensued in July 1865, when he increased his majority by some twenty seats. Gladstone was defeated at Oxford University, in part at least because of his defection to the Liberals, his support for university reform and his involvement in theological disputes. Yet probably the major cause of his defeat was the introduction for the first time of postal voting. In previous elections only those graduates living in or near Oxford had mostly bothered to vote in this non-territorial constituency, few others being willing to undertake a lengthy journey in order to cast their votes. Now, in particular, the large number of graduates serving as clergymen throughout the United Kingdom – who were overwhelmingly Tory – were able to participate, and the turnout rose by some 300 per cent. Gladstone finished up bottom of the poll, but just managed to be elected at South Lancashire, where he came third behind two Tories in a three-member seat. Disraeli had no problems in being re-elected in Buckinghamshire, where he and two other Tories were returned unopposed.

The overall result was Liberals 360, Conservatives 298, but the newly elected MPs were not due to take their seats until November. On 18 October, however, Palmerston died at Brocket Hall, Hertfordshire (the country seat which Lady Palmerston had inherited from her brother, Lord Melbourne), just two days short of his eighty-first birthday. The circumstances of his death are unclear; the death certificate said it was due to pneumonia, but a persistent local rumour had it that he had collapsed while seducing a pretty young chambermaid.[2] His supposed last words – 'Die, my dear doctor! That's the *last* thing I shall do' – are probably apocryphal.

There was never much doubt that Lord John Russell, who had been created Earl Russell some years before and was now aged 73, would succeed to the premiership. Gladstone pre-empted any suggestion that he might himself be chosen by writing immediately to Russell saying, 'Your former place as her Minister, your powers, experience, services, and renown, do not leave room for doubt that you will be sent for.'[3]

Gladstone emphasised that he was not seeking any special place in the new ministry, and would be 'most willing to retire'; he would, however, be 'quite willing' to continue in the 'exact capacity I now fill'. In the event, Russell not only confirmed him as Chancellor, but also appointed him as Leader of the House of Commons, making it crystal clear that he was now the second person in the administration, and his own presumptive successor. Otherwise the cabinet remained unchanged, except that the Earl of Clarendon returned to his former post as Foreign Secretary, now vacated by Russell's promotion.

Russell's overwhelming priority in his second premiership was to secure the passage of a Second Reform Bill, extending the franchise further down the social scale. This he felt would successfully round off his career as a reformist politician. He anticipated that Gladstone would be an enthusiastic supporter in this endeavour, despite his earlier lukewarm attitude to reform. Gladstone, on his adhesion to the Liberals, appeared to have effected a sea change in his position on the issue. Speaking in a debate on an (unsuccessful) private member's bill in 1864, he had electrified the House and made himself the hero of Radical MPs by uttering the following words: 'I venture to say that every man who is not presumably incapacitated by some consideration of personal unfitness or of political danger is morally entitled to come within the pale of the constitution.'[4]

The logic of his words implied that he now supported something approaching universal manhood suffrage, or at the very least household suffrage. In fact, at least in the short term, he intended something a great deal more modest. Put in charge of preparing Russell's bill, he initially thought of lowering the property qualification in borough constituencies from £10 to £6, but took fright when research indicated that this would lead to a working-class majority of voters in more than half the parliamentary constituencies. He therefore proposed that the limit should be set at £7. This infuriated the Radicals, but was still going too far for the more right-wing former Whigs, led by the caustic but brilliant orator Robert Lowe. They were branded as 'Adullamites' in a biblical reference (I Samuel XXII: 1–2) by John Bright, who said of Lowe in a parliamentary debate, 'The Rt. Hon. Gentleman is the first of the new Party who has retired into what maybe called his political cave of Adullam – and he has called about him everyone that was in distress and everyone that was discontented.'[5]

Caught between the disappointment of his main supporters and the obduracy of the Adullamites, who made common cause with the Tories, skilfully led by Disraeli, Gladstone floundered in the numerous debates on the bill. In the second reading debate Disraeli made much of Gladstone's long record as an opponent of reform, quoting at length from his passionate speech against the 1832 Reform Bill in the Oxford Union in 1831. Gladstone was able to retort that 'my youthful mind and imagination were impressed with the same idle and futile fears which still bewilder and distract the mature mind of the right hon. Gentleman', but was unable to arouse much enthusiasm on the Liberal benches. The bill just scraped through its second reading with a majority of five, and no fewer than 35 Adullamites voting with the opposition. Two months later, in June 1866, a hostile amendment was carried during the committee stage, and the government was defeated by 315 to 304, the number of Adullamites having grown to 44. A defiant Russell, supported by Gladstone but only two other cabinet ministers, wanted to ask the Queen for a dissolution and to fight a general election on the issue of reform. They were over-ruled by their colleagues, who felt that 'the apathetic state of the people at that date' ruled out this recourse.[6] And so, on 26 June 1866, a devastated Russell submitted his resignation to the Queen. His second government had lasted a mere 240 days. Gladstone recorded in his diary, 'Finished in Downing Street. Left my keys behind. Somehow it makes a void.'[7]

Queen Victoria reluctantly accepted Russell's resignation, and – as was her wont – sent again for Lord Derby. There was much speculation that rather than again forming a minority government, he would seek to form a coalition with the Adullamites, which would ensure a parliamentary majority. Derby made no such approach, but the Adullamites themselves indicated that they would like to be included, but not under Derby's premiership. They suggested that he should efface himself in favour of a Whig grandee, such as Lord Clarendon or Earl Granville, or if a Tory was to be chosen, his own son Stanley. Derby had no appetite for this, and Disraeli even less so, and he proceeded to form a government which included only one Liberal MP, Michael Morris, who became Solicitor-General for Ireland. It was notably stronger, however, than his two previous administrations, with Stanley taking over from Malmesbury as Foreign Secretary, and the former Lord Robert Cecil, now Viscount Cranborne and soon to be the 3rd Marquess of Salisbury, as Colonial Secretary. A notable recruit was Gladstone's former private secretary, Sir Stafford Northcote, whom Disraeli had persuaded to join the Tories. He became President of the Board of Trade. For the third time, Disraeli became both Chancellor of the Exchequer and Leader of the Commons. He made an important change in his immediate entourage, dispensing with the services of Ralph Earle, whom he had come to see as unreliable. Earle was paid off by being appointed as secretary to the Poor Law Board, at a salary of £1100 per year, and replaced by Montague Corry, described by Robert Blake as

> the perfect choice. He was devoted to Disraeli, highly competent, and devoid of personal ambition. After Mary Anne's death he was to become even more indispensable, managing those tedious domestic matters such as engaging servants and finding houses etc., at which Disraeli was so hopelessly incompetent.[8]

'Monty' Corry remained as Disraeli's right-hand man until the latter's death in 1881, even after he was raised to the peerage, at Disraeli's urgent request to the Queen, as 1st Baron Rowton, in 1880. A passage in *Endymion*, a novel which Disraeli was to publish in 1880, is generally held to refer to Corry, and reveals how highly Disraeli regarded him: 'The relations between a Minister and his secretary are, or at least should be, among the finest that can exist between two individuals. Except the married state, there is none in which so great a confidence is involved, in which more forbearance should be exercised, or more sympathy ought to exist.'[9]

A remarkable change had come over Derby in recent years. Previously a firm opponent of reform, his views had substantially modified in the light of his experience in dealing with the unfortunate consequences for Lancashire of the American Civil War. The cutting off of cotton supplies from the Southern states had led to widespread unemployment in the textile industry which dominated the county, where Derby was the leading landowner. He threw himself into the relief effort, serving as chairman of the Lancashire Relief Committee, to which he devoted at least a day a week of his time, contributing generously to its funds and persuading other wealthy aristocrats to do the same. He found to his surprise that the unemployed men that he met, so far from being potential revolutionaries, were on the whole moderate and reasonable men. Moreover, his friend and shooting companion, Lord Malmesbury, now Lord Privy Seal, had concluded that while the better-off members of the working class were more likely to be Liberal voters, the really poor tended to be deferential to the wealthy and were thus an untapped source of Tory support. Derby's conclusion was that his government should bring to an end the controversy over reform by carrying a measure which went further than Russell's and Gladstone's bill, which they had contrived to defeat. He brooded on bringing the property qualification for urban voters down to £5, but eventually decided that the only logical conclusion was household suffrage, that is that the head of every household should have the vote, whatever his income.

He instructed an initially sceptical Disraeli to draw up a bill to this effect. After two false starts, he produced a draft which ran into fierce opposition within the cabinet, led by Cranborne and the Earl of Carnarvon, the Colonial Secretary. Cranborne was unconvinced of the necessity for reform; no great believer in democracy, he appeared to feel that the settlement reached under the 1832 Reform Bill had produced an almost perfect balance between the different classes of society. The untrammelled power of the aristocracy had been trimmed, and representatives of the middle classes had been admitted into the decision-making process. Cranborne had no objection to working-class representatives also being involved, but did not wish them to be admitted in such numbers as to swamp the interests of the propertied classes. His quasi-Marxist analysis led him to conclude that giving power to the workers would inevitably lead to the despoliation of the other classes. Derby and Disraeli tried to convince him that this threat could be avoided by the introduction of plural voting for the better-off and better-educated classes. Plural voting, they argued, could be made to produce something like 360,000 extra votes to counter-balance the 4,500,000 who would get the vote under household suffrage. The two objectors, together with the War Secretary, General

Jonathan Peel, were only half convinced, but for the moment they held their hand. Two weeks later, however, on 7 March 1867, they stormed out of the cabinet. Cranborne later claimed that they objected not so much to the proposed reforms but to the 'tricky' way in which Derby, and particularly Disraeli, had tried to bounce them through the cabinet. Derby was initially shocked by their departure, exclaiming, 'This is the end of the Conservative Party,'[10] but calmly reshuffled the cabinet and proceeded to the introduction of the bill.

Disraeli, however, only too aware that the government was in a minority of around seventy in the House of Commons, realised that he would need to attract a substantial number of votes from the opposition if he was to get a bill – *any* bill – onto the Statute Book. He looked primarily to the large block of former Radical MPs, led by John Bright, who were much the most enthusiastic supporters of reform and who were conducting a noisy series of public meetings and demonstrations across the country. During the committee stage of the bill he repeatedly accepted amendments moved by them, which often went far beyond the bill's original scope while steadfastly rejecting all the official Liberal amendments moved by Gladstone, which mostly sought to moderate its effect. One consequence was the progressive abandonment by Disraeli of the 'fancy franchises' designed to balance the effect of household suffrage. Initially it was foreseen that they would, collectively, provide for up to four votes each for those with large incomes, degrees or professional qualifications, investments in government bonds, ministers of religion and so on, but it was soon reduced to a maximum of two votes per person, and then the 'fancy franchises' were struck out altogether. In fact Disraeli, who put in a bravura performance, had got carried away by the chase, and was now absolutely determined to get the bill through at whatever cost, in the process humiliating his great rival Gladstone. Derby's health was poor at this time, and he made no attempt to rein in his deputy, leaving him a free hand throughout much of the committee stage. In fact he too lost sight of his original objectives, and was determined, in his own words, to 'dish the Whigs'.

The decisive moment in the committee stage came on 12 April 1867, when Gladstone confidently moved a wrecking amendment, secure in the belief that he would be able to rally the entire opposition behind him. It did not work out that way – the Liberal leader totally failed to appreciate the strength of feeling among Radical MPs, who were now strongly committed to the passage of the bill, and his speech fell sadly flat. He was followed by Disraeli, who made one of the finest and most persuasive speeches of his entire career, much more closely attuned to the mood of the House. When it divided, Gladstone's motion was defeated by 310 to 289, 45 Liberals having voted with the government, while only five Tories, including Cranborne, had sided with the opposition. Gladstone wryly recorded in his diary, 'A smash, perhaps without example'.[11] A triumphant Disraeli looked in briefly at the Carlton Club on his way home, where a large group of his supporters were wildly celebrating. The president of the club, Sir Matthew White Ridley MP, immediately raised his glass to propose a toast, saying, 'Here's to the man who rode the race, who took the time, who kept the time, and who did the trick!'[12]

Disraeli was strongly pressed to stay and sup with his supporters, but as Mary Anne later boasted to a friend,

> 'Dizzy came home to me.' And she then proceeded to describe the dinner; 'I had got him a raised pie from Fortnum and Mason's, and a bottle of champagne and he ate half the pie and drank all the champagne, and then he said, "Why, my dear, you are more like a mistress than a wife." And I could see that she took it as a very high compliment indeed.[13]

The bill finally cleared the Commons on 15 July 1867 and proceeded to the Lords, where Derby, whose health had temporally recovered, took it through without difficulty, conceding only one minor amendment. In the final debate in the Lords, he struck an optimistic note:

> No doubt we are making a great experiment and 'taking a leap in the dark', but I have the greatest confidence in the sound sense of my fellow countrymen, and I entertain a strong hope that the extended franchise which we are now conferring on them will be the means of placing the institutions of this country on a firmer basis, and that the passing of this measure will tend to increase the loyalty and contentment of a great portion of her Majesty's subjects.[14]

It was indeed a 'leap in the dark', particularly for the Tories, who feared that the removal of the plural voting provisions might have resulted in a bill which gave a net advantage to their Liberal opponents. Disraeli moved sharply to introduce a redistribution bill, which was effectively a 'gerrymander' on behalf of the Tories. It provided for the creation of 45 new seats by the removal of one member from boroughs of less than 10,000 inhabitants, of which 25 were allotted to the counties and 15 to larger towns, while the industrial cities of Liverpool, Manchester, Birmingham and Leeds gained a third member, and the University of London one. Moreover, some 700,000 voters were transferred from counties to boroughs, to ensure that the former would remain solidly Tory. Disraeli took good care to ensure that the Boundary Commission was packed with Conservative country gentlemen.

All in all, the passage of the Second Reform Bill was regarded as a triumph for Disraeli, and greatly increased his prestige in his own party. Most Tories were enthused that he had pulled a fast one over their opponents, and his worsting of Gladstone, who was now seen as a hate figure for 'going over to the other side', was particularly welcomed. Very few supported Cranborne, who wrote a bitter article in the *Quarterly Review* comparing Disraeli's cynical behaviour to that of the Whig lords who in 1688 had accepted the favours of James II while negotiating the invasion by William III. The people who were most put out, and indeed felt betrayed, were the Adullamites, who had defeated a bill proposed by their own party, only to see it replaced by a far worse measure, from their point of view, introduced by their former allies.

The passing into law of the Second Reform Bill effectively ended the agitation for parliamentary reform, and the issue now appeared settled for the foreseeable future, even though the franchise in county constituencies remained subject to strict property qualifications. These were not removed until 1884, by a bill introduced by Gladstone's second government. The 1867 act increased the size of the electorate from just over a million to nearly two million, a much greater proportionate increase than the 1832 act, which added a mere 220,000 voters to an electorate of 435,000. Some 16 per cent of the adult population now had the vote, compared to 7 per cent after the 1832 act. Only males were enfranchised, despite an attempt by John Stuart Mill, who was briefly a Liberal MP between 1865 and 1868, to introduce female suffrage. Disraeli was apparently not unsympathetic to his initiative, but did not regard it as practical politics, and neither spoke nor voted on his amendment, which was defeated by 196 votes to 73.

If the passage of the bill was a triumph for Disraeli, it was seen as a disaster for Gladstone, who had been comprehensively outmanoeuvred by his rival, and had disappointed his own party, and especially the Radicals, by his over-cautious approach. Derby himself was greatly impressed by Disraeli's performance, and this probably tilted the balance in his mind when he came to advise Queen Victoria on the question of his successor. When, because of his worsening health, he resigned six months after the royal assent to the bill, he passed over the claims of his own son, Lord Stanley, and recommended Disraeli, who was duly appointed on 27 February 1868. Two months earlier Earl Russell had stood down as leader of the Liberal Party, and was succeeded by Gladstone. It was the first time in many years that both parties were simultaneously led by members of the House of Commons.

# Eight

## Power – at last, 1868–74

In November 1867 Mary Anne Disraeli, then aged 76, fell seriously ill. Her ailment was not diagnosed at the time, but was possibly an early indication of the cancer of the womb which was to kill her five years later. For three days she was in a critical condition, and Disraeli was warned that she would not recover, but she rallied, and Disraeli, who had remained at her bedside, was able to resume his attendance in Parliament. He was genuinely touched when Gladstone, who was on friendly terms with Mary Anne, made a generous and kindly reference to her health. He replied with tears in his eyes, and the following day wrote to the Liberal leader, 'I was incapable yesterday of expressing to you how much I appreciate your considerate sympathy. My wife had always a strong personal regard for you, and being of a vivid and original character, she could comprehend and value your great gifts and qualities.'[1]

Gladstone responded in cordial terms, but these were among the last civil words – certainly the last warm ones – exchanged between the two men. After that, and particularly after the death of Mary Anne, their relationship descended into one of pure hatred. Before Mary Anne was fully recovered Disraeli also fell ill, and was confined to his bed on a different floor of their Grosvenor Gate house. They communicated with each other by notes carried by servants. Disraeli professed himself enchanted by Mary Anne's letters, full of social gossip, which he described as 'the most amusing and charming...I ever had. It beats Horace Walpole and Mme de Sévigné.'[2]

By January 1868, both had recovered, and Disraeli was able to attend the opening of the new parliamentary session. But Derby's health was failing fast, and he was informed by his doctor that there was no prospect of recovery if he remained in office. He wrote to Disraeli on 19 February saying that he intended to resign, and strongly implied that he would recommend him for the succession. Disraeli, who had been waiting for this moment with burning intensity for many years past, replied disingenuously:

> My dearest Lord – I have not sufficient command of myself at this moment to express what I feel about what has happened, and, after all, has happened so rapidly and unexpectedly!
>
> All I can say is that I never contemplated nor desired it. I was entirely content with my position, and all I aspired to was that, after a Government of tolerable length, and at least, fair repute, my retirement from public affairs should have accompanied your own; satisfied that I had enjoyed my opportunity in life, and proud that I had been long confidentially connected with one of the most eminent men of my time, and for whom I entertain profound respect and affection.
>
> I will not shrink from the situation, but I do not underrate its gravity, and mainly count, when you are convalescent, on your guidance and support.[3]

Far from being taken by surprise, Disraeli had in fact been summoned some weeks earlier by the Queen to Osborne House for a two-day stay. On arrival, he had been informed by the Queen's Private Secretary, General Charles Grey, that she intended to make him her First Minister. According to Monty Corry, 'Mr. D. was much struck by the fact that his old rival at Wycombe [who had defeated him in his first electoral contest] should become the bearer of such a message.'[4] As for the Queen, she proved quite unable to overcome her own impatience to convey to Disraeli her happiness that he was to become her first counsellor. Disraeli sent a cryptic note to his wife, saying, 'The most successful visit I ever had: all I could wish and hope.'[5]

Disraeli returned to Osborne on 27 February to kiss hands upon his appointment as Prime Minister, at the age of 63, and 30 years after the humiliation of his catastrophic maiden speech. The Queen was delighted, writing to her eldest daughter, 'Vicky', the Crown Princess of Prussia, 'Mr. Disraeli is Prime Minister! A proud thing for a Man "risen from the people" to have obtained! And I must say – really most loyally; it is his real talent, his good temper and the way in wh. he managed the Reform Bill last year – wh. have brought this about.'[6]

Disraeli made few changes to Derby's cabinet, the most notable being his choice of the little-known George Ward Hunt, previously Financial Secretary to the Treasury, to replace himself as Chancellor of the Exchequer. Commending him to the Queen, he wrote, 'He is more than six feet four inches in stature, but does not look so tall from his proportionate breadth; like St. Peter's no one is aware of his dimensions. But he has the sagacity of the elephant as well as the form.'[7]

He also took the opportunity of dispensing with the services of the 73-year-old Lord Chancellor, Lord Chelmsford, whom he had always found an unpleasant and obstructive colleague. Highly disgruntled, Chelmsford demanded a major honour as recompense for giving up office. Disraeli proposed a GCB (Knight Grand Cross of the Order of the Bath), but Chelmsford made clear that nothing less than an earldom would do. Disraeli forwarded his request to the Queen, commenting, 'It seems impossible that your Majesty can entertain such preposterous claims.'[8] So the poor man was left with nothing more than a burning sense of grievance, which he confided to all and sundry. Through an emissary, Disraeli offered Cranborne back his former post as Secretary of State for India, but to no avail. About to succeed his father as the 3rd Marquess of Salisbury, and still irreconcilable, he wrote contemptuously to a friend, 'Matters seem very critical – a woman on the throne, and a Jew adventurer who found out the secret of getting round her.'[9] The old Marquess's death had another consequence which was to have some political significance. After a decent interval, his much younger widow – Cranborne's stepmother – married Lord Stanley, who had long been her admirer. Disraeli celebrated his success with a grand reception, held in the Foreign Office, by courtesy of Lord Stanley, who continued as Foreign Secretary. It was so much more impressive than 10 Downing Street, which Mary Anne thought so 'dingy and decaying'.[10] Everybody who was anybody, headed by the Prince and Princess of Wales, was in attendance, including Gladstone, as Leader of the Opposition, who – understandably – did not much appear to enjoy the occasion. Disraeli himself seemed a trifle subdued, but cheerfully told his friends that he had at last risen 'to the top of the greasy pole'.

Disraeli did not expect his minority government to last long, but was determined to carry on at least until the new election registers had been compiled, so that the large number of newly enfranchised working-class voters should have the opportunity of showing their gratitude to the party which had given them the vote. So when the government was defeated by 65 votes in a division on a motion moved by Gladstone, on 1 May 1868, barely two months after he had assumed office, he contrived with the Queen that he should neither resign nor should there be an immediate election. It was, instead, determined that this should be deferred until the following November. This was flatly against the view of several senior cabinet ministers, notably Stanley, that the government should have resigned. The relationship between Disraeli and Stanley – previously very close – was slowly beginning to unravel. With the Queen, however, Disraeli's relations became ever closer and closer. In May 1868 she began the custom of sending him freshly cut primroses from the royal gardens, which she continued to do every year until his death, when a simple bunch from her was laid on his coffin. In return, Disraeli presented her with a collected edition of his works, and she responded with her newly published *Leaves from the Journal of Our life in the Highlands*, and was delighted when he addressed her as 'We authors, Ma'am'. It is not, perhaps, going too far to say that Victoria fell in love three times in her life. Firstly with her first Prime Minister, Lord Melbourne, who doubled up as her devoted private secretary. That was more in the way of a 'father and daughter' affair. Then came her overwhelming passion for Prince Albert, whose death she never expected to recover from. Insofar as she eventually did, it was due to Disraeli, to whom she transferred a great deal of her devotion. Some would say that there was a fourth recipient of her love – her Highland servant, John Brown, but that would go well beyond the scope of this book. Disraeli once told Matthew Arnold that 'Everyone likes flattery, and when it comes to Royalty you should lay it on with trowel.'[11] He certainly followed his own precept in his dealings with Victoria, but there is little doubt that he felt a genuine affection and awe for her. He constantly referred to her as the *Faerie Queene*, after the great poetical work by Edmund Spenser, and seemed to picture her as a romantic, almost dreamlike figure.

Disraeli's first government saw the passage of several reforming measures, notably the Corrupt Practices Act, which went a long way towards cleaning up British elections, and in particular provided for disputed election results to be adjudicated by the High Court judges rather than by the House of Commons, which in the vast majority of cases had meant that the majority party prevailed. Other acts passed provided for an end to public executions and the nationalisation of the private telegraph companies – a rare example of a Conservative government extending public ownership. A royal commission on the sanitary laws was appointed, under the chairmanship of Sir Charles Adderley. This did not report until 1871, but it led to extensive public-health reforms introduced by later governments. Yet the parliamentary session was dominated by disputes over Ireland, for the first time since the 1846 famine and the repeal of the Corn Laws. The spark was lit by a series of terrorist acts launched by the Fenian Brotherhood, an Irish Nationalist secret society which had been founded some ten years earlier, but received an injection of strength from a small group of Irish American soldiers who had fought for the North in the US Civil War, which ended in 1865. On demobilisation, they had emigrated to Ireland or England to carry on the struggle against their traditional British oppressors. In December 1867 they exploded a bomb outside the wall of Clerkenwell Prison in London in an attempt to rescue some prisoners. None escaped, but 12 people were killed and 120 injured – and this outrage immediately put the Irish problem high on the political agenda. Disraeli and his colleagues were well aware that land ownership was at the top of the list of Irish Catholic grievances, but sought to provide a sop with the proposal to establish a new Irish university for Catholics, who were excluded from the Anglican-dominated Trinity College, Dublin. Disraeli thought he had cleared the proposal with the future Cardinal Manning, who had just been appointed as Archbishop of Westminster. But the Irish Catholic hierarchy refused to be led by Manning, and strongly objected to the proposal, on the grounds that it did not give the Catholic Church total control over the projected university, and that the funds offered were inadequate.

Gladstone then leapt into the fray, and outbid Disraeli by offering the disestablishment of the Anglican Church of Ireland, which represented only about 10 per cent of the Irish population but was able to impose tithes on both Catholics and Presbyterians, who represented the vast majority. This completely undermined the government's proposal, and the bill was withdrawn, amid much acrimony between Disraeli and

Manning, whom he felt had misled him. He got his own back by basing the profoundly unflattering character Cardinal Grandison in his 1871 novel *Lothair* very obviously on the Roman Catholic prelate.

By proposing disestablishment, Gladstone succeeded in reuniting the Liberal Party, which had been badly split over parliamentary reform, and re-established his position as a resourceful and energetic parliamentary leader. He succeeded in carrying a bill to abolish compulsory church rates, and defeated the government, by a majority of 65, on a resolution to abolish the Anglican establishment in Ireland. Gladstone's initiative was highly popular in the country, appealing especially to Catholics, nonconformists and even those Anglicans who felt that the privileges claimed by their church in Ireland were indefensible. However, it alienated many voters in his South Lancashire constituency, which was heavily populated with Northern Irish Protestants. Disraeli's firm opposition to Gladstone's proposals may have helped consolidate the already strong Anglican support for the Tories. But it offended members of other religious denominations and of none, and was almost certainly an important contributory factor to the Conservative defeat in the November 1868 general election.

This was extremely heavy: the result was Liberals 382, Conservatives 276, a Liberal majority of more than a hundred. Despite his party's great success, Gladstone went down to defeat in the (redistributed) constituency of Lancashire South-West, which had been reduced from three members to two. He finished up in third place, behind two Tories, after conducting a very vigorous campaign. By contrast, he had not set foot in Greenwich (another two-member seat), which he also contested as an 'insurance policy', but managed to claim second place behind a local Liberal alderman. His loss in Lancashire was an unprecedented example of a party leader losing his seat in the context of a national victory for his party. As Roy Jenkins pointed out in his biography,[12] other party leaders (Balfour in 1906, Asquith in 1918 and MacDonald in 1935) also lost their seats in general elections, but in each case their parties had also fared badly. In Gladstone's case his setback was probably due mainly to the redistribution, which had brought many new 'Orange' voters within the new borders while taking largely Catholic areas out. Two other prominent Liberals with Lancashire constituencies – Milner Gibson and the Marquess of Hartington – also lost their seats against the trend, also most likely because of the votes of indignant 'Orangemen'.

Disraeli had no such constituency problems, being once again returned unopposed in Buckinghamshire, along with one other Tory and one Liberal. But the overall election result was a crushing disappointment to him, and an indication that the Tories had not benefited (at least in the short run) from the Reform Bill which he had so skilfully carried through Parliament. Recognising that his government was certain to be defeated in an early parliamentary vote, he broke with precedent and immediately tendered his resignation to the Queen. He had remained at the top of the 'greasy pole' for a mere 278 days, and – at the age of almost 64 – it must have looked to many as though his political career was effectively at an end. Disraeli was not prepared to accept this, and declined the earldom which a tearful Victoria proffered to him. He asked instead for 'one mark of favour': 'Might her husband then hope that your Majesty would be graciously pleased to create [Mrs Disraeli] Viscountess Beaconsfield, [after] a town with which Mr. Disraeli has long been connected and which is the nearest town to his estate in Bucks which is not yet ennobled.'[13]

General Grey thought this a thoroughly bad idea, wrongly predicting that it would expose Mary Anne to 'endless ridicule' if she became a peeress in her own right. He advised instead making Disraeli a Knight Commander of the Bath, which would keep him in the Commons but enable his wife to be addressed as Lady Disraeli. Victoria over-rode her secretary's advice, and two days later Mary Anne learned that she would indeed become Viscountess Beaconsfield.

General Grey's next task was to travel to Gladstone's home at Hawarden to convey to him the Queen's intention of offering him the premiership. The telegram announcing Grey's imminent arrival was delivered as Gladstone was busy felling one of the many trees on his estate. He paused to read the telegram, and then uttered his famous words, 'My mission is to pacify Ireland,'[14] before completing the destruction of the tree. By a strange coincidence, the young Charles Grey had had an early connection with Gladstone as well as with Disraeli. In 1836 he had married Caroline Farquhar some months after she had flatly refused a proposal from Gladstone. Neither man appeared embarrassed by this, and Grey received a warm reception at Hawarden, with Catherine Gladstone insisting that he stayed the night instead of returning to London on the Irish mail train. Grey uttered one word of warning to his host. Victoria, he said, had taken a marked aversion to the former Liberal Foreign Secretary, the Earl of Clarendon. If Gladstone wished to include him in his government, he would need to handle the Queen with exceptional tact. In fact, his audience with the Queen, on 3 December 1868, when he kissed her hand on his appointment, went very well, and he recorded in his diary that he found the Queen 'kind, cheerful, even playful'.[15] She made no great difficulty about Clarendon, but insisted that if Lord Hartington became Chief Secretary of Ireland he should not be accompanied by the German-born Duchess of Manchester, his longstanding mistress (though he was to marry her many years later, after the death of her husband). The Hartington appointment was not made at this time – he was fobbed off instead with the Postmaster-Generalship. Having already served as Secretary for War under Lord Palmerston, he believed this to be somewhat beneath his dignity as the heir to one of the greatest Whig dynasties, the Duchy of Devonshire. It was the first of a series of implied snubs that Gladstone was to deliver to Hartington (known to his colleagues as 'Harty' or 'Harty-Tarty') over the next 18 years, and which he must have regretted when, in 1886, Hartington led a mass defection of former Whigs out of the Liberal Party (see page 187 below).

Gladstone's cabinet included a number of surprise appointments – none more so than his choice of Robert Lowe, the leader of the Adullamites, as Chancellor of the Exchequer, another appointment which he was later to regret. Gladstone no doubt intended this, at least in part, as a demonstration that the split in the Liberal Party over electoral reform had been mended. For the rest, Clarendon was again appointed Foreign Secretary, Henry Bruce (later Lord Aberdare), a mine-owner and steel master from Merthyr, Home Secretary, the Duke of Argyll India Secretary, Lord Granville Colonial Secretary, the Bradford worsted manufacturer W.E. Forster Education Minister, and Edward Cardwell War Secretary. The Radical leader and fanatical devotee of *laissez-faire* John Bright, having declined to serve as a Secretary of State, joined the government as President of the Board of Trade. The elderly Earl Russell was invited to serve as a minister without portfolio, but – probably to Gladstone's relief – ruled himself out. Gladstone, who became Prime Minster some three weeks before his fifty-ninth birthday, was one of the most experienced politicians ever to have made it to 10 Downing Street. An MP for 36 years, he had served as a minister under four different premiers, including 12 years in three different cabinet posts, culminating with a total of over nine years as Chancellor of the Exchequer. The government which he now formed was a blend of traditional Whig aristocrats and thrusting recruits from the manufacturing middle class.

Gladstone was quick to assure himself that – in addition to his cabinet colleagues – God was on his side, and intended him to achieve great things. On 29 December 1868, he noted in his diary, 'This birthday opens my 60th year. I descend the hill of life. It would be a truer figure to say I ascend a steepening path with a burden of ever gathering weight. The Almighty seems to sustain and spare me for some purpose of His own deeply unworthy as I know myself to be. Glory be to his name.'[16]

Gladstone started his premiership with great *brio*, determined to mark each session with a major bill, which he would himself carry through all its stages in the Commons, and which would act as a shop-window for his administration. For the first session he chose the Irish Church Bill, a highly complicated and controversial measure whose purpose was to disestablish and disendow the Church in Ireland, though it made no provision, as some had argued it should, for endowing the Catholic and Presbyterian churches, to which the great majority of Irish adhered. He got it through the Commons, with majorities of over a hundred at all its stages, but had to compromise on its financial terms to carry it through the Lords, where the Tory majority threatened to veto the bill. Gladstone freely admitted during the parliamentary debates that he had changed his views on disestablishment, but clothed his explanation in such lofty terms that he left little doubt in the minds of his listeners that he believed his present position was divinely inspired. This led the Radical politician Henry Labouchere to make his famous remark, often wrongly attributed to Disraeli, that he didn't object to Gladstone always having a card up his sleeve, but merely to his insinuation that the Almighty had put it there.

The Liberals saw the passage of the bill as a great triumph, and Gladstone sought to consolidate his success with a repeat performance in the 1870 session, with the Irish Land Bill. His original aim had been to extend traditional tenants' rights in Ulster to the whole 32 counties of

Ireland, but fierce resistance by Whig landowners in his cabinet forced him to backtrack. The bill as it was presented, and passed, merely gave statutory force to these rights in Ulster, but for the remainder of Ireland, while it provided for compensation to tenants who made improvements to the farms which they rented, did not greatly improve their position *vis-à-vis* their landlords. The bill was passed, and though it had some beneficial effect in Ireland, it did little to remove the causes of rural discontent. Professor Shannon's verdict was that 'It proved to be a boon to the lawyers of Ireland, while the legal wrangles in the land courts poisoned relations between landlords and tenants.'[17]

Meanwhile, other ministers were primarily responsible for carrying measures which contributed to Gladstone's 1868–74 government being seen as a great reforming administration. Chief among these was W.E. Forster's Elementary Education Act of 1870, which aimed to provide primary school education for all children. Alongside the established voluntary schools (most of them provided by the Church of England), local school boards were created to set up state schools, which were required to offer places to all children within their catchment areas. The state also accepted financial responsibility for the voluntary sector, so that school fees were abolished, and the survival, and even expansion, of these schools was guaranteed. Provision was made that no children should be required to undergo religious instruction within the schools from a denomination to which their parents objected. It was therefore prescribed that a daily act of worship in the state schools should be conducted on a non-denominational basis. Initially, it was up to the school boards to decide whether primary education should be compulsory in their areas, but from 1880 it was made compulsory throughout the country. The act was an historic landmark, but was highly controversial, particularly among nonconformists who resented the provision of public money to maintain Anglican schools. It was Gladstone himself who had insisted on this, thus establishing a 'dual system' which has survived to the present day.

Even more controversial was the series of army reforms carried through by Edward Cardwell, the Secretary for War, against determined resistance led by the Army's longstanding Commander-in-Chief, the deeply reactionary Duke of Cambridge. A first cousin of Queen Victoria, he appeared immovable, remaining in office for almost forty years, despite periodic attempts by Liberal ministers to displace him. The hardest fight was over the abolition of the system of purchase for officers' commissions, which had been in force since the seventeenth century. A bill introduced by Cardwell to bring this about was fought every inch of the way by diehard opponents, who filibustered it for several months, to such an extent that even Gladstone doubted whether it would ever be carried, and gave consideration to a compromise measure. But Cardwell battled on, and it eventually obtained its third reading in July 1871, six months after it was first introduced. This was not yet the end of the story. Cambridge organised opposition in the House of Lords, which threw out the bill after two weeks. Cardwell and Gladstone, however, had the last laugh. They took legal advice and discovered that the system could be abolished by royal warrant, and – on her Prime Minister's advice – a deeply reluctant Queen Victoria gave her consent to a measure ending the practice, as from 1 November 1871. *Punch* magazine celebrated the event by publishing a mock advertisement: 'To gallant and stupid young gentlemen: You may buy commissions in the Army up to 31st day of October next. After that you will be driven to the cruel necessity of deserving them.'[18]

Strongly supported by public opinion, alarmed at the overwhelming success of the modernised Prussian Army in wars against Austria (1866) and France (1870–1), Cardwell pressed on with further reforms, but his health suffered badly from the constant struggle in which he was engaged. His wife wrote privately to Gladstone asking if he could be considered for the speakership of the House of Commons, currently vacant, and Victoria – prompted by her cousin, who wanted at all costs to have his minister transferred – also lobbied on his behalf. Gladstone consulted Cardwell, who declined to make the move.

The Ballot Act of 1872 finally established the secret ballot in elections, thereby protecting tenants and employees from intimidation by their landlords or bosses. This measure was twice rejected by the Lords – in 1870 and 1871 – but at the third time of asking they reluctantly gave way. Gladstone had only been a lukewarm supporter of the measure, which was promoted by Forster, but was outraged by the action of the upper house. When it came up for consideration for the third time, he threatened a dissolution if the Lords again defeated the bill, and Disraeli, fearing to fight a general election on this issue, persuaded the Tory peers to let it go through.

The Ballot Act had only a limited effect in England, Wales and Scotland, where such intimidation was limited, but in Ireland it was endemic, and the passage of the act transformed the electoral map. In previous elections all the hundred or so seats had gone to Liberal or Conservative candidates. But in 1874, and even more so in subsequent elections, the great majority of the seats were won by Irish Nationalist or 'Home Rule' candidates, the iron grip which Protestant landlords had held over their Catholic tenants having been manifestly broken. Many of these candidates had originally been Liberals, but under the leadership of Charles Stewart Parnell, the Protestant leader of an overwhelmingly Catholic movement, they were subsequently to organise themselves into an independent 'Irish Party', prepared to offer their support to either the Liberals or the Tories according to how susceptible they appeared to Parnell's demands.

Another measure, about which Gladstone was initially sceptical but which he ended up introducing himself in the Commons, was the University Tests Bill, which removed most of the remaining restrictions on non-Anglicans holding posts in the universities of Oxford and Cambridge. The most difficult legislation, with which Gladstone's involvement was minimal, was on the licensing of public houses. There was a major problem of drunkenness, leading to vigorous demands for temperance reform, particularly among the Liberals' nonconformist supporters. They were, however, split between prohibitionists and advocates of very strict licensing laws. The Home Secretary, Henry Bruce, produced an ambitious Licensing Bill in 1871, which provoked a furious reaction from the drink trade while failing to satisfy the more radical reformers. Bruce eventually withdrew his bill, but tried again a year later, with a much more modest proposal. This was enacted as the Licensing Act 1872, though the fury of the brewers was not assuaged. From that date until the present day, the brewery companies have been heavy contributors to the Conservative Party at every general election.

In foreign policy, Gladstone gave a strong impetus to the cause of international arbitration by agreeing to refer the festering dispute with the United States over the *Alabama* affair to an international tribunal in Geneva. The *Alabama* was a warship built in Liverpool and released to the Confederate navy. It proceeded to wreak havoc, capturing, sinking or burning no fewer than 68 Federal ships before it was itself sunk in June 1864. The US government claimed heavy compensation from Britain, and in September 1872 the tribunal set the amount of compensation to be paid at £3.25 million, about one-third of the US claim. This was an unpopular move with the voters, but it put Anglo–American relations back on a good footing, and probably relieved Gladstone's conscience for the strongly pro-Confederate speech he had made at the outset of the Civil War, and which he later regretted. When war broke out between France and Prussia in 1870, he saw merit on both sides, and was determined to stay neutral, though he signed a treaty with both powers to recognise Belgian neutrality, and prepared to send an expeditionary force of 30,000 men if either side reneged. It was this treaty which was cited in 1914 to justify Britain's declaration of war on Germany. When the 1870 war ended, Gladstone was appalled by Germany's annexation of Alsace–Lorraine, without a plebiscite being held, but was overruled by his cabinet when he proposed to organise a joint protest with other neutral countries. Gladstone was even more upset by the declaration of papal infallibility at the Vatican Council in 1870, which he largely blamed on his former Oxford friend the future Cardinal Manning, who had become a leader of the extreme 'ultramontane' faction in the Roman Catholic Church. Gladstone attempted to mobilise diplomatic opposition by other European governments to the declaration, but had little success.

Gladstone overshadowed all his ministerial colleagues, but was by no means the unchallenged master of his own house. Roy Jenkins aptly described him as pre-eminent, but not predominant, and over several issues he was overruled by his cabinet. Nor was he a great success as Leader of the House of Commons, a role which all prime ministers not in the House of Lords continued to fulfil until the time of Lloyd George. It involved sitting in the House for long hours each day, and being ready to receive representations from other party leaders and groups of MPs, as well as individual members. Gladstone soon acquired a reputation as a poor listener, but very quick to deliver his own views. These were often the result of many hours of careful deliberation on his part, but once he had made up his mind it was extremely difficult to shift him, and he tended to be impatient with the views, however sincerely held, of others. Despite his high moral tone he was also felt by many to be prepared to cut corners and to breach the spirit, if not the letter, of laws or conventions. Twice in 1872 he was arraigned before the House for alleged sharp practice in making public appointments. He appointed Sir Robert Collier (later Lord

Monkswell) to a seat on the Judicial Committee of the Privy Council. The rules stipulated that candidates must have served as a High Court judge in either England or India. Gladstone got round this by arranging for the appointment of Collier to the Puisne bench for a two-day period. He narrowly defeated motions of censure in both Houses of Parliament. A few weeks later he was in similar trouble over an ecclesiastical appointment – the rectorship of Ewelme, an Oxfordshire village with a close connection to the university. According to the statutes, the appointee was required to be an Oxford MA. Gladstone chose to appoint W.W. Harvey, a Fellow of King's College, Cambridge, with whom he had been at Eton. He persuaded Oriel College, Oxford to grant him temporary membership, which after a statutory period of 42 days entitled him to MA status. Roy Jenkins commented, 'Both these incidents were widely regarded as showing that exhaustion combined with an imperious nature were leading Gladstone away from judgment and proportion towards a petulant authoritarianism. They damaged him both inside and outside the government.'[19]

He also experienced difficulties in his dealings with Queen Victoria, whom he tried to chivvy into playing a more active and public role, believing that her decade-long period of grieving for Albert was harmful both to the country and the monarchy. He also tried, with little success, to get her to allow the Prince of Wales to play an active part in public affairs, for example as Viceroy of Ireland. Although he invariably treated her in a respectful way, she soon tired of hearing the earnest arguments which he put to her, and complained that he addressed her like a public meeting. She pined for her beloved Disraeli.

Disraeli had kept a low political profile for the first year or two after his defeat, unsure whether – at the age of 64 – he would be able to stage a comeback. But he was not yet ready to stand down from the Tory leadership, despite the growing dissatisfaction which was being expressed, particularly by his more right-wing followers. The death of Lord Derby in October 1869 and the resignation of Lord Malmesbury as Tory leader in the Lords opened up the possibility that one of his critics would be elevated to this position. Many Tory peers wanted the new Marquess of Salisbury to take over, which would have made Disraeli's position impossible. Salisbury, the former Lord Cranborne, refused to stand, and Lord Cairns, a former Lord Chancellor who was friendly to Disraeli, accepted the position. He gave up, however, in February 1870 after serving for only one session, and Salisbury, who had recently attacked Disraeli in an article in the *Quarterly Review* as 'a mere political gamester', was once again pressed to stand. When he declined, Edward Stanley, now the 15th Earl of Derby, was unanimously elected by the Tory peers. He served for precisely one day before having second thoughts, perhaps concluding that as his views on many issues were closer to the Liberals than his own party he would be an inappropriate choice. To Disraeli's relief, the chalice then passed to the Duke of Richmond, described by Robert Blake as 'an amiable but ineffective nonentity'.[20] He continued to lead the Tories in the House of Lords until 1876, when Disraeli himself went to the upper house, as Lord Beaconsfield.

Early in 1869 Disraeli had settled down to writing a new novel, *Lothair*, the first book he had written since his biography of Lord George Bentinck, published some two decades earlier. He embarked on the project in the deepest secrecy; even his secretary, Monty Corry, remained unaware of what he was doing until shortly before the book's publication, in May 1870. Disraeli's enterprise had apparently been sparked off by the news, which had been sensationally reported, of the conversion to Catholicism of the young and fabulously wealthy 3rd Marquess of Bute. The character of Lothair is based very loosely on Bute, and the novel is a highly melodramatic and colourful account of the struggle between Catholicism and Protestantism for the soul of the protagonist. The publication of *Lothair* was itself a sensation – the first time a former Prime Minister had written a novel (the only subsequent time was in 1880, when Disraeli's last book, *Endymion*, appeared). This was enough in itself to fire public interest, as well as the lively curiosity to find out which public figures appeared – thinly disguised – in his narrative. The book proved to be an out-and-out bestseller, earning Disraeli at least £7500 in royalties over the next six years. In addition, a new edition of his earlier novels brought him in some £3100, bringing his total earnings to at least £10,600 (or some £700,000 in modern terms). Gladstone, who had himself just published a new study of Homer, entitled *Juventus Mundi*, lost little time in reading his rival's work, noting in his diary on 18 May 1870 that he had read 'a spice of *Lothair*'.[21] A week later he recorded, 'Finished *Lothair*',[22] without further comment, though a famous cartoon in *Punch* showed them making dismissive remarks about each other's work. The critical reception of *Lothair* was much less enthusiastic than that of the general public; nearly all the reviews were bad, apart from those in *The Times* and the *Pall Mall Gazette*. His pre-eminent modern biographer, Robert Blake, believes that they were too hard on Disraeli. His considered view was that '*Lothair*, in spite of much careless prose, especially in the earlier chapters, is perhaps the best-constructed work from his pen.'[23]

Many of Disraeli's Tory colleagues took a dim view of his literary activities, believing that he pursued them at the expense of his parliamentary work, and that he had failed to mount an effective challenge to Gladstone. They felt particularly frustrated as the government, after its early bout of legislation, was now beginning to run out of steam, and was internally divided on many issues. On 1 February 1872 a group of eminent grandees met at the Marquess of Exeter's country seat at Burleigh, where, with only two dissenters – Lord John Manners and Sir Stafford Northcote – they agreed that the 15th Earl of Derby would make a more effective leader. The Chief Whip opined that 'his name alone would be worth forty or fifty seats.'[24] According to Blake, 'No one had the nerve to convey these doubts to Disraeli, nor did Derby give the slightest encouragement. But Disraeli knew that there was trouble afoot. The newspapers were full of it, and the rival merits of the two leaders were the subject of much public discussion.'[25]

This came as a wake-up call to Disraeli. He stepped up the frequency and quality of his parliamentary interventions, and was encouraged by a quite unexpected demonstration of public support at a thanksgiving service at St Paul's Cathedral for the recovery of the Prince of Wales from typhoid fever on 27 February 1872. He was loudly cheered by the crowd, who had greeted Gladstone's arrival with stony silence. He now determined to challenge Gladstone on his own ground by addressing, on 3 April, a mass public meeting at the Free Trade Hall in Manchester, the venue of many of the Liberal leader's oratorical triumphs. Here he made perhaps the greatest speech of his life, excoriating the Liberal government and brutally dissecting the full range of its policies, both domestic and foreign. He concluded with a contemptuous dismissal of Gladstone and his colleagues, in a passage which reverberated around the country, and whose striking image entered the political vocabulary:

As I sat opposite the Treasury bench the ministers reminded me of one of those marine landscapes not very uncommon on the coasts of South America. You behold a range of exhausted volcanoes. Not a flame flickers from a single pallid crest. But the situation is still dangerous. There are occasional earthquakes, and ever and anon the dark rumbling of the sea.[26]

Disraeli followed up his Manchester triumph with a similar meeting in London, at the Crystal Palace, on 24 June. Here he made an audacious bid to win the support of working-class voters enfranchised by his 1867 Reform Act, who he claimed were Conservative in the 'purest and loftiest sense'. They were, he said,

proud of belonging to a great country, and wish to maintain its greatness – that they are proud of belonging to an Imperial country, and are resolved to maintain, if they can, their empire – that they believe on the whole that the greatness and the empire of England are to be attributed to the ancient institutions of the land.[27]

This represented Disraeli's attempt to seize the mantle of Lord Palmerston, the great advocate of an aggressive British imperialism, with the implication that Gladstone and his fellow Liberals were incapable of standing up for British interests in the wider world. He tied this to an appeal for continuing social reform, reminding his listeners that the Factory Acts were largely the result of the efforts of the Tory peer Lord Shaftesbury. In pitching his appeal to the 'deferential working class voter', Disraeli launched a strategy which was followed, at least spasmodically, by every subsequent Conservative leader at least until the time of Harold Macmillan, nearly a century later. Two years after his death, *The Times* coined a memorable phrase, 'Angels in Marble' in describing how he had sought to build up a new bedrock of support for his party: 'In the inarticulate mass of the English populace, [Disraeli] discerned the Conservative working man as the sculptor perceives the angel prisoned in a block of marble.'[28]

Mary Anne had accompanied Disraeli to both his great meetings, but shortly afterwards her health began to decline, and she died of cancer aged 80 on 15 December 1872. Disraeli was devastated, but was comforted by the flood of tributes and letters of condolence which flowed in. One from the Queen, recalled that '*Yesterday* was the anniversary of her great loss [Prince Albert],'[29] but Gladstone's, if rather stiff, showed somewhat more empathy:

You and I were, as I believe, married in the same year. It has been permitted to both of us to enjoy a priceless boon through a third of a century. Spared myself the blow which has fallen on you, I can form some conception of what it must have been and be. I do not presume to offer you the consolation, which you will seek from another and higher quarter. I offer only the assurance which all who know you, and all who knew Lady Beaconsfield, and especially those among them who like myself enjoyed for a length of time her marked though unmerited regard, may perhaps tender without impropriety; the assurance that in this trying hour they feel deeply for you and with you.[30]

Disraeli replied more briefly: 'I am much touched by your kind words in my great sorrow. I trust, I earnestly trust, that you may be spared a similar affliction. Marriage is the greatest earthly happiness, when founded on complete sympathy. That hallowed lot was mine, and for a moiety of my existence; and I know it is yours...'[31]

These were the last friendly letters to pass between the two men. Disraeli had not lost only his wife, but her income of some £5000 a year and the house at Grosvenor Gate, which reverted to her husband's heirs. He was forced to move into Edwards's Hotel, off Hanover Square, which he described to friends as 'a cave of despair'.[32] Some 15 years earlier, Mary Anne had written him a letter to be opened in the event of her death. This read,

My own dear Husband – If I should depart this life before you, leave orders that we may be buried in the same grave...God bless you my dearest, kindest. You have been a perfect husband to me. Be put by my side in the same grave. And now farewell...my dear Dizzy. Do not live alone dearest. Someone I earnestly hope you may find as attached to you as your own devoted MARY ANNE.[33]

It was not very long before a candidate presented herself. In June 1873 he received a letter from the wealthy widow of the 7th Earl of Cardigan, who had led the 'Charge of the Light Brigade' at the Battle of Balaclava during the Crimean War. Claiming to have received '12 offers of marriage since Lord Cardigan's death', she now proposed the alliance of 'the greatest man we have in genius and intellect with the wealthiest relict of the staunchest Conservative Peer that ever lived'.[34]

Disraeli was not interested, and by August she was writing again, announcing her forthcoming marriage to a Portuguese aristocrat. Nor did he seriously entertain an offer of marriage from one of the richest women in England, Angela Burdett-Coutts. This may have been because he believed her to be a lesbian, but this did not prevent her, ten years later when she was aged 66, from marrying her 29-year-old protégé, William Bartlett. More likely Disraeli rejected her proposal because he had, at the age of 68, fallen hopelessly in love with the 54-year-old Lady (Selina) Bradford, the mother of two children and already herself a grandmother. She was to be the object of his desire for the rest of his life. There was, however, a major snag. Her husband, the Earl of Bradford, was still very much alive and was a leading Conservative peer, though his main passion in life was horseracing. So Disraeli transferred his attentions to her much older sister, the recently widowed Lady (Anne) Chesterfield (now aged 71), and proposed marriage to her. Realising that this was only a ruse to get nearer to her sister, she declined, but both she and Selina remained close friends of the Tory leader for the rest of his life, while keeping him firmly at arm's length as a potential lover. He sought them out on every possible occasion, and began a long and confidential correspondence with both of them, discussing at length all his political as well as more personal problems. In a way they replaced his sister Sarah in the role of *confidante*. Altogether, he wrote more than eleven hundred letters to Lady Bradford and over five hundred to Lady Chesterfield. Many of these were collected and published in two volumes in 1929, and they remain a highly valuable source for students of Disraeli's later career.[35]

Meanwhile, the government was rocked by a series of scandals, and even Gladstone's titanic energy seemed to be wilting. For a time he was seriously distracted by what Jenkins describes as 'an infatuation' and H.C.J. Matthew as 'a platonic extra-marital affair'. This was with Laura Thistlethwayte, a former courtesan who had made an advantageous marriage to a wealthy but otherwise uninteresting gentleman, Frederick Thistlethwayte. He was the brother of one of her previous clients, who had died in the Crimean War. Gladstone quickly got into the habit of writing long letters to her, and seeking out her company, showing no regard for discretion. He addressed his letters to her as 'Dear Spirit', and ostentatiously wore on the third finger of his right hand a gold ring she had given to him (it appears in several surviving portraits of the then Prime Minister). People began to notice; the new Lord Derby, for example, noted in his journal on 11 December 1869,

Strange story of Gladstone frequenting the company of a Mrs Thistlethwaite [*sic*], a kept woman in her youth, who induced a foolish person with a large fortune to marry her. She has since her marriage taken to religion, and preaches or lectures. This, with her beauty, is the attraction to G and it is characteristic of him to be indifferent to scandal. But I can scarcely believe a report that he is going to pass a week with her and her husband at their country house – she not being received in society.[36]

In his introduction to the *Gladstone Diaries*, Matthew discusses the 'affair' at length, and concludes that 'Laura Thistlethwayte was not Gladstone's mistress in the physical sense … But she fulfilled the other functions of that office.'[37] The relationship was at its most intense in 1869, but it dragged on spasmodically for several more years. It has been compared to Asquith's infatuation with Lady Venetia Stanley, to whom he wrote several indiscreet letters a day at the height of his wartime premiership,[38] but Gladstone managed to keep his feelings under somewhat tighter control. One consequence of his relationship with her is that his night-time activities with street prostitutes tailed off considerably during this period.

If Gladstone's first government began with a bang, it sadly ended with a whimper. He was largely responsible for creating his own troubles. Against the wishes of most of his cabinet, he insisted on bringing in a third Irish measure, the Irish Universities Bill, whose main aim was to open them up to Catholic students. He handled the issue maladroitly, succeeding in antagonising not only the powerful lobby of Trinity College, Dublin but also many secular educationalists and, fatally, the Roman Catholic hierarchy. When the bill came up for its second reading, on 13 March 1873, a large number of Liberals, mostly but not exclusively Irish members, voted against or abstained, and the government was defeated by three votes. Gladstone immediately resigned, and with perhaps indecent haste Queen Victoria invited Disraeli to take his place. Yet the wary Tory leader declined. He had no wish to emulate Lord Derby's experience, on three occasions, of leading a minority government, and was by now confident enough to believe that if he held off until the next general election he would gain an elected majority. It was the last occasion in British history when an opposition leader refused to accept office. Disraeli showed good judgement and immense self-confidence in taking what must have been a difficult decision, though it proved to be the right one. The government limped on for nearly another year, but repeated Conservative successes in by-elections gave it little confidence that it would survive the general election.

In the summer of 1873, Gladstone gave way to pressure from his more Radical MPs and announced himself in favour of extending male household franchise to county constituencies. This smacked too much of democracy for one of the stuffier Whig peers, Lord Ripon, who resigned his post as Lord President of the Council. This triggered a government reshuffle, the most striking feature of which was that Gladstone himself assumed the post of Chancellor of the Exchequer, displacing Robert Lowe, who had greatly disappointed him. Lowe was compensated by the Home Office, Henry Bruce being shifted to replace Ripon. There had already been several important changes in government personnel. Lord Clarendon had died in 1870, and Earl Granville, perhaps Gladstone's closest colleague, had replaced him as Foreign Secretary. John Bright had resigned as President of the Board of Trade in 1871, but returned two years later as Chancellor of the Duchy of Lancaster, and Lord Hartington had – with great reluctance – taken over as Irish Chief Secretary in 1870.

The general election was not due until 1875, but Gladstone decided on a bold stroke, and sought dissolution early in 1874. He made the abolition of income tax the central feature of the Liberal election platform. He managed to persuade himself that it was justified on economic grounds, but in reality it was little more than a blatant electoral bribe, which sat ill with the high moral tone which he habitually adopted. Nor was it successful: Disraeli instantly followed suit, but when he assumed office found it utterly impractical, and the tax has remained the main source of government revenue ever since. During the election campaign Gladstone was extraordinarily passive, speaking at only three meetings, all of them in or near his Greenwich constituency. The election, held in February 1874, produced an overall majority of 50 for the Tories, while Gladstone suffered the indignity of coming second at Greenwich, behind the leading Tory candidate, a brewer. Gladstone wrote to his brother Robertson that 'we have been borne down in a torrent of gin and beer.'[39]

# Nine

# The rise and fall of 'Beaconsfieldism', 1874–81

The general expectation before the 1874 general election was that it would be extremely close, and there was general surprise that it produced much the best result for the Tories since Sir Robert Peel's great victory in 1841. In terms of seats, the outcome was:

| | |
|---|---|
| Conservatives | 350 |
| Liberals | 245 |
| Home Rulers | 57 |

In his analysis of the results, Robert Blake discerned three reasons why the Tories did so much better than expected. The first was bad timing by Gladstone in his choice of the election date. The second was a substantial increase in the number of voters on the electoral register since the previous poll in 1868. This was largely made up of poorer members of the working class who had not yet qualified for inclusion in the election register six years earlier, or had been inadvertently excluded. The third reason was the very great improvement in Conservative organisation, which resulted from Disraeli's comprehensive overhaul of the party. This included the creation of Conservative Central Office, and of the National Union of Conservative Associations, which had ensured that there was an effective local organisation in virtually every constituency.[1] To these may be added the halfhearted campaign mounted by Gladstone, who by now was thoroughly out of sorts with his party and half anxious to return to his Homeric studies. When all the results were declared, he was undecided whether to emulate Disraeli's example in 1868 of prompt resignation, or to follow the earlier practice of waiting to be defeated in a House of Commons vote. The Queen, however, made it quite clear that she was in a hurry for a new government to be formed.

Learning of this, Gladstone hastened to Windsor on 17 February and offered his resignation which was promptly accepted. He cryptically recorded in his diary, 'H.M. very kind; the topics of conversation were of course rather limited.'[2] They included the offer of a peerage, which Gladstone unhesitatingly declined. Victoria let her true feelings be felt in a letter to her eldest daughter Vicky, recalling that Palmerston had warned her that Gladstone was a 'very dangerous man', and adding, 'And so very tyrannical and obstinate, with no knowledge of the world or human nature…a fanatic in religion. All this and much want of regard towards my feelings…led to make him a very dangerous and unsatisfactory Premier.'[3]

She immediately dispatched Henry Ponsonby, who had succeeded General Charles Grey as her private secretary in 1870, to summon Disraeli, who the following day knelt before her and kissed her hand, saying, 'I plight my troth to the kindest of Mistresses.'[4] Disraeli set out to form a compact government – the smallest cabinet since 1832, with 12 members, six from each House. Nine of them had served in his shortlived first government, including Derby, who was again Foreign Secretary. The Chancellor of the Exchequer was Sir Stafford Northcote, the former civil servant who had once been Gladstone's private secretary, while Disraeli's previous Chancellor – the 'elephantine' G.W. Hunt – now became First Lord of the Admiralty. The Home Secretary was a new man, Richard Cross, the most middle-class man of the 12, with a background in local government. As Indian Secretary, Disraeli persisted once again in wanting Salisbury to return, but was pessimistic about the chances of him accepting. Salisbury, indeed, was by no means keen, writing to his wife on 15 February that 'the prospect of having to serve with this man again is like a nightmare.'[5] Disraeli shrewdly enrolled Lady Derby – Salisbury's stepmother, though she was less than six years his senior – as a go-between, and, together with several of his friends, she persuaded him that if he wished to be taken as a serious politician he could not afford to pass up this opportunity yet again. So Salisbury reluctantly accepted, while his close friend and ally, the 4th Earl of Carnarvon, became Colonial Secretary. The Lord Chancellor was

Lord Cairns, and he – together with Derby – made up Disraeli's unofficial 'inner cabinet'. Disraeli's old friend from Young England days, Lord John Manners, became Postmaster-General. Among ministers outside the cabinet, two who later became very prominent were Michael Hicks Beach, the Irish Secretary, and the bookseller W.H. Smith, who was Financial Secretary to the Treasury. Disraeli also found a minor place for his 'favourite', Lord Henry Lennox. This was as First Commissioner of Works, a severe disappointment for Lord Henry, who had – quite unrealistically – expected a post in the cabinet. He accepted, with ill grace, and proved to be a conspicuous failure.

Disraeli took an equal interest in proposing court appointments, and suggested the Earl of Bradford as Master of the Horse. This was reminiscent of French kings ennobling the complaisant husbands of their mistresses, except that the Earl, who was besotted with horses, was well qualified for the post, and Selina never surrendered her virtue to her elderly admirer. At meetings of the cabinet Disraeli proved himself a skilful and alert chairman, but was not particularly active in proposing policy initiatives. This was especially disappointing for the new Home Secretary, Richard Cross, who – writing many years later – recalled that

> From all his speeches I had quite expected that his mind was full of legislative schemes, but such did not prove to be the case; on the contrary he had to rely on the suggestions of his colleagues, and, as they themselves had only just come into office, and that suddenly, there was some difficulty in framing the Queen's speech.[6]

In fact during his second premiership, Disraeli – already aged 69 when appointed, and in poor health – did not prove himself a very energetic figure. He devolved a great deal to his colleagues, worked relatively short hours when the House was not sitting, and spent many of his weekends at aristocratic country house parties, especially if Selina was likely to be among the guests. Even when working on his papers at Hughenden, he was liable to fall into a reverie and moon about her. On 28 July 1874, for example, he wrote to her of his dream of living with her at Hughenden, as he had with Mary Anne: 'Writing in the early hours of morn, passing my day in wood rambles with you or drives to ancient heaths – and in the evening reading to you my mature labours, and profiting by the criticism of your quick wit and taste. Dreams of impossible … yet ineffable bliss.'[7]

As for Gladstone, at 64, he was far fitter and more active, both physically and intellectually, than his rival. He was still capable of very long walks, of thirty miles a day or even more, and regularly indulged his hobby of tree-felling on his Hawarden estate. He inherited this from his brother-in-law, Sir Stephen Glynne, who died on 17 June 1874, having already bought out the interests of other members of the Glynne family. He transferred the legal ownership to his eldest son, Willy, but he and Catherine continued to live there until their deaths. Their second son, the Rev. Stephen Gladstone, was already Rector of Hawarden, and retained the living until 1904, when he moved to Lincolnshire. Having lost his prime ministerial salary of £5000, Gladstone concluded, however, that he could no longer continue to keep up his fashionable London residence, and after having lived for 35 years at various addresses in Carlton House Terrace or Carlton Gardens, he now sold up 11 Carlton House Terrace and moved to a less grand house at 37 Harley Street. Something else Gladstone was determined to give up was the leadership of the Liberal Party. After his unfortunate experience in 1867–8, he had no desire to become Leader of the Opposition again. He was by temperament and conviction much more fitted to be in government than in opposition, as he had revealed in a little-noticed article which he had contributed to the *Quarterly Review* in 1856: 'He must be a very bad minister indeed, who does not do ten times the good to the country when he is in office, that he can do when he is out of it; because he has helps and opportunities which multiply twentyfold, as by a system of wheels and pulleys, his power for doing it.'[8]

At this point Gladstone did not expect ever to be Prime Minister again, and though he intended to remain in Parliament saw his future role primarily as that of a polemicist for the Church of England, while holding himself in reserve to fight for other causes to which he might become committed, if that seemed to be the will of God. He therefore announced his intended resignation at the first meeting of his former cabinet following their electoral defeat. His colleagues unanimously deprecated his decision, and persuaded him to stay on, at least for the first parliamentary session under the new government. Gladstone agreed, and went through the motions of leading the opposition until February 1875, when he insisted on giving up. The Liberal MPs would have been well advised to have chosen one of the more successful and activist former ministers, such as William Forster or Edward Cardwell, to succeed him. Instead, they chose to pick a Whig grandee, and 'Harty Tarty', as much a socialite as a politician, though not without ambition, found himself stepping into the oversized shoes of his predecessor. He shared the party leadership with the former Foreign Secretary Lord Granville, who had been the Liberal leader in the Lords since 1868. Many of Gladstone's colleagues doubted the permanence of Gladstone's retirement, believing that he would soon find some cause to reclaim the leadership. That Gladstone himself half suspected that this might indeed be the case was evidenced by the more than usually convoluted memorandum which he addressed to himself at this time:

> I shall not now resign my seat in Parliament; but after the labour of the last years I require rest particularly mental rest, and my attendance will only be occasional...I do not conceal my hope and expectation that this first step of retirement into the shade will be followed by others accomplishing the work...Deeming myself unable to hold [the party] together from my present position in a manner worthy of it I see how unlikely it is that I should hereafter be able to give any material aid in the adjustment of its difficulties. Yet if such aid should at any time be generally desired with a view to arresting some great evil or procuring for the nation some great good, my willingness to come into counsel for that occasion would follow from all I have said.[9]

One person who strongly regretted his giving up the leadership, and also the house in Carlton House Terrace, was his wife Catherine, who saw her own life diminished by Gladstone's withdrawal. She had not played a great role as a political hostess, but vicariously lived through her husband's public life, and 'could share very little of either his literary interests or his religious enthusiasms'.[10]

Despite Disraeli's apparent lethargy, his government chalked up an impressive legislative record during its first two years in office. The first – and least important – measure introduced was at the direct urging of the Queen, which Disraeli, though he had severe doubts about its wisdom, felt bound to promote. This was the Public Worship Regulation Bill, designed to prohibit 'Romish' practices and rituals in Anglican churches. It was strongly attacked by High churchmen, including Gladstone, who tabled no fewer than six hostile amendments, which enjoyed little support in the Commons. Although Gladstone remained fiercely opposed to Roman Catholicism, it was not their rituals to which he mainly objected, and he was firmly against Parliament legislating to control the practices of the Church of England. Another High churchman who attacked the bill was Lord Salisbury, who had no qualms about criticising a government measure when it was debated in the Lords (collective cabinet responsibility was less rigid in those days, and it was not all that unusual for cabinet members to oppose their colleagues, especially on issues of individual conscience). When the bill was debated in the Commons, Disraeli referred to Salisbury's rumbustious speech, and described him as 'a great master of gibes and flouts and jeers'.[11] The bill, which was effectively unworkable, duly passed into law. Disraeli bore no ill-will towards Salisbury, and privately agreed with his views. This was in fact the last occasion when the two men were to differ publicly. Salisbury found it much more agreeable than he had anticipated to work as Disraeli's colleague, and their relations became steadily warmer throughout the course of his premiership. By contrast, there was a considerable cooling off between Disraeli and Derby, the Prime Minister finding him over-cautious and unsympathetic to many of his own foreign-policy objectives. In addition, Disraeli became wary of the activities of Lady Derby, a formidable political intriguer who was not above leaking government secrets to the press and to their political opponents. Salisbury was progressively to replace Derby as Disraeli's closest political ally.

Richard Cross, the Home Secretary, was the driving force behind most of the other bills which the government pushed through in its first two years of office. He was encouraged, but not especially helped, by the Prime Minister, whose mind, Cross complained, 'was either above or below (whichever way you like to put it) mere questions of detail. When the House was in Committee he was, comparatively speaking, nowhere.'[12]

It was an astonishing burst of legislative activity for a Tory government, though none of the bills was as major as the leading measures carried by the preceding Gladstone government. They included the Artisans' Dwelling Act, the Public Health Act, the Merchant Shipping Act, the Rivers Pollution Act, the Food and Drug Act and the Friendly Societies Act. Particularly important for working-class voters, whom Disraeli was now ardently wooing, were two labour bills – the Employers and Workmen Bill and the Conspiracy and Protection of Property Bill. They legalised peaceful picketing, freed unions from criminal liability for their members' unauthorised behaviour, and put them on an equal footing with employers in negotiating contracts. The unions were delighted, and Disraeli wrote to Lady Chesterfield on 29 June 1875 that the legislation 'will gain and retain for the Conservatives the lasting affection of the working classes'.[13] Another measure passed with electoral support in mind was a Licensing Act, which watered down the provisions of the act passed three years earlier by the Liberals. It was patently a 'thank you' gesture to the brewers for their strong backing in the 1874 election.

Contrary to his relative inactivity in the passage of legislation, Disraeli took a keen interest in foreign affairs, which soon became his main focus. He scored a notable success in November 1876 with the purchase of shares in the Suez Canal Company. Built by the French engineer Ferdinand de Lesseps, the canal had been largely French-owned, except that Khedive Ismail of Egypt had a large minority holding. An incompetent and profligate ruler, he found himself urgently in need of £3–4 million before the end of the month, and on 13 November opened negotiations with two French banks to sell his shares for £4 million. Tipped off by his friend Lionel de Rothschild that the Khedive would prefer to sell to a British buyer, Disraeli, overruling negative advice from Lord Derby, hastened to put the proposition to the cabinet, writing to the Queen in a breathless letter, 'The thing must be done. 'Tis an affair of millions; about four, at least.' In cabinet the Chancellor of the Exchequer, Sir Stafford Northcote, joined with Derby in opposing the deal, but they were outvoted. Speed was of the essence, and Disraeli arranged that Rothschilds would advance the money to the British government until it had been voted on by Parliament, and would undertake the complicated negotiation with the Khedive's representatives. De Lesseps and the French government were furious, but Britain obtained a substantial, though minority, interest in the canal, which was considered vital for its communications with India. Disraeli's prompt action was seen in retrospect as a masterstroke, and his reputation soared. Deeply impressed by the efficiency with which the Rothschilds had handled the negotiation, Disraeli reputedly quipped that if the Almighty had had their assistance it would not have taken Him six days to create the world.

Queen Victoria was delighted by Disraeli's coup, and used the occasion to press a longstanding desire of her own. The creation of the German

Empire, following the Prussian victory over France in the 1870–1 war, meant that there were now three emperors on the European continent, those of Russia, Austria–Hungary and Germany, who were united in a loose alliance, the *Dreikaiserbund*. Victoria chafed at being outranked by her three fellow monarchs, and her dissatisfaction was increased by the realisation that her eldest daughter, Vicky, was herself set to become an empress when her husband Friedrich succeeded the elderly Kaiser, Wilhelm I. She therefore revived a proposal, not previously seriously considered by anyone but herself, that she should be proclaimed Empress of India. She practically forced the decision on Disraeli, who privately thought it unwise, but was temperamentally incapable of denying any sop to her vanity. The last Mughal Emperor, Bahadur Shah II, whose power had been only nominal, was deposed by the British and exiled to Burma in 1858 following the Indian Mutiny, in which he had been an unwilling participant. Disraeli's Royal Titles Bill proposed reviving the title and bestowing it on Victoria, who would subsequently be known as the Queen–Empress. Disraeli badly mishandled the affair, failing to consult the opposition in advance and grossly offending the Prince of Wales, who only read about the proposal, which intimately affected his own future, when it appeared in the newspapers. When the bill reached the House of Commons it was vigorously opposed by the Liberals, with both Gladstone and Robert Lowe to the fore. Lowe was a bitter enemy of Disraeli, whom he felt had double-crossed him, encouraging him to defeat the very moderate Reform Bill of Lord Russell, only to carry the far more radical measure of his own. He now over-reached himself by making a speech at East Retford, in which he claimed that at least two former prime ministers had previously rejected the Queen's request, adding that 'More pliant persons have now been found and I have no doubt the thing will be done.'[14]

Gladstone immediately denied that he had spurned an approach from the Queen, and Disraeli turned the tables on Lowe by revealing in the Commons that he had the Queen's authority to deny that she had ever made any such proposal to previous prime ministers. Lowe was reduced to making an abject apology, and his political career was effectively at an end. He was not included in any of Gladstone's future governments, and retired to the House of Lords, as Viscount

Sherbrooke, in 1880. 'He is in the mud, and I leave him there,' Disraeli wrote to Lady Chesterfield.[15]

Despite dissension in the cabinet – Derby describing the bill as 'an act of folly' – Disraeli pressed ahead, and it finally passed the House of Commons and proceeded to the Lords, where it had a somewhat easier passage. It was, however, vigorously opposed by the Liberal leader, Earl Granville, formerly a favourite of the Queen, who now provoked her lasting rancour. Disraeli was rewarded by the gift from the Queen of a sumptuously illustrated folio volume of Goethe's *Faust*, signed 'V.R. et I.' ('regina et imperatrix') for the first time. The Queen also presided at a celebratory dinner at Windsor, 'where she startled her guests, including Disraeli and Lord George Hamilton, the Undersecretary for India, by wearing masses of jewels given to her by Indian princes and maharajahs'.[16]

Disraeli's health did not improve during the first two years of his second premiership, and he suffered periodic attacks of asthma, bronchitis and gout. Furthermore his eyesight – never very good – was rapidly failing, and he was unable to recognise people unless they stood very close to him. Finally Lady Derby, whom he sometimes still absentmindedly addressed as Lady Salisbury, took him in hand and found an emigré German oculist, who prescribed him the appropriate corrective lenses. This at least meant that he could read again, which he had been unable to do for some time. He depended more and more on Monty Corry to manage the business of government – so much so that the Earl of Carnarvon, the Colonial Secretary, complained that he never saw Disraeli except at cabinet meetings, and that Corry was 'the real Prime Minister'.[17] By the summer of 1876 there was increasing concern about Disraeli's health and his capacity to continue as Prime Minister, and Disraeli sounded out his closest colleagues about his possible retirement. They unanimously advised him to stay, partly because there was no obvious successor apart from Derby, who not only ruled himself out but declared that he would serve under nobody else. Apart from a natural diffidence, Derby was overawed by the prospect of having to deal with the Queen, who was notoriously antipathetic to him. So the advice which he and others offered to Disraeli was that he should retain the premiership but accept the peerage which Victoria had already offered him, and relieve himself from the strain of having to lead the House of Commons, which sat for many more hours each day than the upper house. This was probably the advice which he had wanted to hear. So, on 12 August 1876 Disraeli became the Earl of Beaconsfield, a non-hereditary creation because Disraeli felt that neither of his presumptive heirs, his brother Ralph or his nephew Major Coningsby Disraeli, would enjoy a sufficiently large income to maintain the state of an earldom. Conscious that membership of the upper house would somewhat diminish his authority, Disraeli told a friend, 'I am dead; dead but in the Elysian fields.'[18]

As the new Leader of the Commons, Disraeli had been expected to appoint Gathorne Hardy, his highly combative Secretary of War, but instead he picked the Chancellor of the Exchequer, the more emollient Sir Stafford Northcote. This proved a mistake, as Northcote was quite unable to stand up to Gladstone, who shortly returned to play a leading role in parliamentary debates. His attendance had only been spasmodic since he relinquished the Liberal leadership, but when he was there it was impossible to overlook him. He seated himself prominently on the front bench, usually sitting next to John Bright, and occasionally intervened without warning in debates on fairly minor matters, such as the Regiment Exchange Bill, debated on 15 March 1875. Disraeli in his daily report to the Queen on parliamentary proceedings commented, 'Mr. Gladstone not only appeared but rushed into the debate … The new Members trembled and fluttered like small birds when a hawk is in the air.'[19]

For the most part, however, Gladstone took a holiday from Parliament during the first 18 months after his resignation. His time was much taken up with family affairs, becoming a grandfather for the first time, marrying off his eldest son, Willy, to the grand-daughter of a duke, and burying the closest of his brothers, Robertson, who had looked after the family businesses, and whose demise led to his involvement in unravelling the complications of the family fortunes, now much diminished. His pen did not remain idle. He published yet another work on Homer, and two further pamphlets criticising the Vatican and its ultramontane doctrines, and embarked on a treatise on Hell, which was never finished nor published. His enormous appetite for reading was undiminished, and even included – in an attempt to probe the character and motivations of his great rival – the autobiographical novel of Disraeli's youth, *Vivian Grey*. In his diary, he recorded his verdict: 'The first quarter extremely clever, the rest trash.'[20] Like Disraeli, Gladstone spent much time visiting the country houses of great aristocrats, but his visits were a great deal more purposeful, and designed to further his insatiable curiosity, which led him to visit every county in England and all but two in Scotland. Somewhat surprisingly, given that Irish affairs were to dominate his political interests for the final three decades of his life, he visited the country only once, in 1877, when he stayed for almost a month but visited only three counties, Wicklow, Dublin and Kildare.

Gladstone was called back to the political arena by events a thousand or more miles away, in the European territories of the Ottoman Empire. A series of revolts against Turkish rule broke out in Bosnia–Herzegovina and Bulgaria, and when the Ottomans moved to crush them, Russia threatened war against the Turks. The two small Christian kingdoms of Serbia and Montenegro actually did declare war, no doubt in the hope of annexing territory, but their armies fared badly against the superior Turkish forces. Stories of brutal Turkish massacres, involving as many as 12,000 deaths of men, women and children, were widely reported, particularly in the Liberal-supporting *Daily News*, which overestimated the death toll at 25,000. This caused great indignation to British church-goers, particularly among members of the nonconformist churches, who saw this as a direct attack on the Christian population. Gladstone moved promptly to put himself at the head of the protest movement, rushing out a 10,000-word pamphlet entitled *The Bulgarian Horrors and the Question of the East* on 5 September 1876. Within two days, 22,000 copies were sold, and by the end of the month, 200,000. Gladstone followed this up, on 9 September, when he addressed 10,000 people on Blackheath, in his Greenwich constituency, in continuous heavy rain. Gladstone did not mince his words. The Turks, he wrote, had indulged in 'abominable and bestial lusts', and 'Hell itself might almost blush' at their deeds. But the most memorable passage, which added a new phrase ('bag and baggage') to the English language, was,

> Let the Turks now carry away their abuses in the only possible manner, namely by carrying off themselves. Their Zaptiehs and their Mudirs, their Bimbashis and their Yuzbashis, their Kaimakams and their Pashas, one and all, bag and baggage, shall I hope clear out from the province they have desolated and profaned.[21]

One person who was not in the least impressed was Disraeli, who had already dismissed the reports of Turkish atrocities as 'coffee-house babble'. In a letter to Derby, he described Gladstone's pamphlet as 'passionate and not strong; vindictive and ill-written – that of course. Indeed, in that respect, of all Bulgarian horrors perhaps the greatest'.[22]

This petty and sniggering judgement was quite below the level which one might expect from a senior statesman. It can only be explained by two factors: Disraeli's extreme pro-Turkism, which dated from his youthful voyage to the East, and by his slowly growing hatred for Gladstone, which had now reached its apogee. In a further letter to Derby, he poured out all the venom which had been accumulating through the years: 'Posterity will do justice to that unprincipled maniac – extraordinary mixture of envy, vindictiveness, hypocrisy and superstition; and with one commanding characteristic – whether Prime Minister, or Leader of Opposition, whether preaching, praying, speechifying or scribbling – never a gentleman!'[23]

Publicly he was equally scathing about his great rival, describing him in a speech at Knightsbridge in July 1878 as 'A sophisticated rhetorician, inebriated by the exuberance of his own verbosity, and gifted with an egotistical imagination, that can at all times command an interminable and inconsistent series of arguments to malign his opponents, and glorify himself'.[24]

Gladstone's view of his rival was probably no less unflattering, but he took care never to reveal his feelings in public. From time to time, however, he let himself go in the privacy of his diary, which (unlike modern examples of the genre) was not intended for publication. Only years after Disraeli's death did he allow himself the luxury of criticising him to a few close friends. To Lord Acton he revealed that he regarded Disraeli as 'the worst and most immoral minister since Castlereagh',[25] while to Lord Rendel he said, 'In past times the Tory party had principles by which it would and did stand for bad and for good. All this Disraeli destroyed.'[26]

Neither Disraeli nor Gladstone were fully supported by their party colleagues at this time. Both Derby and Salisbury thought Disraeli unwise to take so blatantly pro-Turkish a line, and wished that he had backed an initiative by the *Dreikaiserbund* to pressurise the Turks into introducing a wide-ranging series of reforms. In the absence of support from Britain and France, who were both invited to sign the so-called

Berlin Memorandum, the Turks blandly ignored the approach of the three emperors. As for the two Liberal leaders, Hartington and Granville, they were deeply embarrassed by Gladstone's activities, which they believed would encourage the Russians to go to war, which in turn would provoke demands for Britain to intervene again on Turkey's side, as in the Crimean War twenty years earlier. The country itself was already deeply split, with the North of England, Scotland and Wales strongly backing Gladstone while London and the south-east were in the grip of anti-Russian 'jingoism', a term coined at this time, probably inspired by a music-hall song: 'We don't want to fight, but, by Jingo, if we do, We've got the ships, we've got the men, we've got the money too. We've fought the Bear before, and while Britons shall be true, The Russians shall not have Constantinople.'[27]

The consequence was that while Gladstone was hailed as a national hero in many provincial cities, his London home was often threatened by demonstrations from an angry mob. Views soon became polarised between supporters of Gladstone and Disraeli, with moderate voices on both sides being effectively drowned out. One person who got carried away by extreme partisanship was Queen Victoria, whose initial position was critical of the Turks but who became so enraged by Gladstone that she swung violently to the other side, revealing her increasing anger in successive letters to Vicky. In these, she described his behaviour as 'most reprehensible and mischievous … shameful, and unjustifiable', referred to 'the disgraceful conduct of that mischief maker and firebrand, Mr. Gladstone', and described him as 'that half madman'.[28]

Disraeli was now threatened by a deep split in his own cabinet. His own pro-Turkish and anti-Russian stance was shared by few of his ministers, though it was enthusiastically seconded by the Queen, who was in favour of publicly warning the Tsar that if he attacked Turkey it would also mean war with Britain. 'Oh, if the Queen were a man,' she wrote, 'she would have liked to go and give those horrid Russians whose word one cannot trust such a beating!' Disraeli had no wish to go as far as this, and instead proposed a conference of the great powers of Europe (Austria–Hungary, Britain, France, Germany, Italy and Russia) to persuade the Turks to reform their administration. The Russian government was unexpectedly willing to go along with this proposal, and itself convened a conclave at its embassy in Constantinople to which the other powers were invited.

Lord Derby, as Foreign Secretary, would have been the obvious person to attend. Disraeli chose instead to send Salisbury, the Indian Secretary, who he thought – wrongly as it soon appeared – was closer to his anti-Russian views. He left for Constantinople in November 1876, stopping off on the way at the main European capitals to discuss the situation. In Berlin he met Bismarck, the German Chancellor, and the Emperor, Wilhelm I, and in Paris, Vienna and Rome had long discussions with the leading political figures. No British politician since the Congress of Vienna, sixty years earlier, had had such extensive contacts with his foreign counterparts. Salisbury's private views at this stage were not very different from Gladstone's. As a dedicated High Church Christian, he was predisposed to take a pro-Russian viewpoint.

At Constantinople, he made common cause with the amiable but artful Russian representative, General Ignatiev, though he subsequently realised that he had been manipulated by him, and his views sharply changed. The conference itself went remarkably smoothly, and an agreed list of demands was presented to the newly enthroned Sultan, Abdulhamid II. These he promptly rejected, and the plenipotentiaries returned home feeling that the venture had been a failure. So, in substance, it had, but for Lord Salisbury it had been a triumphant success, putting him on the map internationally, and he returned home, to his amazement, to a hero's welcome. The subsequent war between Russia and Turkey, which broke out in April 1877, provoked fears that the Russians would occupy Constantinople and seize control of the Dardanelles Straits. The state of British public opinion, whipped up by Gladstone's campaign, made it impossible for the government to intervene on Turkey's side, but Disraeli, backed by Salisbury, now demanded that a fleet be sent to the Dardanelles to warn the Russians off. A majority of the cabinet, however, led by the peace-loving Derby, refused to agree. For some months both Derby and his wife had been regularly leaking news of cabinet discussions to the Russian ambassador, Count Shuvalov, who was desperate to avoid a widening of hostilities and who was attempting to be a restraining influence on his own government and on the Tsar, Alexander II. The Turkish resistance to the Russian advance was more determined than had been expected, and the Tsar's troops were held up for several months before the town of Plevna. By January 1878, however, they were approaching the gates of Constantinople, and Disraeli – under great pressure from the warlike Queen – now insisted on the dispatch of the fleet, the voting of a war credit of £6 million, and the opening of discussions with Austria–Hungary on joint steps to resist the Russian advance. Derby and Carnarvon, the Colonial Secretary, immediately resigned in protest, though Derby was induced to withdraw his resignation, only to renew it some weeks later when he was replaced as Foreign Secretary by Salisbury. This was the final break between Disraeli and a man who had once been his devoted follower, and remained his closest political associate for many years. Apart from their now gaping policy differences, Derby was enraged that Disraeli promoted his younger brother, Frederick Stanley, with whom he did not get on, to cabinet rank in the resulting reshuffle, a blatant attempt to keep the influential electoral interest of the Derby family, which dominated Lancashire politics, on side. Within two years, Derby was to break with the Tories, and subsequently served under Gladstone as Colonial Secretary.

The Russians halted before Constantinople, and on 31 January 1878 signed an armistice with the Turks at Adrianople (now known as Edirne), and a few weeks later imposed stiff peace terms under the Treaty of San Stefano. This was a suburb of Constantinople, now known as Yesipoy, and the site of Istanbul's airport. The central provision of the treaty was the creation of a large Bulgaria, as an independent state, stretching from the Black Sea to the Aegean, and including virtually the whole of Macedonia. The universal assumption was that it would, effectively, be a Russian satellite, giving the Tsar an outlet to the Aegean Sea, and an open door to Constantinople and the Dardanelles. Serbia and Montenegro both gained territory, as did Russia itself, which annexed large stretches of the Ottoman Empire at the eastern end of the Black Sea, as well as the southern part of Bessarabia. The British government's reaction was that the treaty breached the terms of the Treaty of Paris, which ended the Crimean War, and that it should not be ratified unless its terms were approved by all the signatories of the earlier treaty. When Russia sent an evasive answer, Lord Salisbury resolved personally to take the matter in hand, and took the most decisive step of his career. His formal appointment as Foreign Secretary was not due to take effect until 2 April 1878, but on the evening of 29 March, returning home from a dinner party, he retired to his study, and without any help or consultation with Foreign Office staff, composed a circular which a subsequent Prime Minister, Lord Rosebery, described as one of 'the historic State Papers of the English language'. With Disraeli's strong support, it was approved by the cabinet the following morning, and went out to the capitals of the five other powers. The circular made clear that each and every one of the provisions of the San Stefano Treaty must be re-examined at a congress of the European powers, and left little doubt in the minds of its readers that British military intervention would follow if Russia did not agree to this. Salisbury followed up the circular with secret negotiations with the Turks for the transfer of Cyprus to Britain, to provide a suitable base for such intervention either immediately or in the future. The circular had the effect of stiffening the other powers, notably Austria–Hungary, and Russia climbed down and agreed to the summoning of the Congress of Berlin, which assembled on 13 June 1878. In the meantime, the cabinet had also voted to call up the reserves and to transfer troops from India to Malta, from where they could more readily intervene in the Balkans. There was a dramatic swing of public opinion, the balance of which now turned against Gladstone and in favour of standing up to the Russians. The humorous magazine *Punch*, however, took a different view, publishing a parody of the 'Jingo' song: 'We don't want to go to war, For, by Jingo, if we do, We may lose our ships, and lose our men, And what's worse, lose our money too.'[29]

The Queen, fearful for Disraeli's health, was extremely reluctant to let him travel to Berlin for the congress, but he insisted on going. In fact – having switched to a new doctor who specialised in homeopathic treatment – he was feeling better than for a long time past. So he travelled leisurely over a four-day period, accompanied by Salisbury, and turned out to be the star of the conference, along with Bismarck, who presided, and was regarded as an 'honest broker', as Germany had no direct territorial interest in the outcome of the negotiations. Intrigued by Disraeli's reputation, his exotic appearance and his fame as a novelist, the cream of European society which flocked to Berlin, as it had to Vienna sixty years earlier, was entranced by the British premier, his congeniality, sparkling wit and clear-sighted objectives. He made an immediately good impression on Bismarck, whom he had previously met 16 years earlier in London, when neither man had taken much notice of each other. There was much apprehension among Disraeli's entourage as to his ability to make himself understood in French, the *lingua franca* of diplomatic negotiation. Disraeli had prepared to deliver his opening address in French, but Lord Odo Russell, the British ambassador to Berlin, tactfully approached him, saying that the assembled plenipotentiaries would be disappointed if he did so. 'They know,' he said, 'that they have here in you the greatest master of English oratory, and are looking forward to your speech in English as the intellectual treat of their lives.'[30]

Disraeli took the hint, and the delegates had no difficulty in comprehending his message. This was notably light in detail, which he left to Salisbury to fill in, but the general thrust of the British case was clear. It comprised three objectives: to maximise the extent to which the Turkish position in Europe could be maintained, to minimise the size of Russian (and Bulgarian) gains, and to secure material advantages for Britain, notably the annexation of Cyprus. Salisbury now totally shared Disraeli's aims, but, annoyed at being upstaged by his boss, complained in a letter to his wife, 'What with deafness, ignorance of French and Bismarck's extraordinary mode of speech, Beaconsfield has [only] the dimmest idea of what is going on, understands everything crossways and imagines a perpetual conspiracy.'[31]

Bismarck, however, told one of his aides, Count von Radowitz, 'In spite of his fantastic novel-writing, he is a capable statesman. It was easy to transact business with him: in a quarter of an hour you knew exactly how you stood with him, the limits to which he was prepared to go were exactly defined, and a rapid summary soon put a point on matters.'[32]

In fact, Disraeli and Salisbury had a symbiotic relationship at the congress. Without Disraeli's prestige and panache, the British would not have carried weight; without Salisbury's attention to detail their aspirations would not have been turned into concrete results. At one moment when the Russian delegation (Shuvalov and the 80-year-old Chancellor Gorchakov) refused to accept Disraeli's demand that Turkish Thrace, promised to Bulgaria but hankered after by Greece, should be retained by the Ottomans, Disraeli threatened to walk out, and ostentatiously asked Monty Corry to summon a special train. Bismarck, sensing that he was not bluffing, then leaned hard on the Russians, and, fortuitously, word arrived from the court at St Petersburg agreeing to the concession. The congress sat for exactly a month, ending on 13 July 1878, with the signature of a treaty replacing that of San Stefano. The central provision was the cutting down to size of the large Bulgaria promised by the earlier treaty. All the non-Bulgarian-speaking areas were excluded, it lost its access to the Aegean Sea, and the remainder of the country was divided into two, the southern half, known as eastern Roumelia, remaining under Turkish control. Russia retained the territories it had sought to annex, while Austria–Hungary was allowed to occupy Bosnia–Herzogovina, and the British occupation of Cyprus was confirmed. Neither of these virtual annexations proved of much benefit to the occupiers: Austrian rule in Bosnia led to the assassination of the Archduke Franz-Ferdinand in Sarajevo in 1914, setting off the First World War, while Britain stored up future trouble for itself in Cyprus, leading to a bloody struggle for independence, which was granted only in 1959. Yet these events were far in the future, and the outcome of the congress was seen as a triumph, both for the Austrian Chancellor, Count Andrassy, and for Disraeli. He returned in triumph to London, where he and Salisbury were widely feted, claiming to have brought back 'Peace with Honour', a claim repeated by Neville Chamberlain, with a great deal less justification, on his return from Munich sixty years later. A delighted Queen Victoria wanted to make Disraeli a duke, but he refused, though he accepted the Garter, on condition that it was also bestowed on Salisbury. As for Bismarck, he shrugged off congratulations for his masterful chairmanship of the Congress, saying, '*Der alte Jude. Das ist der Mann*' ('The old Jew. That's the man.')

The Congress of Berlin was without doubt the crowning achievement of Disraeli's career, albeit a late blooming. He was now wildly popular, and most historians have assumed, not necessarily correctly, that had he opted to call a general election in its immediate aftermath he would have won a sweeping majority. On 11 August the idea was discussed in cabinet, but – as the Parliament still had three years to run, and the Tories complacently assumed that their newly won popularity would continue indefinitely – it was rejected. So Lord Beaconsfield, now aged nearly 74, remained in office, largely resting on his laurels, and taking few new political initiatives during the remainder of his premiership. His expansive imperial policies continued, however, leading to two disasters – in Zululand and Afghanistan – which largely took the bloom off his reputation. Both wars were provoked by the recklessness of British generals or administrators on the spot, but

Disraeli and his government got the blame for both humiliating setbacks. These were at Isandlwana, on 22 January 1879, where a British Army led by Lord Chelmsford was wiped out by the Zulu King, Cetewayo, and at Kabul, where the entire British mission was massacred in September of the same year. The Zulu War eventually ended in a British victory and annexation of the territory. The Third Afghan War, however, ended with a complete withdrawal of British forces from the country. Neither conflict brought any credit to Britain or to the Beaconsfield government.

Gladstone, who had been one of very few British politicians not to hail the Berlin settlement as a triumph, kept up his criticism of his opponent, declaring at a meeting in Oxford that his object in 18 months of passionate campaigning had been 'to counter-work as well as I could what I believe to be the purpose of Lord Beaconsfield'.[33] He dubbed the premier's adventurous foreign policy 'Beaconsfieldism', and made it clear that he regarded it as vainglorious and contrary to the country's best interest. Never having established what he regarded as a satisfactory relationship with his Greenwich constituency, Gladstone announced that he would not contest the seat again, but let it be known that he was open to offers from other constituencies. He was approached by Liberals in Leeds, a large urban constituency regarded as a safe Liberal seat, and expressed interest without actually committing himself. Another offer came from the Earl of Rosebery, a major Scottish landowner and one of the richest men in the country, thanks to his marriage to a great heiress, Hannah de Rothschild. Rosebery suggested he should contest the county constituency of Midlothian (otherwise known as Edinburghshire), which incorporated the hinterland of the Scottish capital and was dominated by the Rosebery family seat of Dalmeny. He intimated that he would be responsible for Gladstone's election expenses, and that the former Liberal leader would be welcome to base himself at Dalmeny. The fact that the seat was currently represented by a Tory, the Earl of Dalkeith, would not be a problem, Rosebery insisted, offering evidence to Gladstone that he could expect very strong support in the constituency, which had only a small electorate. Dalkeith was the son and heir of the Duke of Buccleuch, a colleague of Gladstone in Peel's cabinet and an old friend of his, but this did not appear to deter Gladstone, who accepted the offer with alacrity.

Gladstone embarked on his famous 'Midlothian campaign' on 24 November 1879, taking a train from Liverpool to Edinburgh, with stops on the way at Carlisle, where he addressed a crowd of 500, Hawick (4000) and Galashiels (8000). In the following week, he addressed nine further meetings in the constituency, and in Edinburgh, with audiences ranging up to 20,000, being received everywhere with great enthusiasm. He remained in Scotland for a second week, speaking in Inverkeithing, Dunfermline, Aberfeldy, Perth (twice), Motherwell and Hamilton, as well as a whole series of meetings in Glasgow. He then returned by train to his home at Hawarden, again addressing crowds at intermediate stops at Carlisle, Preston, Wigan, Warrington and Chester. Gladstone meticulously recorded in his diary that a total of 86,930 persons had attended his meetings. Roy Jenkins wryly comments that 'As a less friendly observer also calculated that he had delivered himself of 85,840 words during this fortnight, there was a close balance between output and audience.'[34]

Nothing remotely resembling this had ever been seen in British politics. No previous politician had ever before mounted such a tour, which was not even during an actual election campaign, and Gladstone's venture created a national sensation. Every word of his major speeches was reported in the national newspapers, and this was clearly a large part of Gladstone's motivation. During his speeches he had subjected every aspect of Beaconsfield's policies to an astringent examination, not excluding his 'debauching of the public finances', turning a surplus of £6 million bequeathed by the Gladstone government into a deficit of £8 million. His greatest moral fervour, however, was reserved for the victims of Beaconsfield's colonial wars. He referred to ten thousand Zulus, slaughtered 'for no other offence than their attempt to defend against your artillery with their naked bodies, their hearths and home, their wives and families ...',[35] while asserting that 'the sanctity of life in the hill villages of Afghanistan, among the winter snows, is as inviolable in the eyes of Almighty God as can be your own.'[36]

Gladstone held no official position other than as a member of parliament, but his doings now totally overshadowed those of any of his colleagues, most notably the Marquess of Hartington, the Leader of the Opposition. Hartington had every expectation of becoming the next Liberal Prime Minister, and he is recorded as having consulted Lord Granville and W.E.

Forster in October 1879 on the possibility that Gladstone might consent to serve under him as Chancellor of the Exchequer should the Liberals win the next general election. This was not expected until some time in 1881, but on 8 March 1880, Disraeli, made overconfident by two unexpected Tory by-election victories, declared an immediate election. Gladstone once more took the train to Scotland, and repeated his triumphant progress of barely four months earlier. His speeches totally dominated the campaign, in which a weary Disraeli took no part, unwisely following a tradition that peers did not participate in election campaigns. The Tory leader in the Commons, Sir Stafford Northcote, though a highly capable minister, was a poor speaker, and made very little impact, so the Conservative case virtually went by default. Hartington campaigned energetically, actually addressing more meetings than Gladstone, but these were far less fully reported. In every respect, the election was a triumph for Gladstone, who was comfortably elected, both in Midlothian and in Leeds, where he was also nominated as a candidate. He chose to represent Midlothian, and the Leeds seat went to his youngest son, Herbert Gladstone, in a subsequent by-election. The overall election result was:

| | |
|---|---|
| Liberals | 353 (+103) |
| Conservatives | 238 (−113) |
| Home Rulers | 61 (+10) |

Openly, Disraeli took this heavy defeat with admirable aplomb, but he let loose his bitter disappointment in private letters to Lady Bradford. He found the whole business of preparing a resignation honours list highly disagreeable, telling Selina, 'My room is filled with beggars, mournful and indignant, and my desk is covered with letters like a snow storm. It is the last and least glorious exercise of power.'[37]

He was, however, determined to show his gratitude to his devoted private secretary, Monty Corry. Not only did he recommend a reluctant Queen to make him a peer, he wrote to an elderly, wealthy yet childless aunt of Corry's, Lady Charlotte Lyster, begging her to make him her heir, so that he would have an estate and an income worthy of the honour which he was proposing. She readily agreed, and Corry became Lord Rowton, subsequently famous for his philanthropic activities, including the endowment of 'Rowton houses', low-rent accommodation for poor single men. Victoria was devastated by the election result, telling

Ponsonby, regarding Gladstone, that she would 'sooner *abdicate* than send for or have any *communication* with *that half mad firebrand* who wd soon ruin everything and be a *Dictator*'.[38]

She was relieved when Disraeli, in submitting his resignation, recommended her to send for Lord Hartington, who, he said, was 'in his heart a Conservative, a gentleman, and very straightforward in his conduct'. 'Harty Tarty' was promptly summoned, and was invited by the Queen to form a government, but said that he thought it would be impossible unless Gladstone was willing to serve under him. She instructed him to ask his former leader outright if he would accept *any* subordinate role, and then to report back to her. Gladstone refused point-blank, and then added insult to injury by suggesting that the Queen had been wrong to send for Hartington, as he, Gladstone, had resigned the party leadership to Granville. He nevertheless made it clear that he would not serve under him either. Gladstone later justified his action in a letter to a friend claiming that he had acted in accord with 'the just expectations of the country' that he should assume the premiership, and he had 'done the work' of dislodging the Beaconsfield government, something which he had described in his diary as 'A great election of God'. 'Besides,' he added, 'as the head of a previous ministry, and as still in full activity, I should have been strangely placed as the subordinate of one twenty years my junior and comparatively little tested in public life.'[39]

Hartington and Granville accordingly returned together to Windsor, and explained as gently as they could that the Queen had no option but to turn to Gladstone. And so, on 23 April 1880 – more than a month after the general election – Victoria finally received him at Windsor – coldly but politely – and he kissed hands on becoming Prime Minister for the second time. Once again Vicky, as her *confidante*, was told that it was 'hardly possible to believe…I had felt so sure that he could not return and it is a bitter trial for there is no more disagreeable Minister to have to deal with.'[40]

Gladstone, who had written to Granville and Hartington to express his sense of 'the high honour and patriotism with which they had acted', was in no hurry to show his gratitude, at least to Hartington. He might have expected to be offered the effective number-two position in the new government, as Chancellor of the Exchequer. In fact, he was fobbed off with the Indian Secretaryship, Gladstone retaining the chancellorship for himself. Granville again became Foreign Secretary, and most of the other principal offices were conferred on Whig grandees, such as Lord Kimberley as Colonial Secretary, Earl Spencer as Lord President of the Council and the Duke of Argyll as Lord Privy Seal. Sir William Harcourt, an able and combative parliamentarian, was Home Secretary, and Erskine Childers Secretary of War, while W.E. Forster became Chief Secretary for Ireland. Edward Cardwell, one of the great successes of Gladstone's first government and now in the House of Lords, was discarded, ostensibly on health grounds, though in a spirited letter to the Prime Minister he claimed that he was fully fit. There remained what to do about the large number of youngish Radical MPs who had been elected in the Liberal landslide. Two of them were seen as exceptionally promising. One was Joseph Chamberlain, a self-made businessman from Birmingham, where he had been an outstanding Mayor. He had built up an extraordinarily effective political machine which had swept the Liberals to power virtually across the whole of the West Midlands. The other was his close associate Sir Charles Dilke, seen as even more talented but whose prospects were damaged by his well-known republican views. The Queen would accept Dilke only for a junior office, and that only if he renounced his views – which he reluctantly did, and became Under-secretary to Granville at the Foreign Office. Gladstone had intended Chamberlain also only for a junior post, but gave way to Radical pressure and finally chose him as President of the Board of Trade. Gladstone offered the post of Under-secretary at the India Office to Lord Rosebery, but – disappointed not to have been included in the cabinet – he declined, saying he did not want to appear to be receiving a pay-off for his role in the Midlothian campaign. Altogether the cabinet had 14 members, of whom eight were in the Commons.

Gladstone's view that the sweeping Liberal victory was a direct result of his own sustained attacks on Disraeli's foreign and imperial policies was generally accepted, both by the newspapers at the time and by many historians. Disraeli, however, took the late-twentieth-century view that 'it's the economy, stupid', pointing out that the election came in the wake of an industrial recession and six successive bad harvests. There is now no way of telling, but it seems likely that his explanation came a bit nearer the mark. After his resignation, he continued to lead the Conservative Party, with the unanimous support of his leading colleagues, though he pointed out that before long they would have to look to more youthful leadership. He was to survive leaving office by only a year, or, to be more precise, 363 days. He remained in close contact with the Queen, sending her 22 letters and staying as a guest at Windsor Castle on three different occasions, the Queen undoubtedly behaving in an unconstitutional way by consulting him on political issues, which she should only have discussed with the current Prime Minister. But his main energies were devoted to literary work. He completed a political novel, *Endymion*, the bulk of which he had composed several years earlier, and which was a great success when it was published in November 1880, netting him £10,000, believed to be the largest amount ever paid for a work of fiction by that time. He then embarked on yet another novel, *Falconet*, a really vicious attack on Gladstone, who was unmistakably clearly the model for the main character, and to whom Disraeli now habitually referred as the 'AV' ('Arch Villain') in his regular correspondence with Lady Bradford and her sister. He completed only nine chapters and the beginning of a tenth, which were published in three instalments in *The Times* in 1905, and reprinted as an appendix to the great biography by Monypenny and Buckle.

Disraeli's health held up quite well during the first eleven months of his retirement, but the winter of 1880–1 was exceptionally cold, and he suffered a severe attack of bronchitis in March 1881, soon after moving into his newly acquired London residence at 19 Curzon Street. For several weeks he was confined to bed, gradually growing weaker, an agitated Queen frequently enquiring for news, and many wellwishers calling at Curzon Street to convey their best hopes for his recovery, which daily became less likely. These included Gladstone, who on 29 March recorded a visit in his diary, adding, 'May the Almighty be near his pillow.'[41] As the end approached, the Queen also proposed a visit, but Disraeli, whose mordant humour had not yet deserted him, replied, 'No it is better not. She would only ask me to take a message to Albert.' He finally succumbed on 19 April 1881, his last recorded words being, 'I had rather live but I am not afraid to die.'[42] He had lived for 76 years and 119 days, and his two premierships had totalled six years and 39 days. The Queen demanded a grand state funeral at Westminster Abbey, which Gladstone had already proposed, but Disraeli's will clearly stated, 'I DESIRE and DIRECT that I may be buried in the same Vault in the Churchyard of Hughenden in which the remains of my late dear Wife Mary Anne Disraeli created in her own right Viscountess of Beaconsfield were placed and that my funeral may be conducted with the same simplicity as hers was.'[43]

So, on 26 April the whole political and fashionable world, led by the Prince of Wales and his brothers, descended on the small Buckinghamshire village which had been his main home for nearly thirty-five years to pay their last respects. There were only two notable absentees. One was the Queen, who was advised that protocol precluded her from attending the funeral of one of her subjects. But she travelled to Hughenden a few days later to lay flowers on his coffin, and paid for the erection of a marble monument to him in the Hughenden church. The other prominent non-attender was Gladstone, who felt he would be accused of humbug if he came, and pleaded overwork as an excuse, which was widely received with derision. He made up for this by paying a fine tribute to his rival, emphasising in particular his great courage, when the Commons resumed its sittings two weeks later, while frankly acknowledging that he had been 'separated from Lord Beaconsfield by longer and larger differences than, perhaps ever separated two persons brought into constant contact in the transaction of Public Business'.[44]

Yet the occasion caused him great anguish: he had sleepless nights, and suffered severe diarrhoea in the days leading up to what proved to be the most difficult speech of his entire career. He managed to give a performance which rose well above damning with faint praise, but which, as numerous entries in his diary illustrated, was quite contrary to his private views.

# *Ten*

# Gladstone alone,
# 1881–98

G ladstone survived Disraeli by 17 years, for the first 13 of which he continued to lead the Liberal Party, and he was to form two further governments, making him the only person in history to have become Prime Minister four times. There was no one to replace Disraeli as his sworn enemy, but perhaps an even more formidable rival for political power now emerged in the shape of the 3rd Marquess of Salisbury. No match for Gladstone as an orator, and sitting in a different parliamentary chamber, there were few direct encounters between the two men, Gladstone being effectively allowed a free run in the Commons, where the Tories were still led Sir Stafford Northcote, dubbed by Roy Jenkins 'a sheep in sheep's clothing'.[1] Yet Salisbury proved a determined opponent, with a shrewd sense of political realities, and – while lacking the tactical facility of Disraeli – showed himself to be a master strategist who in the end succeeded in thwarting the Liberal leader's most cherished objectives. There was no personal ill feeling between the two men, who shared the same High Church views, though these brought comfort and calm to the Tory leader and – all too often – only *angst* to his Liberal counterpart. They had, indeed, been very friendly for many years; Gladstone had often visited Hatfield House as a guest of the Marquess, and earlier of his father. Salisbury was the spokesmen for the high aristocratic Tories, but had very little in common with them. He abhorred 'country sports' – hunting, shooting and fishing – and had markedly intellectual tastes. Salisbury saw it as his mission to defend the interests of the landed classes, which he saw as the backbone of the country, together with the monarchy and the established Church. He saw all three as threatened by 'change', but he was not a fanatical opponent of change at any price. Rather, he saw it as something which should be resisted, delayed, but – if inevitable – accepted and if possible modified to yield the least damaging result. The biggest threat he saw was the growing Radical element within the Liberal Party. The Whigs, he felt, were basically on his side, and he saw their partnership with the Radicals as an historical aberration. The class interest of the Whigs was identical to that of the Tories, in his view, and his long-term strategy was to seek to detach them from the Liberal Party.

The Gladstone who returned to office in 1880 was a different character from the one who had been defeated in 1874. In the words of the Gladstonian scholar Eugenio Biagini, his 'semi retirement' in 1875 had 'marked a watershed in his career from the executive politician of the Peelite tradition to the charismatic leader of a new and more democratic age'.[2] Gladstone's later career was, in fact, the prototype on which Max Weber based his famous theory of charisma in politics. Previously, essentially a cautious politician, Gladstone now increasingly threw caution to the wind, depended more and more on his own whims rather than on the counsel of colleagues, and became much more 'left wing' as he grew older, though still insisting that he was not an egalitarian. His reputation with the poor and the working class soared, but he was increasingly seen by 'men of property' as a dangerous demagogue.

Unlike his first administration, Gladstone's second government was not hailed as a great reforming ministry, though it did pass the 1884 Reform Bill, which effectively completed the work of the 1867 act, by introducing male household suffrage to county as well as borough constituencies. Lord Salisbury, formerly a stubborn opponent of reform who had resigned from the Derby–Disraeli government in protest against the 1867 Reform Bill, threatened to defeat the new bill in the Lords. Yet, after negotiation with Gladstone he agreed to let it through, provided it was accompanied by a redistribution of seats, which saw the replacement of almost all the two-member seats by single-member constituencies. As he foresaw, but the Liberals did not, this proved greatly to the advantage of the Tories.

At the outset of the government, in April 1880, the now 70-year-old Gladstone, who initially saw his premiership as only a stopgap arrangement for a year or two at most, concentrated on foreign affairs, determined to put an end to Disraeli's adventurism, and to curb the excesses of his imperialism. Gladstone's mentor in foreign affairs had been Lord Aberdeen, whose pacific approach to potential conflicts, based on a strong preference for diplomatic negotiation rather than sabre-rattling, had greatly influenced him. He had, accordingly, set out six principles of correct international behaviour in a speech in Midlothian, on 27 November 1879.[3] In practice, he found these principles more difficult to apply than he had imagined, and his determination to prevent further imperialist expansion proved elusive. Nowhere was this more so than in relations with Egypt, where British influence continued to grow following Disraeli's purchase of the Suez Canal shares, so that it was fast becoming a British protectorate, though it remained technically part of the Ottoman Empire. Gladstone initially encouraged nationalist sentiment in Egypt, but reluctantly agreed to the bombardment of Alexandria by a British fleet in June 1882 after riots had broken out, and then to a full-scale invasion after it had been demanded by all his cabinet ministers except John Bright, who resigned in protest. The country was completely in British hands by September 1882, and the nationalist leader, Arabi Pasha, was deported and imprisoned in the Seychelles. Unfortunately, the British commitment did not end there. Sudan, an Egyptian dependency, was the scene of a rebellion by a fanatical Muslim leader, known as the Mahdi, and General Charles Gordon was dispatched with a small force to rescue isolated Egyptian garrisons in the country and evacuate them. Gordon, a hero of the Crimean and Chinese Wars, exceeded his instructions and established himself in Khartoum, where he hoped to keep the Mahdi's army at bay. Instead, he was besieged there, and his situation became progressively more hopeless. For long Gladstone resisted pressure to send a relief force, but when he finally agreed it was too late, and in January 1885 the force arrived in Khartoum two days after it had been over-run, and Gordon and all his troops killed. Gladstone's reputation was badly damaged; he survived a Commons censure motion by only 14 votes. The Tories gleefully reversed the acronym GOM (Grand Old Man) by which he was becoming widely known, to MOG (Murderer of Gordon).

When Gladstone returned to power in 1880 he had not expected that Ireland would again be the dominant issue facing his government, but so it proved. His 1870 Irish Land Act had failed to dampen discontent, and rural violence had greatly increased. Meanwhile, Nationalist leader Charles Stewart Parnell had built up a formable electoral machine which had made a virtual clean sweep of the Irish constituencies outside Ulster, with an insistent demand for Home Rule. Gladstone's response was two-fold; he introduced another Land Bill, which went a great deal further towards meeting Irish demands than his earlier measure, and accompanied this with a Coercion Bill, giving the Viceroy powers to detain people indefinitely without bringing them to trial. Parnell and several of his associates were arrested and held in Kilmainham jail for several months. Eventually a deal was struck under which Parnell and his followers effectively agreed publicly to oppose the violence of the Fenians in exchange for policy concessions by Gladstone. The Irish Secretary, W.E. Forster, did not agree with the deal, which was popularly known as 'the Treaty of Kilmainham', and submitted his resignation. He was replaced by Lord Frederick Cavendish, Hartington's younger brother, who was married to Catherine Gladstone's niece and was accustomed to addressing Gladstone as 'Uncle Willy'. Later, in December 1882, there was a more comprehensive cabinet reshuffle, with Gladstone relinquishing the chancellorship to Erskine Childers, and the 15th Earl of Derby, who had crossed the floor of the House of Lords from the Tory benches two years earlier, replacing Lord Kimberley as Colonial Secretary. Kimberley moved to the India Office, in place of Hartington, who went to the War Office, in place of Childers.

Lord Frederick Cavendish had less than a week to enjoy his new post. On 6 May 1882, while walking in Phoenix Park, Dublin, he was assassinated by Fenians, together with his Permanent Under-secretary, T.H. Burke. Gladstone was severely shaken by this event, but probably concluded about this time that Home Rule was the only viable long-term solution for Ireland, though he did not reveal this to any of his colleagues. In the meantime, an even stronger Coercion Bill was passed. This upset Parnell and his party, previously allied to the Liberals, and in June 1885 they voted with the Tories to defeat the budget. Gladstone immediately resigned, and Salisbury formed a minority Tory government. A relieved Victoria then offered Gladstone an earldom, which he unhesitatingly rejected. In November 1885, Salisbury called a general election, in which he failed to win a majority, the result being:

| | |
|---|---|
| Liberals | 334 |
| Conservatives | 250 |
| Home Rulers | 86 |

The Tory leader remained in office with the support of the Parnellites. At around this time, Gladstone approached Arthur Balfour, Salisbury's nephew, to see whether a bipartisan agreement on some measure of Home Rule might be reached. Salisbury flatly refused, and Gladstone's youngest son Herbert then leaked to the press that his father was converted to Home Rule.

This was good enough for the Parnellites, and they promptly abandoned their temporary alliance with the Tories, defeating the government in the Queen's Speech debate on 27 January 1886. Salisbury resigned, and Victoria, anxious to avoid a third Gladstone government at all costs, put out feelers to George Goschen, a former Liberal cabinet minister who now often voted with the Tories, to see if he would head a coalition government. Goschen refused, and after three days she bowed to the inevitable, and sent her secretary to call on Gladstone with 'the Queen's Commission', which, as he recorded in his diary, 'I at once accepted.'[4] He had difficulty in forming the government: several prominent Whigs, led by Lord Hartington, whom Gladstone had treated so insensitively in the past, and including both Derby and Goschen, refused to serve, because of their strong opposition to Home Rule. Two leading Radicals, Joseph Chamberlain and Sir George Trevelyan, accepted office, but resigned soon after for the same reason. Victoria continued to make difficulties, turning down Gladstone's first two choices for the Foreign Office, Lord Granville and the Earl of Kimberley, and insisting instead on the young Earl of Rosebery. Undeterred, Gladstone pressed ahead, and introduced his Home Rule Bill in April 1886. After 16 days of debate, it was defeated by 30 votes on the second reading, on 8 June 1886, with only two-thirds of Liberal MPs voting with the government. Gladstone immediately asked for, and was granted, a dissolution, and went down to heavy defeat in the subsequent general election, which produced the following result:

| | |
|---|---|
| Conservatives | 316 |
| Liberals | 190 |
| Irish Nationalists | 85 |
| Liberal Unionists | 79 |

The Liberal Unionists, who included a large element of the former Whigs as well as Joseph Chamberlain's formidable Birmingham-based group of Radicals, threw in their lot with the Conservatives, with whom they eventually merged to form the Conservative and Unionist Party. Gladstone's third government had lasted a mere 169 days, and Salisbury became Prime Minister for the second time, with a large majority. Many of the Liberals who stayed loyal nevertheless blamed Gladstone for the recklessness with which he had split his party. They agreed with him in principle on Home Rule, but did not believe that its importance outweighed all other considerations. They felt that he should not have sprung the issue on the party without spending a great deal more time in gentle persuasion. This, however, was not the way of the older Gladstone, who, in Lord Randolph Churchill's words, had become 'an old man in a hurry'.[5] Salisbury was triumphant: his aim of separating most of the more prominent Whigs from the Liberal Party had been achieved. The simultaneous departure of so many Radicals, led by Joseph Chamberlain, was an additional bonus which he had never foreseen. The motives of the defectors were undoubtedly mixed. Many of the grander Whigs held extensive estates in Ireland, of which they were absentee landlords. The Devonshire family, for example, of which Hartington was the heir, owned 60,000 acres in Waterford and County Cork. They undoubtedly feared that they would be expropriated if an Irish House of Commons, dominated by Catholic small farmers, was brought into existence. Hartington himself would only have been human if he had been influenced, at least in part, and however unconsciously, by his repeatedly scurvy treatment at the hands of Gladstone. Others, including the dissident Radicals, had no selfish interest in opposing the Liberal leader, and objected on grounds of public policy.

The now 76-year-old Gladstone had no thought of retiring, but sat out the six years of Salisbury's second term as Leader of the Opposition, continuing to make Home Rule his over-riding priority, and forming a close alliance with the Irish Nationalists, sometimes using Parnell's mistress, Kathy O'Shea, as a go-between. When, in November 1890, Kathy's husband, Captain W.H. O'Shea MP, cited Parnell as a co-respondent in his divorce case, Gladstone sanctimoniously threw up his hands in horror, though he was well aware of what had been going on. He urged Parnell to retire temporarily from public life, and withheld his support when Parnell's Catholic supporters turned on him. Parnell, a broken man, died within the year, aged 46. The GOM's abandonment of Parnell, and the consequent fatal split in the Irish Nationalist Party, was highly damaging to the Home Rule cause. A string of by-election successes had led to high hopes of a massive Liberal victory at the forthcoming general election, with a majority large enough to secure not only the passage of a bill through the Commons but also to deter the Lords from applying a veto. In the event, some 355 supporters of Home Rule were returned in the 1892 election, and 315 opponents – a clear majority, but a bitter disappointment after the earlier high hopes. This was the last general election which Gladstone fought, and he was again returned for Midlothian. The overall result was:

| | |
|---|---|
| Liberals | 270 |
| Conservatives | 268 |
| Liberal Unionists | 47 |
| Irish Nationalists | 81 |
| Others | 4 |

Salisbury resigned, and on August 1892, aged 82, Gladstone embarked on his fourth government. Queen Victoria had contemplated a last-ditch attempt to avoid having 'that dangerous old fanatic thrust down her throat'[6] by sending for Lord Rosebery instead, but had been dissuaded by her secretary, Henry Ponsonby, who argued that this would be a useless and indeed counter-productive gesture.[7] Gladstone himself was in a poor physical condition, having suffered a serious injury to his 'left and only serviceable eye' during the election campaign, when, he recorded in his diary, 'a middle aged bony woman' threw a 'hard baked little gingerbread say 1½ inch across…with great force and skill about two yards off me'.[8] This badly affected his reading ability for several weeks, and his vision was permanently impaired. Then a few weeks later he was knocked down by a 'dangerous cow' on his Hawarden estate.

The Liberals were in a minority, but were strongly backed by the Irish Nationalists, even though they were themselves divided between pro- and anti-Parnellite factions. Gladstone's last government included three subsequent Liberal prime ministers – Rosebery, Henry Campbell-Bannerman and H.H. Asquith, but his closest associate was John Morley, the Irish Chief Secretary, who was later to write his biography in three extensive volumes. His last premiership lasted for one year and 199 days, and was totally dominated by the issue of Home Rule. Gladstone received little support from his cabinet colleagues, only two of whom – Morley and Lord Spencer, a former Irish Viceroy – were wholeheartedly behind his efforts. Spencer was known as the 'Red Earl', not on account of any left-wing views but because of his bright red beard. The two most senior figures – Harcourt, the Chancellor of the Exchequer, and Rosebery, the Foreign Secretary – were determinedly obstructive, while most of the rest of the cabinet were sullenly resentful that what they regarded as a quixotic enterprise should take precedence over all other government business. Gladstone himself was far from optimistic about the outcome, and, now half blind as well as half deaf, had serious misgivings about his own capacity, confiding to his diary, 'Frankly from the condition *(now)* of my senses, I am no longer fit for public life; yet bidden to walk in it. "Lead thou me on."'[9]

Yet he rose sublimely to the occasion, Jenkins commenting that 'Even among his bitterest opponents, there was a sense of witnessing a magnificent last performance by a unique creature, the like of whom would never be seen again.'[10]

Virtually singlehandedly, Gladstone assumed the entire burden of carrying the bill through the Commons, speaking frequently and impressively at all stages – nine days of debate at second reading, 53 days for the committee stage, nine for the report stage, and three for third reading, altogether the greater part of 82 sittings of the House. In the end, the bill was passed by a majority of 34. The House of Lords was not impressed, and certainly not overawed. It spent only four days on the bill, and then rejected it by 419 votes to 41, one of the most one-sided votes in its entire history. The opposition to the bill was led, with great fervour, by Hartington, who, on the death of his father in 1891, had become the 8th Duke of Devonshire. The Lords did not stop at that, going on to defeat or truncate several other Liberal bills over the following months. Gladstone was indignant that the Tory leader, Lord Salisbury, should take such liberties with the programme of a recently elected government, and proposed to his colleagues that an immediate election should be fought on a 'peers versus people' prospectus, and that – in the event of victory – the bill should be reintroduced. The cabinet, sensing – probably correctly – that this was a recipe for electoral disaster, unanimously turned him down.

Increasingly after that Gladstone was at odds with a majority of his cabinet colleagues, and it seemed only a matter of time before he would stand down. The issue on which he chose to go was naval rearmament. While preoccupied by the Home Rule Bill, and distracted and saddened by the sudden and tragic deaths of both his doctor and his valet, he had failed to take account of the rising tide of anxiety about the reinforcement of both the French and Russian fleets, and early indications that the young and impetuous German Kaiser, Wilhelm II, intended to build his own Grand Fleet. (Wilhelm had succeeded his father, the 'liberal' Frederick III and husband of Victoria's daughter Vicky, who ruled for only 99 days in 1888 before dying of cancer, aged 56.) The Admiralty proposed a large increase in its estimates, strongly backed by the Queen. She wrote a letter to Gladstone which she insisted should be read to the whole cabinet. Gladstone was appalled by the Admiralty's demands, which offended against both his hatred of militarism and his continuing determination to keep budgetary expenditure under the strictest control. He made it clear to his cabinet colleagues that he regarded it as a matter of confidence, and when a vote was taken on 9 January 1894 on the Admiralty's demands he was shocked to find himself in a minority of 13 to 3. He declined to resign on the spot, but indicated that he would probably do so at the end of the parliamentary session in February 1894. Meanwhile, he left for a month-long visit to Biarritz to commune with his family, his secretary and a few close friends. He left Harcourt to lead the House of Commons in his absence.

As the session neared its end it became clear that the House of Lords was bent on emasculating each of the three bills which had – apart from the Home Rule Bill – occupied most of the Commons' time in the preceding year. Gladstone toyed with the idea of reviving his plan to precipitate a 'peers versus people' election, while putting off a final decision on naval rearmament. It was immediately clear, however, that none of his cabinet colleagues would agree to this, and he returned to London, where the cabinet agreed to withdraw one of the three bills, but to accept 'under protest' the Lords' amendments to the other two. Gladstone attended his final cabinet on 1 March 1894, the last of 556 cabinet meetings he had chaired. It was a sad and disconcerting occasion, dubbed by Gladstone in his diary as 'the blubbering cabinet'.[11] As the senior minister present, Kimberley attempted to pay a heartfelt tribute to the retiring premier, but broke down in tears after a few sentences. Then Harcourt, who aspired to be the GOM's successor and had for long been scarcely able to contain his impatience for him to go, produced a lengthy memorandum, which, also sobbing, he proceeded to read out. Described by Shannon as 'an embarrassingly pompous *éloge*', Gladstone himself later referred to it as 'nine-tenths buncrum' (*sic!*).[12] Morley wrote in his diary that Harcourt's words were 'horrid, grotesque, nauseous, almost obscene'. Gladstone, he recorded, 'sat quite composed and still. The emotion of the Cabinet did not gain him for an instant … [he] went slowly out of one door, while we with downcast looks and oppressed hearts filed out by the other, much as men walk away from the graveside.'[13]

Following the meeting, Gladstone went to the House of Commons, where he spoke for the last time. Without mentioning his intended resignation, he announced that the government was accepting 'under protest', the Lords' amendments to the Local Government Bill. He coupled this with a warning that if, as seemed likely, the Lords had abandoned their traditional 'reserve and circumspection' then the conflict between them and the elected house 'when once raised must [in due course] go forward to an issue'.[14] It was a fair warning, which the Lords were to ignore when, 15 years later, they voted down Lloyd George's 'People's Budget', leading to the clipping of their powers by the 1911 Parliament Act. The following day, 2 March 1894, Gladstone travelled to Windsor to deliver his formal letter of resignation to the Queen, having already told her informally of his intentions at an audience in Buckingham Palace on 28 February.

The Queen, who treated Gladstone in the churlish way to which she had become accustomed, did not ask his advice on the succession. If she had, he would have proposed Lord Spencer; the choice of Liberal MPs would probably have been Sir William Harcourt. But, showing remarkably poor judgement, she chose instead the Earl of Rosebery, who turned out to be one of Britain's least successful premiers. She had been flattered and charmed by this glamorous Scottish aristocrat, and totally failed to discern his volatile and basically unstable temperament. Gladstone left office on 2 March 1894, in his eighty-fifth year. In total, he had been Prime Minister for 12 years and 126 days, then the fourth-longest in British history, though he was subsequently overtaken by Salisbury. The day after leaving office he received a letter from the Queen which contained not a single word of appreciation for his long years of service as her Prime Minister. He regarded this as the final insult, complaining in his diary that he had been dismissed with 'the same brevity … used in settling a tradesman's bill'.[15]

Windsor Castle, 3rd March 1894

Though the Queen has already accepted Mr. Gladstone's resignation and has taken leave of him, she does not like to leave his letter tendering his resignation unanswered. She therefore writes these few lines to say that she thinks, after so many years of arduous labour and responsibility, he is right in wishing to be relieved at his age of these arduous duties, and she trusts [he will] be able to enjoy peace and quiet, with his excellent and devoted wife, in health and happiness, and that his eyesight may improve.

The Queen would gladly have offered a peerage to Mr. Gladstone, but she knows he would not accept it.[16]

Gladstone lived for another four years and 78 days after his final resignation. Despite his poor eyesight and growing deafness, he remained extremely active, for at least the first two or three years. He never again set foot in the House of Commons, but retained his seat until the general election of 1893, when he was not a candidate. Though he was privately highly critical of Rosebery's premiership, he made no major public intervention until 24 September 1896. He then mounted a platform in Liverpool and delivered to a vast audience an address of one hour and twenty minutes, denouncing Turkish massacres of Christians in Armenia and demanding that the British government, now again led by Lord Salisbury, should take action against the Turks. It was a re-run of his condemnation of the Bulgarian massacres a decade earlier. Gladstone's words had no discernible influence on the Turks nor on Salisbury's government. Yet they had a devastating effect on the now deeply divided Liberal Party. Within 12 days Rosebery resigned as its leader, describing Gladstone's speech as 'the last straw on his back', and complaining that it would enable 'discontented Liberals to pelt him with Gladstone's authority'.[17] He stood down in favour of Harcourt, who lasted only two years before also resigning in a huff, making way for a much more low-key, but more mature and more rational successor, Sir Henry Campbell-Bannerman, who had been War Secretary under Gladstone. After many vicissitudes, he was able eventually to lead the Liberal Party into its greatest election victory, in 1906.

For the most part, Gladstone concentrated on his literary work, publishing his translation of the *Odes of Horace*, on which he had been working during his final premiership, but then had the choice of embarking on two major enterprises. One was to write his autobiography, for which – through the good offices of the Scottish–American millionaire and philanthropist Andrew Carnegie – he was offered the then unheard-of sum of $100,000, far surpassing the lifetime literary earnings of Disraeli. Gladstone was tempted, but decided to give priority to his other project, making only desultory progress on his autobiography, and not committing himself to any publisher. He devoted himself instead to editing the complete works of Bishop Joseph Butler, a noted eighteenth-century theologian, who had greatly influenced Gladstone in his youth and on whom he had been working, on and off, since 1846. In 1896 the edition was published in two volumes, together with a bulky 150,000-word tome of Gladstone's own interpretations, entitled *Studies Subsidiary to the Works of Bishop Butler*.

He continued to brood, both in his diary and his autobiographical writings, about Victoria's hostility to him, declaring that he was himself 'conscious without mistrust of having invariably rendered to her the best service that I could'.[18] He speculated that the root cause of her disapproval must have been the rumours about his 'rescue work' and his well-known association with Mrs Thistlethwayte, whose death in May 1894 was not noted in his diary. 'Statements,' he wrote, 'whether true or false must have been carried to her ears which in her view required (and not merely allowed) the mode of proceeding that was actually adopted.'[19]

The GOM sadly concluded that Victoria's attitude to him was analogous to his own towards the mule who had carried him on an uncomfortable 400-mile tour of Sicily some 56 years earlier: 'I had been on the back of the beast for many scores of hours. It had done me no wrong. It had rendered me much valuable service. But...I could not get up the smallest shred of feeling for the brute. I could neither love nor like it. What the Sicilian mule was to me I have been to the Queen.'[20]

Gladstone kept up the daily record of his activities and thoughts in his diary until 23 May 1894, when he underwent a cataract operation, almost 69 years since he began his marathon diary. He never resumed his daily habit, but made a few spasmodic entries, concluding the diary on his eighty-seventh birthday, 17 December 1896. He then rounded off the 41 octavo volumes with a brief 'Retrospect' of what he described as his 'long and tangled life'. Ten days earlier, he had written out and signed, in the presence of his son Stephen, a solemn 'Declaration' of his marital fidelity:

> With reference to rumours which I believe were at one time afloat, though I know not with what degree … of currency: and also with reference to the times when I shall not be here to answer for myself: I desire to record my solemn declaration and assurance, as in the sight of God and before His judgment seat, that at no period of my life have I been guilty of the act that is known as that of infidelity to the marriage bed.
>
> I limit myself to this negation, and I record it with my dear Son Stephen, both as the eldest surviving of our sons, and as my pastor. It will be for him to retain or use it, confidentially unless necessity should require more, which is unlikely: and in any case making it known to his brothers. WEG Dec. 7 1896.[21]

It is not known if Gladstone continued his encounters with prostitutes after his final retirement, but it seems unlikely. The last occasion recorded in his diary was on 24 February 1894, just a week before his resignation. After that he spent relatively little time in London, retreating to Hawarden, and staying during his London visits chiefly in the Carlton Gardens home of Lord Rendel, a former Liberal MP, whose daughter Maud had married Gladstone's son Henry Neville. Rendel, who had been ennobled by Gladstone in his resignation honours list, proved to be a generous host, who each winter put his luxurious villa in Cannes at the disposal of Gladstone and an extended family group. During the last four years of his life, Gladstone, who did not retain the services of a secretary, became very dependent on the help of his family. His daughter Mary Drew, who was married to a clergyman, acted as secretary to both her parents, and continued to live in their home after her marriage, her husband working as a curate under Stephen Gladstone, and later succeeding him as Rector of Hawarden. Other family members, including in-laws, were regularly co-opted to assist him in many ways and to accompany the family in their visits to Cannes and to Bournemouth, where Gladstone went to convalesce on several occasions.

In 1895 Gladstone gave £40,000 (estimated to be equivalent to £3.42 million today) to endow a residential library and study centre, known as St

Deniol's Library, in Hawarden village. Despite his advanced age, he personally transported most of his own 32,000 books to their new home a quarter of a mile away, using his wheelbarrow. The library, renamed Gladstone's Library in 2010, is considered an important research library in Wales, with over 250,000 items, mostly in the arts, humanities and theology.

Gladstone continued to be troubled by his hearing and eyesight, but his general health remained good for a man of his age, though he appeared increasingly frail, and Catherine even more so. Then, in the autumn of 1897, he suffered a severe attack of facial neuralgia, and remained in great pain throughout much of the coming winter, which he spent at Rendel's villa in Cannes. He returned from there to Bournemouth in March 1898, where he was diagnosed with cancer. Four days later he was transferred to Hawarden, where he died, surrounded by nine members of his family and three doctors, at 5 a.m. on Ascension Day, 19 May 1898. He had lived for 88 years and 141 days. Unlike Disraeli, Gladstone received a state funeral and was buried in Westminster Abbey, after his body had lain in state in Westminster Hall, where an estimated 250,000 people had filed past during two days. His grave, where, as he had prescribed in his will, he was joined by Catherine two years later, is overlooked by statues of Peel and Disraeli, his mentor and his bitter rival.

There were no flowers from Queen Victoria. Indeed, when she heard that the Prince of Wales (later Edward VII), and his son, the Duke of York (later George V), had been among the ten pallbearers, she telegraphed the Prince reproaching him, and asked him if there were any precedents, and on whose advice he and the Duke had acted. The Prince telegraphed back that 'there were no precedents and he took no advice – the circumstances were unprecedented, and he would and should never forget what a friend to Royalty Mr. G. had been.'[22]

Gladstone was certainly one of the most remarkable men ever to serve in 10 Downing Street. The sheer length of his political career was in itself daunting. Over 62 years as an MP (narrowly second only to Churchill among prime ministers), 27 years as a minister, he spanned the period between George Canning, whom he knew as a young man, and Asquith, who served in his last cabinet. He transformed the office of Chancellor of the Exchequer, was the first politician to campaign actively throughout the whole country, and was the virtual creator of the modern Liberal Party.

He then badly split it, by driving out most of the former Whigs, while compensating by building up a great bond of trust among working-class voters. The effect of this was probably to delay the creation of a viable Labour or socialist party until after his death, while this development occurred notably earlier in most other Western European countries. Regarded as 'mad' by Queen Victoria, many of his Liberal colleagues thought that he had lost all sense of proportion over Ireland, and that the strength and persistence of his commitment to Home Rule was a grave error. Nevertheless, if his efforts had been crowned with success, more than a century of turmoil, including two long periods of terrorist and counter-terrorist violence would have been avoided, and Ireland would conceivably have remained within a devolved or federal United Kingdom. Gladstone was, more than any other British leader, strongly and publicly motivated by his Christian beliefs, which were undoubtedly sincere, though he was not above cutting corners and indulging in sharp practice from time to time. Disraeli should not be taken at his word when he complained that 'he did not have a single redeeming defect'.[23] Nor would it be true to picture Gladstone as consistently solemn and humourless. He had a lively sense of fun, and his speeches, though over-long, were enlivened by flashes of wit, which were not, however, the equal of those of his more mercurial rival. Perhaps, above all, Gladstone should be seen as an archetypal figure of the Victorian age, though he was never appreciated by its figurehead, whose interests he had tried so devotedly and so unrewardingly to serve.

# *Eleven*

# The final reckoning

'Dizzy is a charlatan and knows it. Gladstone is a charlatan and doesn't know it.' The verdict of Thomas Carlyle, the Scottish essayist and historian, does less than total justice to both men.[1] Yet it encapsulates the main criticism made against each man by their critics: that Gladstone was a hypocrite and Disraeli unprincipled. The charge against Gladstone, which was often levelled, particularly by his Tory opponents in the later stages of his political career, was that the high moral standards which he propagated were not sincerely held. Yet even the briefest perusal of his diaries, which were not written for publication, can leave no doubt in any reader's mind that he was very strongly committed to the Christian beliefs he put forward, though equally aware of the extent to which he failed to live up to them. The worst that can be said of Gladstone in this respect is that he too readily presumed that actions he decided upon for selfish or mundane reasons were, in fact, the will of God. He seldom set out with the deliberate intention to deceive others; all too often he succeeded in deceiving himself. His Christian faith did not make Gladstone a particularly serene or contented man, but it gave him great force and self-confidence, and the courage to stick to his guns even when circumstances combined against him.

That Disraeli lacked principle seems evident from his opportunistic and generally disreputable conduct as a young man, and the eagerness with which he was prepared to embrace free trade *after* his destruction of Sir Robert Peel. Yet his attack on Peel was based more on the fact that Peel's government had reneged on the programme on which it had won the 1841 election rather than on the issue of free trade versus protectionism *per se*. In his later career, Disraeli probably showed as much consistency as most other politicians in sticking to policy positions which he had adopted. In defence of Disraeli, it could be argued that he looked upon himself as an artist, and thus absolved from following the rules of conduct which applied to ordinary mortals. However, his pre-eminent modern biographer, Robert Blake, who as a Tory life peer was predisposed to favour him, states unequivocally that 'Disraeli *was* an adventurer' and that 'Morally and intellectually Gladstone was his superior.'[2] The truth about Disraeli is that he was a great romantic, seeing himself as a Byronic figure. He romanticised his own ancestry, he romanticised the Jewish race, he romanticised the aristocracy, he romanticised the working classes, rural England and even the Queen. Where others might have seen a short, dumpy, plain and self-indulgent woman, of limited judgement and imagination, he saw 'the Faerie Queene', and endowed her with infinite qualities.

Religion was important to both men, though in very different ways. Gladstone could hardly have been more devout, but Disraeli confessed to Edward Henry Stanley that he was 'personally incapable of religious belief'.[3] Nevertheless, he took Christianity extremely seriously, always stressing its Judaic origins. He regarded Christianity, Jonathan Parry argues, as 'Judaism perfected',[4] stressing that both Jesus and the Virgin Mary were Jews. 'Half Christendom worships a Jewess and the other half a Jew,' says a character in his novel *Tancred*.[5] In the same book, he remarks that 'The Roman church had been founded by a Hebrew when the English were tattooed savages.'[6] Disraeli's interest in religion was largely of an anthropological nature, though he also saw it as a means of giving cohesion to a society. He was a practising Anglican, regularly attending church services at Hughenden, where he was the patron of the local church. He strongly defended the establishment and the privileges of the Church of England, which he rightly saw as a bastion of the Conservative Party. The publication of Charles Darwin's *On the Origin of Species* and *The Descent of Man,* with their implied rejection of the literal truth of the Bible, disturbed both men. Gladstone felt that he lacked the 'physical knowledge to deal with the Darwinian question'.[7] Yet he wrote in his diary, on 17 January 1872, that it had not been 'given to Mr. Darwin ... to sweep away that fabric of belief which has stood the handling of 1800 years and of stronger men than any now alive'.[8]

Disraeli's rejection of Darwin's findings was earlier and more definite, if less well considered. Speaking in 1864 at a debate in the Sheldonian Theatre in Oxford, in support of Bishop Samuel Wilberforce, he declared, 'The question is this – Is man an ape or an angel? My Lord, I am on the side of the angels.'[9]

Various characteristics of the two men have often been compared and contrasted. Both of them became prominent primarily because of their oratory, though their styles were very different. Gladstone's speeches largely consisted of building up a logical argument, step by step, and enunciated with great force, aided by his splendid presence and flashing eyes. He always spoke with great optimism, appealing to the better selves of his auditors. His main defect was that he almost always went on for too long, though at his many public meetings he normally succeeded in retaining the attention of his audience until the very end. As a performer at mass meetings, either outdoors or indoors, he was without a rival; within the Chamber of the Commons, he was still highly formidable, and clearly superior to all others except Disraeli, who was arguably his equal and in some respects his superior. The Tory leader's speeches were more subtle and complex, relying more on wit, irony and paradox. He was much more of a debater than his rival. A more 'destructive' speaker, he mercilessly cut down his victims, of whom Peel was merely the most prominent. He was a more complete 'parliamentarian' than Gladstone, having a much surer grasp of parliamentary tactics.

As a minister, Gladstone proved by far the more effective. In Robert Blake's words,

> The most ardent admirer of Disraeli must concede that Gladstone was more thorough, more knowledgeable, more energetic, better briefed. One has only to contrast the slapdash nature of Disraeli's first budget (1852), in which he muddled up all the income tax schedules, with the immensely competent, carefully planned first budget of Gladstone the following year.[10]

Gladstone excelled at introducing, and carrying through, major pieces of legislation in the House of Commons, both as Prime Minister and earlier as a departmental minister. Apart from his masterly handling of the 1867 Reform Bill, Disraeli took little responsibility for legislation.

All the important bills passed by his second government were steered through Parliament by other ministers, with the Prime Minister being virtually 'absent', as his Home Secretary Richard Cross caustically noted. In fairness to Disraeli, it should be noted that he was much more of an opposition politician than his rival. He led the Conservatives in the House of Commons for 28 years, and for only nine of these was he in office, holding only one post, as Chancellor of the Exchequer, before assuming the premiership. By contrast, Gladstone held six different posts (including nine years as Chancellor) before forming his first government in 1868, and was sitting on the government benches for the great majority of his time in Parliament. Moreover, when Disraeli finally achieved office with power in 1874, he was an old and often sick man. He was only too aware of this, and confessed in one of his many letters to Lady Bradford that the opportunity had come to him 'too late'. As Leader of the Opposition, however, he proved superior to Gladstone, who had a very unhappy time opposing the Derby–Disraeli government of 1866–8, when he was frequently humiliated by Disraeli.

Gladstone had evident difficulty in treating his ministerial colleagues on anything like terms of equality. Two of them he looked up to – Peel, whom he hero-worshipped, and Aberdeen, under whom he served twice, both when the latter was Foreign Secretary and Prime Minister. Each of these men acted to some extent as his exemplars, the former regarding taxation and trade policy, the latter in foreign relations. Yet he badly mishandled his relations with several of his own subordinate ministers, especially Hartington, but also the two Radicals Joseph Chamberlain and Sir Charles Dilke. All three turned against him in 1886 when he opted for Irish Home Rule. By contrast, Disraeli took care to act considerately towards all his ministers, and, as we have seen, persistently wooed Salisbury, even though in both his former identities as Lord Robert Cecil and Viscount Cranborne he had been his sternest critic. His eventual falling out with the 15th Earl of Derby was due to developing policy differences rather than ill-will on the part of either man. As well as getting on better with his fellow ministers, Disraeli was much more adept at charming his acquaintances, especially if they were women. Jennie Jerome, the American wife of Lord Randolph Churchill and mother of Winston Churchill, wrote in her *Reminisces* that 'when I left the dining room after sitting next to Gladstone I thought he was the cleverest man in England. But when I sat next to Disraeli, I left feeling that I was the cleverest woman.'[11]

Both Disraeli and Gladstone were prolific authors, and in terms of quantity their output was probably about equal. Yet the quality, the nature and the purpose of their works were quite different. The majority of Disraeli's work was fiction, in one form or another. It was written to entertain, to project himself and, not least, to make money. Only the three novels which he wrote in the 1840s – *Coningsby, Sybil* and *Tancred* – had an additional purpose, to give an airing to Disraeli's newly formulated ideas on politics, social reform and religion. They were probably his best works. Literary critics have generally been unkind about Disraeli's novels, saying that the plots tended to be too melodramatic and that his characterisation was poor. Disraeli probably recognised this, and based many of his characters on real persons, taking little trouble to disguise their identity. There were few contemporary public figures who could not easily recognise themselves in one or more of his novels, which did not necessarily endear the author to them. Nevertheless, most of Disraeli's work was highly readable, and often amusing. The same cannot, unfortunately, be said of Gladstone's works, which covered a large range of topics – religious, historical, political and literary. His language was often turgid, his sentences far too complex and long. An exception were polemical pamphlets written in the white heat of the moment, condemning apparent scandals or atrocities, such as the Neapolitan prison system in 1850 and the Turkish massacres and the declaration of papal infallibility in the 1870s. These were much more direct and simple, were widely read, and proved highly influential. That Disraeli produced many more striking phrases and memorable quotes is evidenced by *The Oxford Dictionary of Quotations*. In the current edition, he has 95 entries, against 18 for Gladstone.

The deaths of Disraeli and of Gladstone did not end their influence, which in some respects continues to the present day. Gladstone is remembered for putting the nation's finances in good order, for establishing the chancellorship of the exchequer as the second post in the government, for his love of liberty and close sympathy for the peoples of subject nations (including the Irish), for his advocacy of international arbitration, and his preference for pursuing a peaceful, non-expansionist foreign policy. He became a hero to many people both inside and outside the Liberal Party, and proved an inspiration to generations of Liberal, and later Labour, politicians. Inevitably, however, with the passage of years his memory has faded, and there are nowadays perhaps only a few veterans of the Liberal Democratic Party who feel any personal affinity with him. Disraeli's posthumous fame has been more enduring, particularly within the ranks of the Conservative Party, which has come to revere him as their founding father, airbrushing Peel, the actual founder of the party, from its history. Many Conservatives credit him with bequeathing them an electoral platform, which has brought them lasting success – combining a muscular foreign policy with promises of social reform at home. In practice, Disraeli was not much of a social reformer himself – the reforms passed by his second government being the work of other ministers. It was his novels – particularly *Sybil or the Two Nations* – which gave him the reputation for being sympathetic to the poor and the working class. This tradition drove successive party leaders, up to and including Macmillan and Heath, and was constantly fostered by an influential group of Tory MPs, known as the One Nation Group. It was, however, firmly repudiated by Margaret Thatcher, but appeared to be revived by David Cameron, with his advocacy of 'progressive conservatism' and the 'Big Society' as Leader of the Opposition. Since becoming Prime Minister in 2010, however, he has disappointed many of his supporters, and was taken aback in October 2012 when, at the annual conference of the Labour Party in Manchester, Ed Miliband made an audacious bid to seize the mantle of Disraeli for his own party. Referring directly to Disraeli's great speech of 1872, also in Manchester, he claimed that Labour was now the 'one-nation' party. It is a remarkable tribute to the durability of Disraeli's legacy that over a hundred and thirty years after his death both leading political parties are now claiming to be his legitimate heir.

# Notes

References to Monypenny and Buckle (1929 edition), *The Life of Benjamin Disraeli, Earl of Beaconsfield* are shown below as 'MB'. Those to the *Gladstone Diaries* as 'GD', to Benjamin Disraeli (1982), *Letters 1815–81* as 'BDL' and to *Parliamentary Debates* as 'PD'. Other sources listed are as shown in the Select bibliography.

## Prologue, The night of 16–17 December 1852

1  PD, 17 December 1852.

## Chapter 1, Benjamin Disraeli, early life, 1804–41

1  Ogden (2004).
2  Blake (1966), p. 7.
3  Ibid., p. 12.
4  Ibid., p. 17.
5  Bradford (1982), pp. 215–19.
6  Weintraub (1993), p. 38.
7  Ibid., p. 44.
8  Bradford (1982), p. 14.
9  Blake (1966), pp. 772–8.
10  Bradford (1982), p. 14.
11  MB, I, p. 73.
12  Flavin (2005), p. 15.
13  Blake (1966), p. 48.
14  Hibbert (2005), p. 53.
15  Weintraub (1993), p. 87.
16  Ibid., p. 143.
17  BDL, I, p. 198.

18  B. and S. Disraeli (1983).
19  MB, I, pp. 258–9.
20  Ibid., I, p. 282.
21  Ibid., I, pp. 287–8, quoting *The Courier*, 6 May 1835.
22  Blake (1966), p. 126.
23  Aldous (2006), p. 11.
24  Sykes (1928), p. 42.
25  Weintraub (1993), p. 13.
26  Ibid., pp. 170–1.
27  Hibbert (ed.) (1981), p. 148.
28  PD, 7 December 1837.
29  MB, I, p. 412.
30  BDL, I, p. 276, 5 June 1883.
31  Langley (2003), p. 86. The original is in the Hughenden Papers, Box 4, A/I/583.
32  Blake (1966), p. 161.
33  Ibid., p. 162.
34  Weintraub (1993), p. 177.
35  Ibid., p. 5.

## Chapter 2, William Ewart Gladstone, early life, 1809–41

1   Matthew (1986), p. 3.
2   Checkland (1971), pp. 14–15.
3   Ibid., pp. 414–15.
4   Ibid., p. 31.
5   Ibid., p. 33.
6   Ibid., p. 38.
7   Matthew (1986), p. 4.
8   Ibid., p. 6.
9   Ibid., p. 7.
10  Morley (1905), I, pp. 12–13.
11  Ibid., I, p. 15.
12  Jenkins (1995), p. 12.
13  Ibid., p. 13.
14  Ibid., p. 18.
15  Matthew (1986), p. 7.
16  Morley (1905), I, p. 14.
17  Matthew (2004c).
18  Morley (1905), I, p. 52.
19  GD, 21 February 1829.
20  Shannon (1982), p. 25.
21  GD, 29 March 1830.
22  GD, 24 March 1830.

23  Morley (1905), I, p. 80.
24  Shannon (1982), p. 35.
25  GD, 17 January 1832.
26  Morley (1905), I, p. 89.
27  Checkland (1971), p. 277.
28  Morley (1905), I, p. 23.
29  Checkland (1971), pp. 161–2.
30  Matthew (1986), p. 31.
31  Ibid., p. 90.
32  Shannon (1982), p. 63.
33  Ibid., p. 64.
34  Matthew (2004c).
35  Matthew (1986), p. 53.

**Chapter 3, Peel and the great Tory split, 1841–7**

1  Wilson (1977), p. 45.
2  Gash (1976), p. 123.
3  Hibbert (ed.) (1981), pp. 163–4.
4  Gash (1976), p. 207.
5  Bradford (1982), p. 113.
6  Blake (1966), p. 164.
7  Ibid., p. 165
8  Weintraub (1993), p. 200.
9  MB, I, p. 520.
10  Hibbert (2005), p. 155.
11  Disraeli, Benjamin (1954), *Sybil*, II, Chapter 5.
12  Jenkins (1995), p. 106.
13  Somervell (1926), p. 54.
14  PD, 4 February 1843.
15  Morley (1905), I, p. 311.
16  PD, 22 January 1846.
17  Ibid.
18  Ibid.
19  Gash (1976), p. 275.
20  Blake (1969), p. 15.
21  PD, 15 May 1846.
22  Ibid.
23  Ibid.
24  Blake (1966), p. 239.
25  Ibid.
26  PD, 18 June 1846.
27  Hilton (1998), p. 147.

## Chapter 4, Party realignment, 1847–52

1   Jenkins (1995), p. 87.
2   Shannon (1982), p. 201.
3   Checkland (1971), p. 358.
4   National Trust (1997), p. 5.
5   Morley (1905), II, pp. 715–16.
6   PD, 17 December 1847.
7   Macintyre (2004).
8   Weintraub (1993), p. 289.
9   Ibid., p. 294.
10  Jenkins (1995), p. 86.
11  Ibid.
12  Matthew (1986), pp. 74–5.
13  Gladstone (1851).
14  Shannon (1982), pp. 230–1.
15  Checkland (1971), p. 354.
16  Jenkins (1995), p. 99.
17  Shannon (1982), p. 215.
18  GD, IV, p. 144.
19  Checkland (1971), p. 367.
20  GD, 3 January 1881.
21  Shannon (1982), pp. 221–2.
22  Ibid.
23  GD, 13 December 1851.
24  Blake (1966), p. 285.
25  Lytton (1852).
26  PD, 24 April 1844.
27  Blake (1966), p. 26.
28  Weintraub (1993), p. 301.
29  Ibid., p. 302.
30  Ibid., p. 284.
31  Blake (1966), p. 30.
32  Weintraub (1993), p. 293.
33  MB, II, p. 1269.
34  Ibid.
35  PD, 24 June 1850.
36  Weintraub (1993), p. 314.
37  Chambers (2004), p. 343.
38  Weintraub (1993), p. 314.
39  Ibid., p. 317.
40  PD, House of Lords, November 1852.
41  MB, I, p. 1239.
42  Ibid.

43  *The Times*, 22 November 1852.
44  Blake (1966), p. 343.
45  Ibid.
46  PD, 16 December 1852.

## Chapter 5, The Palmerston era begins, 1853–8

1   Hibbert (2005), p. 269.
2   Ibid.
3   Weintraub (1993), p. 317.
4   Ibid.
5   Ibid.
6   Ibid.
7   Ibid. p. 345.
8   Blake (1966), p. 347.
9   Jenkins (1995), p. 143.
10  Weintraub (1993), p. 324.
11  GD, 9 December 1852.
12  GD, IV, p. 477.
13  Matthew (1986), p. 81.
14  Jenkins (1995), p. 149.
15  PD, 18 April 1853.
16  Shannon (1982), p. 272.
17  Fulford (ed.) (1968), p. 542.
18  Morley (1905), p. 469.
19  Shannon (1982), p. 272.
20  Greville (1888), VI, p. 419.
21  GD, IV, p. 525.
22  Shannon (1982), p. 274.
23  Chambers (2004).
24  Chamberlain (1903), p. 478
25  Shannon (1982), p. 286.
26  Ibid., p. 302.
27  Ibid.
28  Ibid., p. 300.
29  Ibid., p. 306.
30  Weintraub (1993), p. 242.
31  Morley (1905), I, p. 563.
32  GD, 14 February 1857.
33  Jenkins (1995), p. 183.
34  Weintraub (1993), p. 334.
35  Ibid., pp. 333–4.
36  Blake (1966), p. 353.

37  Ibid., p. 354.
38  Weintraub (1993), p. 345.
39  Ibid., p. 359.
40  Bradford (1982), p. 246.
41  Miller (2004).
42  Bradford (1982), pp. 322–3.
43  Weintraub (1993), p. 347.
44  McDowell (2004).
45  Chambers (2004), p. 440.

## Chapter 6, Derby again, but then 'Pam' goes on and on…, 1858–65

1   Blake (1966), p. 379.
2   MB, II, pp. 1557–8.
3   Magnus (1954), p. 134.
4   MB, II, pp. 1558–9.
5   Shannon (1982), p. 356.
6   Ibid., p. 357.
7   Weintraub (1993), p. 373.
8   Blake (1966), p. 401.
9   Ibid., p. 402.
10  MB, II, pp. 1635–7.
11  Shannon (1982), p. 383.
12  Ibid., p. 386.
13  Jenkins (2001), p. 912.
14  Jenkins (1998), p. 6.
15  Jenkins (1995), p. 216.
16  Speech at Edinburgh, 29 November 1876.
17  *The Times*, 9 October 1862.
18  Jenkins (1995), p. 238.
19  Magnus (1954), p. 152.
20  Jenkins (1995), p. 239.
21  Weintraub (1993), pp. 282–3.
22  Ibid.
23  Ibid., p. 282.
24  Ibid.
25  Ibid., p. 285.
26  Ibid.
27  Ibid., p. 420.
28  Ibid.
29  Ibid.
30  Ibid.
31  Ibid., pp. 419–36.
32  Ibid., p. 436.

## Chapter 7, The struggle for reform, 1865–8

1 Seton-Watson (1935).
2 Aldous (2006), p. 152.
3 Morley (1905), II, p. 151.
4 PD, 11 May 1864.
5 Ibid., 13 March 1866.
6 Shannon (1999), p. 23.
7 GD, 6 July 1866.
8 Blake (1966), pp. 448–9.
9 Disraeli, Benjamin (1927), *Endymion*.
10 Blake (1966), p. 379.
11 GD, 12 April 1867.
12 MB, II, p. 267.
13 Kebbel (1907), p. 40.
14 PD, House of Lords, 6 August 1867.

## Chapter 8, Power – at last, 1868–74

1 MB, II, p. 304.
2 Ibid., p. 306.
3 Ibid., p. 319.
4 Ibid., p. 321.
5 Ibid.
6 Blake (1966), p. 487.
7 Ibid., pp. 488–9.
8 Ibid., p. 488.
9 Weintraub (1993), p. 489.
10 Jenkins (1995), p. 276.
11 Weintraub (1993), p. 547.
12 Jenkins (1995), p. 287.
13 Weintraub (1993), p. 474.
14 First cited in *The National Review*, June 1898.
15 GD, VII, p. 43.
16 Ibid., 29 December 1868.
17 Shannon (1999), p. 85.
18 Bond (2004).
19 Jenkins (1995), p. 370.
20 Blake (1966), p. 516.
21 GD, 18 May 1870.
22 Ibid., 25 May 1870.
23 Blake (1966), p. 520.
24 Ibid., p. 521.

25 Ibid.
26 MB, II, pp. 530–1.
27 Blake (1966), p. 523.
28 *The Times*, 18 April 1883.
29 Weintraub (1993), p. 508.
30 MB, II, p. 570.
31 Ibid.
32 Weintraub (1993), p. 510.
33 MB, II.
34 Blake (1966), p. 531.
35 Zetland (ed.) (1929).
36 Vincent (1978), p. 346.
37 Matthew (1986), p. 242.
38 Leonard (2004), pp. 63, 68.
39 Matthew (2004c).

## Chapter 9, The rise and fall of 'Beaconsfieldism', 1874–81

1 Blake (1966), pp. 535–7.
2 GD, VII, p. 464.
3 Fulford (ed.) (1976), p. 128.
4 Bradford (1982), p. 305.
5 Roberts (1999), p. 131.
6 Cross (1903), p. 3.
7 Bradford (1982), p. 315.
8 Gladstone (1856), pp. 521–70.
9 Shannon (1999), p. 153.
10 Ibid., p. 155.
11 PD, 5 August 1874.
12 Weintraub (1993), p. 529.
13 Zetland (ed.) (1929), I, p. 260.
14 Bradford (1982), p. 331.
15 Zetland (ed.) (1929), I, letter dated 5 May 1875.
16 Weintraub (1993), pp. 572–3.
17 Ibid., p. 530.
18 Bradford (1982), p. 334.
19 Matthew (1986), p. 223.
20 GD, 7 March 1874.
21 Gladstone (1876).
22 Letter to Lord Derby, 8 September 1876.
23 Magnus (1954), p. 245.
24 Speech at Knightsbridge, 27 July 1878.
25 Blake (1966), p. 607.
26 Ibid.

27  Song by George William Hunt, written *c.*1878.
28  Blake (1966), p.605.
29  Weintraub (1993), p.590.
30  Ibid., p.593.
31  Ibid.
32  Seton-Watson (1935), p.439.
33  Speech at Oxford, January 1878.
34  Jenkins (1995), p.428.
35  Morley (1905), II, p.595.
36  Ibid.
37  MB, II, p.1403.
38  Ponsonby (1942), p.184.
39  Shannon (1999), p.247.
40  Fulford (ed.) (1981), p.75.
41  GD, 29 March 1880.
42  Blake (1966), p.748.
43  Ibid., p.751.
44  PD, 9 May 1881.


## Chapter 10, Gladstone alone, 1881–98

1   Jenkins (1995), p.445.
2   Biagini (1998), p.201.
3   Matthew (2004c).
4   GD, XI, p.484.
5   Speech at South Paddington, 19 January 1886.
6   Ponsonby (1942), pp.216–17.
7   Ibid.
8   Matthew (1995), p.328.
9   GD, XIII, p.43.
10  Jenkins (1995), p.603.
11  GD
12  Shannon (1999), p.562.
13  Matthew (1995), p.355.
14  Jenkins (1995), p.617.
15  GD.
16  Fulford (ed.) (1968), 3rd Series, II, pp.372–3.
17  Jenkins (1995), p.628.
18  GD.
19  Shannon (1999), p.576.
20  GD, XIII, p.403.
21  Matthew (1995), p.377.
22  Ibid., p.385.
23  Wintle and Kenin (1978), p.334.

## Chapter 11, The final reckoning

1   Cited by Gladstone's secretary, Edward Hamilton, in his diary, 7 May 1883. See Bahlman (ed.) (1972).
2   Blake (1966), pp. 757, 765.
3   Parry (2004).
4   Ibid.
5   Disraeli (1919).
6   Ibid.
7   Shannon (1999), p. 117.
8   GD, 17 January 1872.
9   Bradford (1982), p. 255.
10  Blake (1966), p. 26.
11  Churchill (1908), p. 207.

# Select bibliography

Aldous, Richard (2006), *The Lion and the Unicorn: Gladstone vs. Disraeli*, London.

Bahlman, D.W.R. (ed.) (1972), *The Diary of Sir Edward Walter Hamilton 1880–85*, Oxford.

Biagini, Eugenio (1998), 'William Ewart Gladstone', in Robert Eccleshall and Graham Walker (eds), *Biographical Dictionary of British Prime Ministers*, London.

— (2000), *Gladstone*, London.

Bigham, Clive (1924), *The Prime Ministers of Britain 1721–1921*, London.

Blake, Robert (1966), *Disraeli*, London.

— (1969), *Disraeli and Gladstone* (Leslie Stephen Lecture), Cambridge.

— (1992), *Gladstone, Disraeli and Queen Victoria* (Romanes Lecture), Oxford.

Bond, Brian (2004), 'Cardwell, Edward, first Viscount Cardwell (1813–86)', in *Oxford Dictionary of National Biography*, Oxford.

Bradford, Sarah (1982), *Disraeli*, London.

Campbell, John (2009), *Pistols at Dawn: Two hundred years of political rivalry from Pitt and Fox to Blair and Brown*, London.

Chamberlain, Muriel (1983), *Lord Aberdeen*, London.

Chambers, James (2004), *Palmerston: The people's darling*, London.

Checkland, S.G. (1971), *The Gladstones 1764–1851*, London.

Churchill, Lady Randolph (1908), *Reminiscences*, London.

Clarke, Peter (1992), *A Question of Leadership: From Gladstone to Thatcher*, London.

Conacher, J.B. (1968), *The Aberdeen Coalition 1852–55*, Cambridge.

Cross, Viscount (1903), *A Political History*, London.

Disraeli, Benjamin (1872), *Lord George Bentinck, A Political Biography*, London.

— (1919), *Tancred or The New Crusade*, London.

— (1927), *Coningsby*, London.

— (1927), *Contarini Fleming: A psychological auto-biography*, London.

— (1927), *Endymion*, London.

— (1927), *Lothair*, London.

— (1927), *Vivian Grey*, London.

— (1954), *Sybil or The Two Nations*, Harmondsworth.

— (1982), *Letters 1815–81*, ed. J.A.W. Gunn, John Matthews, Donald M. Schurman, M.G. Wiebe and others (the series is continuing, and nine volumes had appeared by 2012, taking the correspondence up until 1867. Several more volumes are expected to appear over the next half dozen years), Toronto.

Disraeli, Benjamin and Sarah Disraeli (1983), *A Year at Hartlebury or The Election*, London.

Englefield, Dermot, Jean Seaton and Isobel White (1995), *Facts about the British Prime Ministers*, New York.

Feuchtwanger, E. (1975), *Gladstone*, London.

FitzGerald, S.V. (2004), 'Cross, Richard Assheton, first Viscount Cross (1823–1914)', in *Oxford Dictionary of National Biography*, Oxford.

Flavin, Michael (2005), *Benjamin Disraeli: The novel as political discourse*, Brighton.

Fulford, Roger (ed.) (1968), *Dearest Mama: Letters between Queen Victoria and the Crown Princess of Prussia*, London.

— (1976), *Darling Child: Private correspondence of Queen Victoria and the Crown Princess of Prussia 1871–8*, London.

— (1981), *Beloved Mama: Private correspondence of Queen Victoria and the German Crown Princess*, London.

Gash, Norman (1976), *Peel*, London.

Gilliland, J. (2004), 'Opdebeck, Lady Susan Harriet Catherine [formerly Countess of Lincoln] (1814–89)', in *Oxford Dictionary of National Biography*, Oxford.

Gladstone, William Ewart (1838), *The State in its Relations with the Church*, 2 vols, London.

— (1840), *Church Principles Considered in their Results*, London.

— (1856), 'The declining efficiency of Parliament', in *Quarterly Review*, June– September 1856, London.

— (1869), *Homeric Synchronism: An enquiry into the time and place of Homer*, London.

— (1876), *The Bulgarian Horrors and the Question of the East*, London.

— (1896), *The Odes of Horace*, London.

— (ed.) (1896), *The Works of Joseph Butler*, 2 vols, London.

— (1896), *Studies Subsidiary to the Works of Bishop Butler*, London.

— (1968–94), *The Gladstone Diaries: With cabinet minutes and prime-ministerial correspondence*, eds M.R.D. Foot and H.C.G. Matthew, 14 vols, Oxford.

Greville, Charles (1888), *The Greville Memoirs*, London.

Hawkins, Angus (2004), 'Stanley, Edward George Geoffrey Smith, fourteenth Earl of Derby 1799–1869', in *Oxford Dictionary of National Biography*, Oxford.

Hibbert, Christopher (2005), *Disraeli, A Personal History*, London.

— (ed.) (1981), *Greville's England*, London.

Hilton, Boyd (1998), 'Benjamin Disraeli, First Earl of Beaconsfield', in Robert Eccleshall and Graham Walker (eds), *Biographical Dictionary of British Prime Ministers*, London.

Hurd, Douglas (2007), *Robert Peel: A biography*, London.

Iremonger, Lucille (1970), *The Fiery Chariot*, London.

Isba, Anne (2006), *Gladstone and Women*, London.

Jenkins, Roy (1995), *Gladstone*, London.

— (1998), *The Chancellors*, London.

— (2001), *Churchill*, London.

Jones, Gareth H. (2004), 'Copley, John Singleton, Baron Lyndhurst (1772–1863)', in *Oxford Dictionary of National Biography*, Oxford.

Jones, Wilbur Devereux (1956), *Lord Derby and Victorian Conservatism*, London.

Kebbel, T.E. (1907), *Lord Beaconsfield and other Tory Memories*, London.

Kennedy, A.L. (1953), *Salisbury, 1830–1905: Portrait of a statesman*, London.

Langley, Helen (ed.) (2003), *Benjamin Disraeli, Earl of Beaconsfield: Scenes from an extraordinary life*, Oxford.

Leonard, Dick (2004), *A Century of Premiers: Salisbury to Blair*, London.

— (2008), *Nineteenth-Century British Premiers: Pitt to Rosebery*, London.

Macintyre, Angus (2004), 'Bentinck, Lord (William) George Frederic Cavendish, Scott (1802–48)', in *Oxford Dictionary of National Biography*, Oxford.

Magnus, Philip (1954), *Gladstone*, London.

Matthew, H.C.G. (1986), *Gladstone 1809–74*, Oxford.

— (1995), *Gladstone 1875–98*, Oxford.

— (2004a), 'Gladstone, Catherine (1812–1900)', in *Oxford Dictionary of National Biography*, Oxford.

— (2004b), 'Gladstone, Sir John, first baronet (1764–1851)', in *Oxford Dictionary of National Biography*, Oxford.

— (2004c), 'Gladstone, William Ewart (1809–98)', in *Oxford Dictionary of National Biography*, Oxford.

Maurois, André (1978), *Vie de Disraeli*, Paris.

McDowell, R.B. (2004), 'Burgh, Ulrick John de, first Marquess of Clanricarde (1802–74)', in *Oxford Dictionary of National Biography*, Oxford.

McKenzie, Robert and Allan Silver (1968), *Angels in Marble: Working class Conservatives in urban England*, London.

McKinstry, Leo (2005), *Rosebery: Statesman in turmoil*, London.

Miller, Mary S. (2004), 'Earle, Ralph Alexander (1835–79)', in *Oxford Dictionary of National Biography*, Oxford.

Mitchell, L.G. (1997), *Lord Melbourne 1779–1848*, London.

Monypenny, W.F. and G.F. Buckle (1910–20), *The Life of Benjamin Disraeli, Earl of Beaconsfield*, 6 vols, London (republished 1929, unabridged, in two large volumes, London).

Morley, John (1905), *Life of Gladstone*, 3 vols, London.

National Trust (1997), *Hughenden Manor*, London.

Ogden, James (2004), 'D'Israeli, Isaac (1768–1848)', in *Oxford Dictionary of National Biography*, Oxford.

Parry, Jonathan (2004a), 'Cavendish, Spencer, Marquess of Hartington and eighth Duke of Devonshire (1833–1908)', in *Oxford Dictionary of National Biography*, Oxford.

— (2004b), 'Disraeli, Benjamin, Earl of Beaconsfield', in *Oxford Dictionary of National Biography*, Oxford.

Ponsonby, A. (1942), *Henry Ponsonby, Queen Victoria's private secretary: His life from his letters*, London.

Prest, John (1972), *Lord John Russell*, London.

Rhodes James, Robert (1963), *Rosebery*, London.

Ridley, Jane (2004), 'Disraeli, Mary Anne, Viscountess Beaconsfield (1792–1872)', in *Oxford Dictionary of National Biography*, Oxford.

Robbins, Keith (1979), *John Bright*, London.

Roberts, Andrew (1999), *Salisbury: Victorian Titan*, London.

Seton-Watson, R.W. (1935), *Disraeli, Gladstone and the Eastern Question*, London.

Shannon, Richard (1982), *Gladstone*, vol. 1: *Peel's Inheritor, 1809–65*, London.

— (1999), *Gladstone*, vol. 2: *Heroic Minister, 1865–98*, London.

Sherer, Paul (1999), *Lord John Russell*, London.

Somervell, D.C. (1926), *Disraeli and Gladstone*, New York.

Steele, David (2004), 'Stanley, Edward Henry, fifteenth Earl of Derby (1826–93)', in *Oxford Dictionary of National Biography*, Oxford.

Sykes, James (1928), *Mary Anne Disraeli: The story of Viscountess Beaconsfield*, London.

Veysey, A. Geoffrey (2004), 'Glynne, Sir Stephen Richard, ninth baronet (1807–74)', in *Oxford Dictionary of National Biography*, Oxford.

Vincent, John (1990), *Disraeli*, Oxford.

— (ed.) (1978), *Disraeli, Derby and the Conservative Party: Journals and Memoirs of Edward Henry, Lord Stanley, 1849–69*, London.

Weintraub, Stanley (1993), *Disraeli*, London.

Wilson, Harold (1977), *A Prime Minister on Prime Ministers*, London.

Wintle, Justin and Kenin, Richard (eds) (1978), *Dictionary of Biographical Quotations*, London.

Zetland, 2nd Marquess of (ed.) (1929), *The Letters of Disraeli to Lady Bradford and Lady Chesterfield*, 2 vols, London.

# Index

Also by Dick Leonard

*A History of British Prime Ministers: Walpole to Cameron*

*The Routledge Guide to the European Union*
(with Robert Taylor)

*A Century of Premiers: Salisbury to Blair*

*Nineteenth Century British Premiers: Pitt to Rosebery*

*Eighteenth Century British Premiers: Walpole to the Younger Pitt*

*The Economist Guide to the European Union*
(ten editions)

*Elections in Britain* (five editions)

*Guide to the General Election*

*Paying for Party Politics*

*Crosland and New Labour* (edited)

*The Socialist Agenda: Crosland's Legacy*
(edited with David Lipsey)

*World Atlas of Elections* (edited with Richard Natkiel)

*The Backbencher and Parliament*
(edited with Val Herman)

*The Pro-European Reader* (edited with Mark Leonard)

*The Future of Socialism* by Anthony Crosland
(edited fiftieth anniversary edition, 2006)

Rising parliamentary star: Disraeli in the 1840s (by Sir Francis Grant).

Gladstone aged 30, in 1839: already an ex-minister, and shortly to join Peel's second government (by Heinrich Müller).

Mary Anne Disraeli, who married Disraeli, 12 years her junior, in August 1839, a year after the death of her first husband (by François Rochard).

Gladstone's wife Catherine Glynne, pictured around 1860, when she was aged 48 (by Mayall).

Sir Robert Peel, at the height of his power, as Prime Minister in 1842 (by William Salter).

*left* The Duke of Wellington. He was Sir Robert Peel's predecessor as Tory leader and Prime Minister, and subsequently served under him as Foreign Secretary (after John Wood).

*below* Lord Aberdeen, Gladstone's boss in 1835, when he was War and Colonial Secretary, and again in 1853–55, when he was Prime Minister and Gladstone Chancellor of the Exchequer (by John Partridge).

Gladstone, the mature politician in 1859, when he became Chancellor for the third time, under Lord Palmerston (by George Frederick Watts).

Disraeli in 1868, when he became Prime Minister for the first time (by W. and D. Downey).

Leading politicians in the 1860s: *clockwise from top left*, Lord John Russell, Gladstone, 14th Earl of Derby, John Bright, Lord Palmerston.

Gladstone's first cabinet, formed in 1868: he is seated in the foreground on the right, the bearded Marquess of Hartington is standing on the left (by Lowes Cato Dickinson).

Disraeli's leading cabinet colleagues, 1876: standing, from left, 15th Earl of Derby, Lord Cairns, Sir Stafford Northcote, Gathorne Hardy; sitting, Disraeli, 3rd Marquess of Salisbury.

*above* Gladstone's leading colleagues in opposition, 1876: front row, Gladstone, Earl Granville; second row, John Bright, William Forster; third row, Lord Selborne, Robert Lowe, Marquess of Hartington.

*right* Cartoon by John Tenniel published in *Punch* on 14 May 1870. The two men are shown looking disdainfully at each other's recently published books.

"CRITICS"

*(Who have not exactly "failed in literature and art.")*
—*See Mr. D.'s New Work*

MR. G-D-S-T-NE. *"Hm!—Flippant!"*  MR. D-S-R-LI. *"Ha!—Prosy!"*

*left* Laura Thistlethwayte, ex-courtesan and Gladstone's close friend from 1864 (by Girard).

*below* Selina Bradford, Disraeli's last great (but unrequited) love (after Sir Francis Grant).

Queen Victoria, who presented Disraeli a copy of this portrait to hang in the dining room at Hughenden Manor (after Heinrich von Angeli).

Hughenden Manor, as it appeared in the year of Disraeli's death, 1881.

Disraeli relaxes with friends in the garden of Hughenden Manor during his second premiership, in 1874. Seated on the left is Selina, Countess of Bradford, behind her is Montague Corry, Disraeli's secretary, the Earl of Bradford is in the middle of the back row.

Gladstone, aged 79, accompanied by his wife Catherine, eldest son Willy and several grandchildren, fells a tree at Hawarden in 1888.

The 5th Earl of Rosebery, who sponsored Gladstone in his Midlothian constituency, served under him as Foreign Secretary and succeeded him as Prime Minister in 1894 (by Elliott and Fry).

Milton Keynes UK
Ingram Content Group UK Ltd.
UKHW021003110724
445435UK00004B/84

9 781784 536374